Charles R. Ball

The apostle of the Gentiles

His life and letters

Charles R. Ball

The apostle of the Gentiles
His life and letters

ISBN/EAN: 9783741183140

Manufactured in Europe, USA, Canada, Australia, Japa

Cover: Foto ©Lupo / pixelio.de

Manufactured and distributed by brebook publishing software
(www.brebook.com)

Charles R. Ball

The apostle of the Gentiles

THE

APOSTLE OF THE GENTILES.

His Life and Letters.

BY THE

REV. CHARLES R. BALL, M.A.,

VICAR OF S. PAUL'S, PETERBOROUGH,
AUTHOR OF "THE PROMISED SEED," AND
"LESSONS ON OUR LORD'S MINISTRY."

Published under the Direction of the Tract Committee.

LONDON:
SOCIETY FOR PROMOTING CHRISTIAN KNOWLEDGE,
NORTHUMBERLAND AVENUE, CHARING CROSS, W.C.;
43 QUEEN VICTORIA STREET, E.C.;
26 ST. GEORGE'S PLACE, HYDE PARK CORNER, S.W.
BRIGHTON: 135, NORTH STREET.
NEW YORK: E. & J. B. YOUNG & CO.
1885.

"CHRIST! I am Christ's! and let the name suffice you,
   Ay, for me too He greatly hath sufficed;
Lo with no winning words I would entice you,
   Paul has no honour and no friend but Christ.

Yea thro' life, death, thro' sorrow and thro' sinning
   He shall suffice me, for He hath sufficed;
Christ is the end, for Christ is the beginning,
   Christ the beginning, for the end is Christ."

PREFACE.

THIS Book has been written in the hope that it may serve to interest the young, and those who have but little time for reading, in the Life and Writings of S. Paul; and thus serve as an introduction to the many more valuable and important works on the same subject.

The writer wishes to express his acknowledgements of the abundant help he has received from Dr. Farrar's Life and Work of S. Paul, Conybeare and Howson's well-known work on the same subjects, from Professor Westcott's "Historic Faith," and last, and above all, from "The Unity of the New Testament" and "The Epistle to the Hebrews" by the late Rev. F. D. Maurice.

Lent 1885.

CONTENTS.

CHAPTER		PAGE
I.	S. Paul's early life and education	7
II.	Saul the Persecutor	13
III.	The Conversion and Baptism of S. Paul	20
IV.	S. Paul's call to the Apostolate	27
V.	S. Paul's mission as an Apostle	34
VI.	S. Paul's method as an Evangelist	40
VII.	S. Paul's great Controversy	48
VIII.	S. Paul before Kings and Rulers	57
IX.	S. Paul's Voyage and first Imprisonment	66
X.	S. Paul's last Imprisonment and Martyrdom	75
XI.	The Epistles of S. Paul to the Thessalonians	85
XII.	,, ,, (*continued*)	91
XIII.	The 1st Epistle of S. Paul to the Corinthians	98
XIV.	,, ,, (*continued*)	106
XV.	,, ,, ,,	115
XVI.	The 2nd Epistle of S. Paul to the Corinthians	122
XVII.	,, ,, (*continued*)	129
XVIII.	,, ,, ,,	136
XIX.	The Epistle of S. Paul to the Galatians	143
XX.	,, ,, (*continued*)	150
XXI.	The Epistle of S. Paul to the Romans	157
XXII.	,, ,, (*continued*)	163
XXIII.	,, ,, ,,	169
XXIV.	,, ,, ,,	175
XXV.	The Epistle of S. Paul to the Philippians	182

CONTENTS.

CHAPTER		PAGE
XXVI.	The Epistle of S. Paul to the Colossians.	190
XXVII.	,, ,, (*continued*)	198
XXVIII.	,, ,, ,,	205
XXIX.	The Epistle of S. Paul to Philemon	213
XXX.	The Epistle of S. Paul to the Ephesians	220
XXXI.	,, ,, (*continued*)	227
XXXII.	,, ,, ,,	235
XXXIII.	,, ,, ,,	242
XXXIV.	The 1st Epistle of S. Paul to Timothy	250
XXXV.	The Epistle of S. Paul to Titus	256
XXXVI.	The 2nd Epistle of S. Paul to Timothy	264
XXXVII.	The Epistle to the Hebrews	272
XXXVIII.	,, ,, (*continued*)	279
XXXIX.	,, ,, ,,	287
XL.	,, ,, ,,	295
XLI.	,, ,, ,,	303

CHAPTER I.

S. PAUL'S EARLY LIFE AND EDUCATION.

IN the following pages I hope to be able to tell you something about S. Paul, something about the man himself, something about his work, and about his preparation for that work: and especially I hope to be able to give you some idea of the letters which he was inspired to write, letters which have instructed and comforted sixty generations of Christians.

Such a subject as this ought to be interesting, and I will do my best to make it interesting.

It is really almost impossible to reckon up the debt of gratitude which under God's providence we owe to S. Paul. It is hardly too much to say that if it had not been for S. Paul, the Christian Religion and the Catholic Church would have been very different from what they are.

The Christian Church, in its framework, in its extent, in its practical teaching, owes its existing form in great measure to the force of character, the genius, and devotion of this great Apostle.

To his keen and many-sided intellect we owe the systematic statement of the truths of Christianity in their relation to one another.

To his spiritual insight, to his indomitable courage and persistence we owe it, that the Religion of Jesus was freed from the weight of Jewish observances and the yoke of the Mosaic law which at one time threatened to crush out its life.

The Emperor Augustus was said to have boasted that he found Rome a city of brick, and left it a city of marble.

It might almost seem that the Christian community as S. Paul found it might have become little more than a Jewish sect, a sect which possibly might not have survived the destruction of Jerusalem; Christianity, as S. Paul left it, was in a fair way of becoming the Religion of the Roman world, and was seen to possess the elements of a universal Religion.

It was only natural that as S. Paul was especially called to be the Apostle of the Gentiles, his training should have been different from that of the other apostles, whose mission was primarily to the chosen people.

The future Apostle and organizer of the Church was born, so it would appear, about seven years before the birth of our Saviour. He was born at Tarsus, the chief city of the Province of Cilicia, "a citizen," as he himself tells us, "of no mean city."

Tarsus was a great commercial city, like Liverpool or Glasgow: but it was more than that, it was something like what we should call a University town, like Oxford or Cambridge, or Edinburgh, being the seat of a famous school of learning.

But though Tarsus itself was no mean city, Cilicia, the Province of which it was the capital, had a not very enviable reputation.

The birth of Saul at Tarsus determined the trade which the future Apostle was taught, and by which in after days he supplied his scanty needs.

The manufacture of the rough cloth made from goat's hair, which was used for making tents, was the staple trade of Tarsus, and was the handicraft which Saul learnt.

You must not, however, suppose from this that Saul's parents belonged to the poorer class of people. It was the general practice of Jewish parents, of whatever rank, to teach their sons a trade. Indeed, it was a common saying that a father who did not teach his son a trade, taught him to be a thief.

But although born in a heathen city, the abode of Grecian learning and Grecian vice, the young Saul was brought up as a strict and conscientious Jew. His parents were strict Jews, his father was a Pharisee. Under their training Saul grew up to be a thorough-going Jew, a Jew in sympathy, a Jew in nationality, a Jew in faith, or as he himself describes it, " a Hebrew of the Hebrews."

But besides being a citizen of the commonwealth of Israel, he was also a citizen of Rome. This privilege, of which the future Apostle often availed himself, was acquired or inherited by his father, and was by him transmitted to his son, who was, as he proudly asserts, "free born."

The childhood and boyhood of the future Apostle, allowing for the difference of time and country, would not be so very different from the life of an English boy now. He would be taught, as we are, the old Bible stories; he would learn about Adam and Eve, Cain and Abel, about the Flood, and Noah's ark, about Joseph and his brethren; he would read with especial pride and delight the exploits of his namesake Saul, and Jonathan, the heroes of his own tribe of Benjamin. He would also very probably learn by heart, as English boys and girls should be encouraged to do, portions of Holy Scripture.

We may think of Saul as walking through the busy streets, under the care of a slave, who was called the Pædagogue, or boy-leader, to the Synagogue School, and there sitting cross-legged on the floor, with other children, receiving the elements of learning.

At the age of thirteen the young Saul, like other Jewish boys, would undergo a ceremony which in some respects answered to Confirmation with us, and became, as the phrase was, "a son of the Law"; and as he was probably intended for the profession of a Rabbi, or Teacher of the Law, he would be entered as a student in the School of some great Doctor of the Law.

The young student of Tarsus was according'y sent to Jerusalem, and became one of the scholars of Gamaliel.

We all know what an important epoch it is in an English boy's life when he goes up to London for the first time: so we can easily imagine what this first visit to Jerusalem must have been to Saul. But Jerusalem would be to him far more than London would be to us, it would be more what a visit to Rome would be to an ardent Roman Catholic boy. It was not only the capital City of his nation, but the one place which God had chosen to place His Name there. It was "the Holy City," "the Perfection of Beauty," "the Joy of the whole Earth."

Saul was very fortunate in having such a master as Gamaliel, for he was one of the wisest and most liberal, as well as one of the most learned of the Jewish Rabbis. The advantages of a Jerusalem education in the School of Gamaliel were not thrown away upon Saul. The future apostle became an eager and earnest student.

He tells us himself (Gal. i. 14) that he advanced in the Jews' religion beyond many of his own age among his countrymen, being more exceedingly zealous for the traditions of his fathers.

The effects of this study are more or less apparent in every epistle which he wrote.

The argument which he uses in the Epistle to the Galatians, for instance, "Now to Abraham were the promises made, and to his seed : He saith not, And to seeds, as of many, but as of one, And to thy Seed, which is Christ" (Gal. iii. 16), and the allegorical interpretation of the story of Sarah and Hagar, as typifying the Christian and Jewish Covenants, would never have occurred to one who had not been thoroughly imbued with Rabbinical teaching.

But Saul was a great deal more than a diligent student, he was most earnestly religious; as far as the righteousness of the Law was concerned, he was blameless ; he lived in all good conscience towards God.

Yet his was too great a soul to find a lasting peace, or a solid satisfaction, in endeavouring to work out a righteousness of his own. This righteousness brought no peace to him. The Law of God, which he knew to be holy, and just and good, was no way of life to him, but rather the way of death.

It is interesting to think, as one of the ablest writers on the life of S. Paul has pointed out, that while the young student from Tarsus was passing through the Schools of Jerusalem, and winning golden opinions from his teachers, there were boys growing up on the shores of the sea of Galilee, mending their father's nets, with whom he was afterwards to be brought into fellowship as apostles of a new faith, and servants of the same Master: and still more, that while Saul was studying at Jerusalem, One was growing up in the seclusion of a country village, in whom he was afterwards to recognize the long-expected Messiah of his people; the Power of God, and the Wisdom of God.

It is hardly likely that Saul remained at Jerusalem during the years of our Lord's ministry. If he had actually seen our Saviour, and heard him speak; still more if he had been present at the meeting of the Council of the Elders which condemned him to death, he would have made some allusion to it in his speeches, or his letters.

Many things might have called him away from Jerusalem at that time. He might have been sent by the Jewish Sanhedrim on a distant mission; or family affairs might have called him to Tarsus.

We only know for certain that at the time that S. Stephen was exercising his ministry at Jerusalem, Saul had returned, and was known as an ardent disciple of Judaism, an eager controversialist, and afterwards a pitiless persecutor of the followers of Jesus.

It will be necessary now to give an outline sketch of the history of the Christian Church up to this time; but this must be done in another chapter.

CHAPTER II.

SAUL THE PERSECUTOR.

WHEN Saul returned to Jerusalem,—for, as I have said, it is hardly likely that he was there at the time of the crucifixion of our Lord,—he would find the whole aspect of affairs changed.

His friends, no doubt, would cluster round him, and tell him about what had happened during his absence. They would tell him about the Prophet of Galilee, the Nazarene as they would call him, about his revolutionary teaching and extravagant pretensions, and how he had been condemned and put to death.

They would have to tell him also that the disciples of this man were inclined to be troublesome; that they had succeeded in persuading many of the people that the crucified Nazarene was the Christ, that he had risen from the dead, and had bestowed new and strange gifts upon his followers.

Yes, great events had indeed happened; far greater than Saul and his friends would allow to themselves; far greater even than the apostles themselves dreamt of.

Outwardly, no doubt, things remained much the same, the Holy City, the Temple, the Schools of the Rabbis were the same: but in reality it was a new world to which Saul had returned. There were new forces at work which would soon overthrow the existing religions and institutions of the world, and shape the destinies of mankind. The Stone which was to break in pieces the kingdoms of the world, was already cut without hands out of the mountain. The grain of mustard-seed had been sown in the field of the world, the leaven had been hidden in the three measures of meal.

But we must go back a little and endeavour to understand what it was that had happened, to picture to ourselves what had been the history of the Christian Church up to this time.

This history is contained, as you know, in the Acts of the Apostles.

This most interesting and instructive book, which contains the sole record of the beginnings of the Christian Church, has been well called "the Gospel of the Holy Spirit."

On the surface, it is the history of the actings of Apostles, beneath the surface it is the record of the working of the Holy Ghost in the Church, and in the world.

I dare say you have noticed in the two books of the New Testament which we owe to S. Luke—the third Gospel and the Acts of the Apostles—what a prominent place is occupied by the Ascension of our Lord. The Gospel ends with the Ascension, the Acts begins with it. It was the finishing of one part of the Divine plan, the beginning of another.

The history of the origin and growth of the Christian Church starts from AN OPENED HEAVEN, AND AN ASCENDED CHRIST. Soon we read of the descent of the Holy Ghost out of that opened heaven, the Gift of that ascended Christ.

There have been two supreme moments in the history of the human race. One was THE INCARNATION, and the other was THE DESCENT OF THE

HOLY GHOST. The one was the birthday of a restored humanity; the other was the birthday of the Universal Church.

Now, looking again at the inspired record, what do we see beyond the special and passing manifestations of the day of Pentecost, as to the nature and appearance of this Church?

Well, we see a Society of men and women, united in a common faith; bound together by sacramental ordinances; a Society animated with a new life, dwelt in by an unseen Presence, giving out a sort of spiritual radiance, surrounded, as it were, by a supernatural atmosphere, possessing and exercising new powers.

We look again, and we see this Society ever growing in numbers, increasing in reputation with the people, and adapting itself to its growing needs. And we ask ourselves, what is the secret of this growth? what is the explanation of that spiritual attraction which is drawing hundreds of men and women to it?

It was not any special eloquence in the preaching of the Apostles, that seems to have been of the simplest and plainest kind. It was not even, I think, the miracles which they wrought. These indeed served to call attention to the new Society, and to prepare men's minds to recognize a divine power at work within it. No! it was the power of this hidden life; it was the shining of this spiritual light; it was this surrounding atmosphere of peace and holiness which drew people to it.

Those who witnessed the life of the first believers could not help themselves, they were drawn by an unseen power, they were led by an unseen hand. Christ had said, "I, if I be lifted up from the earth, will draw all men unto me," and He was doing it.

This was the secret of the Church's growth. It was not so much what the Apostles and first believers did or said, but what *they were*, that made it grow.

It grew because it lived, it grew by the power of its hidden life.

It was against this Society with its outward witness to Jesus as the Christ, and its inner life in the Holy Ghost, that Saul came into conflict.

To him this new doctrine was the abandonment of the faith and hope of Israel, a pestilent heresy that must be stamped out: to him the Christians were a set of ignoble fanatics, renegades from their faith, rebels against God.

But we must trace more clearly the way in which this conflict was brought about.

To meet a temporary necessity which the rapid growth of the new Society called forth, seven officers had been appointed.

The first of these was Stephen. Higher work was soon found for him than that for which he had been first appointed, and we find him engaged in active work as a preacher and a disputant in the synagogues of the foreign Jews at Jerusalem.

The preaching of S. Stephen took a wider range than any that had yet been taken. He was beginning to see, as no Christian teacher had hitherto seen, that the life of Christ's Church was not bound up in the life of Judaism; that the old order of the Mosaic Dispensation would pass away, and yield place to the new order of Christianity; that the old Jerusalem would pass away, while the new Jerusalem, the Church of the living God, would remain for ever.

This new departure in the teaching of the Christian Church raised to a white heat the already excited indignation of the Sadducean party; and at the same time roused the sleeping fanaticism of the Pharisees, among whom Saul of Tarsus, whose career we have been following, stood out in the front rank.

When S. Stephen disputed in the synagogue of the Cilicians—you remember that Tarsus was the capital of Cilicia—he doubtless found his most formidable antagonist in this profound scholar, this skilled controversialist, this pupil of the great Gamaliel.

When the hurried judgment of the Sanhedrim condemned him to death, Saul gave his voice against him. When the witnesses at whose testimony he was condemned, and who by the law were required to cast the first stone at the condemned man, laid aside their outer robes for this purpose, they placed them at a young man's feet whose name was Saul.

The martyrdom of S. Stephen was the signal for the breaking out of a cruel and deadly persecution against the disciples of Jesus: and in this persecution the prime mover, the inquisitor and persecutor in chief, was Saul.

But it is very clear that the holy martyr's death made a profound impression upon him, however much he might try and shake it off. Indeed, it has been suggested that it was to throw off this impression that made Saul plunge into a still deeper and fiercer persecution of the new sect.

Not content with ravaging the Church at Jerusalem and its neighbourhood, he followed the Christian believers to strange cities, and did his best to make them blaspheme that worthy Name for which they suffered.

Among these "strange cities" was Damascus, where was a large colony of Jews, and also, as it would seem, a considerable number of the hated and despised synagogue of the Nazarenes.

Armed with full authority from the High Priest as Inquisitor-in-chief, and accompanied by a considerable escort, Saul commenced his journey.

Damascus was about 150 miles from Jerusalem, and, at the ordinary rate of travelling, the journey thither would occupy nearly a week.

We can hardly doubt that as he rode along, the terrible scenes in which he had been engaged, and above all the scenes outside Jerusalem, when Stephen the Nazarene fell beneath the crushing stones of his murderers, must have been constantly before his mind. The angelic face of the first martyr of Jesus would haunt him day and night, his dying words would ring perpetually in his ears. What if, after all, the Nazarene were right, and he were wrong! What if, after all, he were fighting against God! What if, after all this, Jesus of Nazareth were indeed the Christ!

The journey was nearly over: Damascus, perhaps, in sight. It was *noon*. At this hour travellers in that burning climate always rest: but there was no rest for Saul. The fire of hatred which burned in his heart would not let him rest. He hurried on. Then suddenly he was arrested in his course. A light more dazzling than the noonday sun shone about him. He fell prostrate to the earth in terror and confusion, and heard a voice, the sound of which was heard by all, but the words of which were heard by him alone, saying to him, "Saul, Saul, why persecutest thou me?"

Fancy the suddenness and the awfulness of this! The Persecutor met on the way by Him whose servants he was persecuting. To feel in a moment that he was wrong, that his life was wrong, that he was doing wrong, that he was indeed fighting against God, persecuting the Saviour of the world: what a fearful spiritual experience this was for a man to undergo.

This sudden revulsion of feeling and thought is more than we can possibly conceive of. Only, indeed, those whose experience has approached that of Saul, can form any idea of the conflict which must have raged within him. We can only record the fact, we can only ponder his words—"And he, trembling and astonished, said, Lord, what wilt Thou have me to do?"

This was the "Conversion," the turning of S. Paul.

Yet you will notice that the Lord did not tell him what he would have him to do.

He only made clear to him one step at a time. "Go into the city," the Lord said to him, "and it shall be told thee what thou must do."

Thus Christ led him step by step: and even thus will He lead us.

It was better so for him, and it is better so for us.

> "I do not ask to see
> The distant scene; one step enough for me."

CHAPTER III.

THE CONVERSION AND BAPTISM OF S. PAUL.

HE Conversion of Saul was the most wonderful and the most important event in the history of the Christian Church, as well as the highest triumph of divine grace.

When we think of what Saul was, and what by God's grace he came to be; when we think of what his Conversion involved, both to himself and to the world, we are struck with amazement.

Among the external evidences for the truth of the Christian Religion, the conversion of its chief persecutor into its most famous Apostle is one of the most striking.

To begin with, he had everything to lose and nothing to gain, as far as worldly things were concerned. It is not as if he passed from a negative Judaism to a negative Christianity. He passed, at a bound, from the fiercest opposition to the most absolute devotion to the cause of Christ. "Saul rose another man: he had fallen in death, he rose in life; he had fallen a proud intolerant Jew, he rose a humble broken-hearted Christian."

What power, short of the reality of the appearance of Jesus to him, what less than the flashing upon his soul of conviction, as complete as it was sudden, could have changed such a man in such a way!

Think also of the wonderful importance of the Conversion of Saul as affecting the destinies of the Christian Church.

The preaching of S. Stephen, and the persecution which followed his martyrdom, marked the beginning of a new epoch in the history of the Church.

The Gospel was about to obtain a wider proclamation. The members of the Christian Society, driven from Jerusalem by persecution, went everywhere preaching the word. The centre of Christian life and activity would soon be shifted from Jerusalem to a Gentile city. Congregations of Gentile believers would soon be springing up in the great cities of the world; and the Christian community, the Body of Christ, would have to meet these altered conditions of its existence.

But a movement such as this would require the most careful guidance, this ever-widening field would demand the most skilful tillage. Questions would inevitably arise as to the relations between these Communities of Gentile Christians, and the Central Body of the Church at Jerusalem, which would need a master mind to grapple with, and a master's hand to set at rest. To steer the ship of the Church through such perilous straits, through such hidden shoals, would require a pilot specially trained and qualified.

No one of the original Twelve Apostles was specially gifted, by education or by training, for such exceptional work. Such special work required a special agent; and such an agent was found by God's providence by the Conversion of Saul.

Here was the chosen vessel of God, the Apostle of the Gentiles. Here was the man who was chosen by God to guide the Church in the perilous times that were at hand; who was chosen to take the helm when the vessel of the Church floated out from the sheltering shores of Palestine into the vast ocean of the world.

But we must now return to the history as S. Luke relates it, and see what followed upon this appearance of Christ to Saul on the road to Damascus.

Acts ix. 8: And Saul arose from the earth; and when his eyes were opened, he saw nothing: and they led him by the hand, and brought him into Damascus. And he was three days without sight, and did neither eat nor drink.

When Saul, trembling and astonished, rose from the earth and opened his eyes, all was dark around him: he was blind, blind with excess of light. His companions had to lead him by the hand into the city.

What a different entrance into Damascus from what he had looked forward to. He passed through its gate, not as a dreaded Inquisitor, but as a poor humbled, blinded man, through the street which was called Straight, to the house of Judas.

Saul was still, no doubt, accompanied by the officers of the High Priest; he had still in his possession the High Priest's commission to summon the Christians before his Court: but in conviction, in heart and conscience, he was himself a Christian.

We should have liked to have heard what he said to his companions about the change which had come over him; with what words he gave up his letters of authority. We cannot help wondering what his companions had to say; but we can picture their dismay, their bewilderment, at the inexplicable delusion that had possessed their leader, and at this unexpected ending to their mission.

But not a word of all this is told us. We only know that the blindness continued for three days, at any rate for part of three days, and that during that time he neither ate nor drank.

I do not think we are meant to understand from this that Saul set himself to fast, that he of set purpose abstained from the food which he craved for. Rather it is implied, that so terrible was the mental struggle through which he was passing, so great the tempest raised in his mind by conflicting waves of thought, that he had no heart to eat and drink, nor indeed any consciousness that he needed food.

It must have been a terrible three days. Of course he would get no sympathy from his companions: but he prayed in silence and alone, and his prayers were heard.

A special vision was granted, in which he saw a man named Ananias coming into his darkened room, and putting his hands upon him, that he might receive his sight.

Acts ix. 10: Now there was a certain disciple at Damascus named Ananias; and the Lord said unto him in a vision, Ananias. And he said, Behold I am here, Lord. And the Lord said unto him, Arise, and go to the street which is called Straight and enquire in the house of Judas for one named Saul, a man of Tarsus, for behold he prayeth; and he hath seen a man named Ananias coming in, and laying his hands on him that he might receive his sight. But Ananias answered, Lord, I have heard from many of this man, how much evil he did to thy saints at Jerusalem: and here he hath authority from the chief priests to bind all that call upon thy Name. But the Lord said unto him, Go thy way, for he is a chosen vessel unto me to bear my Name before the Gentiles, and kings, and the children of Israel: for I will show him how many things he must suffer for my Name's sake. And Ananias departed, and entered into the house; and laying his hands on him said, Brother Saul, the Lord, even Jesus who appeared unto thee in the way which thou camest, hath sent me that thou mayest receive thy sight, and be filled with the Holy Ghost. And straightway there fell from his eyes as it were scales, and he received his sight; and he arose and was baptized; and he took food and was strengthened. And he was certain days with the disciples which were at Damascus.

There are many things which strike us as we read this beautiful and touching story.

And, first of all, we are struck with the way in which the narrative brings out the reality of Christ's presence in His Church, and the nearness of Jesus to His disciples and to all men.

Christ plans and arranges. He speaks and acts as One who is actually and really present. Here, at any rate, there is nothing to countenance the notion of His having departed to some far-off heaven, and committed the care of His Church to the hands of another.

It is, indeed, through the Holy Spirit that Christ is present in His Church. But that Holy Spirit is the Spirit of Christ. The Holy Spirit has not come to take the place of an absent Christ, but to bring about His presence. We are not the less living in the Kingdom of Christ, because we are living under the dispensation of the Spirit.

And then, again, how beautiful is the way in which the truth is brought out, that Christ sees, and watches, and listens to men. He knew Saul's name; He knew the city where he was born; He knew the name of the man in whose house he was lodging; He knew the name of the street; He knew exactly what Saul had seen in his vision; He knew that he had been praying; He knew for what he had been praying.

Of course there is nothing really strange in all this. He who knows all things, knows everything.

But how it brings the truth home to us: how it brings home to us that Jesus knows all about us, knows where we live, knows where we are lodging, knows what we are thinking about, knows when we pray, and what we pray for; knows also how we pray, or whether we pray at all!

There is another thing, of a very different kind, that strikes us when we read in this narrative how Saul was baptized, how Ananias said to him, "Arise, and be baptized and wash away thy sins, calling on the name of the Lord"; and that is how very important, how very indispensable in Christ's eyes, is the Sacrament of Holy Baptism.

Surely if in any case baptism might be thought superfluous and unnecessary, it would be in this case. Here was a man separated to God, from his mother's womb, to whom Jesus had Himself appeared, a man whom He had chosen to be His Apostle, a man who was to occupy altogether an exceptional position in His Church; a man, too, who for the whole of his apostolic career was protesting against the bondage of external ordinances, and vindicating the spirituality of the Gospel.

If Baptism were, what some people are very fond of calling it, merely "an ordinance," merely an outward sign or badge, conferring no real grace, admitting to no spiritual privileges, would such a man as Saul have submitted to it; or would it have been required in his case?

But if Baptism is the sign and instrument of a new birth, if it does confer grace, and admit us to the Kingdom of Christ, then it was as necessary for Saul as for the humblest believer; and in being baptized he was not submitting to a mere external ordinance; but humbly and thankfully receiving a Sacrament of God's grace.

CHAPTER IV.

S. PAUL'S CALL TO THE APOSTOLATE.

IN our last chapter we saw how Saul, converted as he was to Christ by a miracle of God's grace, was received into the Body of Christ's Church by Holy Baptism.

Saul was now not only by inward conviction, and the direct call of Christ, but also formally by the washing of the new birth, a Christian. Old things had passed away, all things were become new. His former life was a thing of the past, his old self was dead. He was a new man, with new hopes, new interests, with new friends.

It was indeed a passing from darkness into light, and that, not from abstract darkness to abstract light; but from an actual darkness to actual light. From the darkness of hatred to the light of love, real human love; from the darkness of a religion of proud self-righteousness and bitter exclusiveness, to the light of a religion of sweet reasonableness and universal love; from the company of bigots and persecutors to the disciples of the meek and lowly Jesus.

We can easily imagine how Saul would enjoy the friendly sympathy which the Christian believers at Antioch, assured as they would be by the testimony of Ananias, would show during the certain days that he remained with them.

We know from his writings that Saul was a man of a warm and affectionate nature, that he yearned for love and sympathy. He would welcome as a foretaste of friendship and Christian fellowship in years to come, the thankful wondering joy with which the disciples at Antioch would show their delight at the Conversion of their expected persecutor. What his own joy and thankfulness were we may gather from what, many years later, he wrote to his friend and disciple Timothy.

1 *Tim.* i. 12: I thank Him that enabled me, even Christ Jesus our Lord, for that He counted me faithful, appointing me to His service; though I was before a blasphemer, and a persecutor and injurious: howbeit I obtained mercy, because I did it ignorantly in unbelief . . . . that in me, as chief, might Jesus Christ show forth all His long-suffering, for an ensample of them which should hereafter believe on Him unto eternal life.

At this point we must read the account which S. Paul gives in his Epistle to the Galatians of this period of his life.

Gal. i. 13: Ye have heard of my manner of life in time past in the Jews' religion, how that beyond measure I persecuted the Church of God, and made havock of it: and I advanced in the Jews' religion beyond many of mine own age among my countrymen, being more exceedingly zealous for the traditions of my fathers. But when it was the good pleasure of God, who separated me, even from my mother's womb, and called me through his grace, to reveal His Son in me, that I might preach him among the Gentiles; immediately I conferred not with flesh and blood: neither went I up to Jerusalem to them which were apostles before me, but I went away into Arabia; and again I returned unto Damascus.

In this passage you see S. Paul speaks of a journey to Arabia immediately after his conversion: but there is no trace of this journey in the history as given by S. Luke in the Acts. And the difficulty arises as to where in the narrative we are to insert it. Was it before or after what we read in the 20th verse of the 9th chapter—that straightway in the synagogues he proclaimed Jesus that He is the Son of God? In other words, which came first, the preaching, or the visit to Arabia?

Different people will always take different views about this. It seems to me far more likely—though this view is by no means universally taken—that a man, such as Saul was, would have felt the necessity of a period of quiet before he began to proclaim the truth against which, up to a few days previously, he had been so fiercely fighting.

It was a very different case from a man who, before his conscious conversion to Christ, held the truth implicitly. There would seem almost something unbecoming in a man one day furiously inveighing against some system, and almost the next day fervently supporting it.

Besides, though Saul was convinced at once and for ever that Jesus was the Son of God; yet he needed time for thought and prayer and self-converse before he could grasp the whole bearings of the truth that had been flashed upon his mind, before he could arrange and harmonize his convictions.

It was, then, if this view be correct, to obtain this quiet time for study, for thought, for prayer, rather than to preach the Gospel, that Saul took his journey to Arabia. The expression "Arabia" was used very vaguely: but it is open to us to believe that he bent his steps to Mount Sinai, the Mount of God, the spot where the Law, to the study of which his whole previous life had been devoted, was given; the spot where Elijah in the crisis of his stormy life betook himself, and where he heard the still small voice of God.

Wherever the scene of his retreat was, doubtless Saul also heard the same still small voice speaking in his heart: just as each one of us may hear it, if we only listen. Here, too, perhaps it was that he "was caught up into Paradise and heard unspeakable words which it is not lawful for a man to utter." Here it was, we may suppose, that the Gospel which he afterwards preached " came to him through revelation of Jesus Christ."

It is not necessary to suppose that he remained three whole years in Arabia. One whole year and parts of two others would quite satisfy the expression according to Jewish usage.

Strengthened, then, by this period of quiet thought and prayer, and equipped for his work by " visions and revelations of the Lord," Saul returned to Damascus, and, to continue in the words of the sacred historian,—

Acts ix. 20: Straightway in the synagogues he proclaimed Jesus, that He is the Son of God, and all that heard him were amazed, and said, Is not this he that in Jerusalem made havock of them which called on this name? and he had come hither for this intent, that he might bring them bound before the chief priests. But Saul increased the more in strength, and confounded the Jews which dwelt at Damascus, proving that this is the Christ. And when many days were fulfilled, the Jews took counsel together to kill him; but their plot became known to Saul. And they watched the gates also day and night that they might kill him: but his disciples took him by night, and let him down through the wall, lowering him in a basket. And when he was come to Jerusalem he assayed to join himself to the disciples, and they were all afraid of him, not believing that he was a disciple. But Barnabas took him and brought him to the apostles . . . . . And he was with them going in and going out at Jerusalem, preaching boldly in the name of the Lord: and he spake and disputed against the Grecian Jews; but they went about to kill him. And when the brethren knew it, they brought him down to Cæsarea, and sent him forth to Tarsus.

When, at the time of his "wonderful Conversion," Saul said to his Lord, "What wilt Thou have me to do?" he laid down the principle on which his whole after life and ministry was based.

The words of a well-known hymn may well be taken as descriptive of S. Paul's feelings at this crisis of his spiritual history:—

> Lead, kindly Light, amid the encircling gloom,
>   Lead Thou me on;
> The night is dark, and I am far from home,
>   Lead Thou me on.
> Keep Thou my feet; I do not ask to see
> The distant scene; one step enough for me.
>
> I was not ever thus, nor prayed that Thou
>   Shouldst lead me on;
> I loved to choose and see my path; but now
>   Lead Thou me on.
> I loved the garish day, and, spite of fears,
> Pride ruled my will: remember not past years.
>
> So long Thy power hath blest me, sure it still
>   Will lead me on
> O'er moor and fen, o'er crag and torrent, till
>   The night is gone,
> And with the morn those angel faces smile,
> Which I have loved long since, and lost awhile.

After his "retreat" in Arabia, Saul returned to Damascus. If we are right in supposing that he had not yet borne witness to Christ at Damascus, he would naturally desire to proclaim to the Jews of that city that Gospel which he had found to be "the power of God unto salvation."

He may also have wished to follow back the clue of God's guiding Providence by returning to the place where the Lord had appeared to him.

On his arrival at Damascus he began to proclaim the Gospel, of the power of which he was himself such a wonderful instance. His preaching was probably of the simplest description; indeed, he would only have to tell his own story, in order to bring conviction to the hearts of all who were not hardened against the truth.

But the more successful his witness was, the greater was the opposition which it roused. That opposition increased to persecution, and would have ended in his murder if his own special converts had not taken measures to ensure his safety. Here is his own account of the matter:—" In Damascus the governor guarded the city in order to take me, and through a window was I let down in a basket by the wall, and escaped his hands." (2 Cor. xi. 32, 33.)

We can hardly help pausing for a moment to reflect what that journey to Jerusalem must have been to the new convert. With what profound emotion he would pass the place where the Lord had appeared unto him! How the whole scene would come back to him!

We cannot be surprised that the Christian community at Jerusalem should regard Saul with suspicion and dislike. Nor is it strange that it was S. Barnabas, the Son of Consolation, that was the first to give him the right hand of fellowship, and to welcome him as a brother in Christ.

It is of this visit that Saul afterwards wrote:—

Gal. i. 18: Then after three years I went up to Jerusalem to visit Kephas, and tarried with him fifteen days. But other of the apostles saw I none, save James the Lord's brother.

During this time, short as it appears to have been, Saul boldly proclaimed the truth in the synagogues of the foreign Jews, and carried on the work which Stephen had begun. But his work was soon cut short; the Jews, worsted in argument, betook themselves to their accustomed weapons of persecution.

And then following the advice of the brethren, in which Saul would recognize the guiding of his Master's hand, he went to his early home at Tarsus. There he waited, not idly or uselessly you may be sure, but patiently till a further call should come, and the Lord's will concerning him be further manifested.

What this call was, and how it came to him, we shall see in the next chapter.

CHAPTER V.

THE "MISSION" OF S. PAUL.

WE left Saul at Tarsus waiting for his final call; waiting till the Lord's will respecting him should be made clear.

We must now see in what shape the call came, and what were the circumstances which led to it.

The martyrdom of S. Stephen had been, as we have seen, the signal for a fierce persecution against the Church in Jerusalem, and so we read that—

Acts xi. 19: They therefore that were scattered abroad upon the tribulation that arose about Stephen, travelled as far as Phœnicia, and Cyprus, and Antioch, speaking the word to none save only to Jews. But there were some of them, men of Cyprus and Cyrene, who, when they were come to Antioch, spake unto the Greeks also, preaching the Lord Jesus. And the hand of the Lord was with them: and a great number that believed turned unto the Lord. And the report concerning them came to the ears of the Church which was in Jerusalem: and they sent forth Barnabas as far as Antioch: who, when he was come, and had seen the grace of God, was glad; and he exhorted them all, that with purpose of heart they would cleave unto the Lord: for he was a good man, and full of the Holy Ghost, and of faith: and much people was added unto the Lord. And he went forth to Tarsus to seek for Saul: and when he had found him, he brought him to Antioch. And it came to pass that even for a whole year they were gathered together with the Church, and taught much people; and that the disciples were called Christians first in Antioch.

Thus it was that the call to a special field of labour in the Lord's Vineyard came to Saul at Tarsus.

He would not thrust himself into a field of work, without being quite sure whether it was the special field for which his Lord intended him.

And so also we may be sure, if we have really given ourselves to Christ, if we have said from our hearts, "Lord, what wilt Thou have me to do?" that the Lord's will concerning us will be made known somehow.

If we wait in faith and humility, the way will be made plain to us. The call may come in many different ways. It may come by the invitation of a friend, as it did to Saul at Tarsus: it may come at the solicitation of strangers, as it did to S. Peter at Joppa: it may come from the bent and inclination of our own minds: it may come by the force of circumstances, as again and again it came to S. Paul in his after life.

The great thing is to have faith, to believe that we have a call; patience to wait for its coming; courage to follow it when it does come.

But now let us be sure that we quite understand S. Luke's narrative which we have just read.

The Christian believers who first ventured to preach the Gospel to the heathen at Antioch, and who were so unexpectedly and abundantly blessed in their work, were simple lay-folk as we should call them, holding no special office in the Christian Community.

But we must never allow ourselves to forget that Christ had sent His Church, not merely to convince men's minds and to influence their lives, but to make them citizens of His Kingdom. The life of Christianity was a corporate life. Believers were not so many separate units, but members of a Body or Society, a Society which had, in the very nature of things, a framework, an organized system.

The first adherents to the faith at Jerusalem not only believed certain truths, and acknowledged Jesus to be the Christ, but continued steadfastly in the fellowship of the Apostles, and in the breaking of the Bread, and in the Prayers.

So when tidings of what was going on at Antioch came to the Church at Jerusalem, the head-quarters of the Christian Society, they sent thither S. Barnabas, one of their leading men, to superintend the work which was going on.

When S. Barnabas reached Antioch and saw the extent and the reality of the work which was in progress, he felt that he could not cope with the work single-handed. There was one man, he felt, who both by special calling and special gifts could give him the help he required, and that man was Saul.

To Saul the invitation of Barnabas to go with him to Antioch came as the voice of the Master Himself, the voice for which he had been waiting.

S. Luke does not devote many words to the work which Barnabas and Saul carried on together at Antioch. He only says:—" For a whole year they were gathered together with the Church, and taught much people. And the disciples were called Christians first at Antioch." But enough is said to show us what sort of work it was. It was, then, a work of teaching, rather than of preaching. It was rather the work of commissioners organizing a lately conquered province, than that of generals advancing to new conquests.

And the result of their labours was that the scattered believers in Christ at Antioch were consolidated into a Church, a Society which, though containing Jews, was not Jewish. Thus the community of believers stood out in the sight of the people of Antioch, as a distinct and independent organization. And the new Society required a new name: so the people of Antioch, who seem to have had a fancy for giving nicknames, called the members of this new Society Christians, i.e. followers of Christus, or Christ.

But the time had now come when "a new departure" in the extension of the Church was to be made, when a great step in advance would be taken.

Saul had not yet received his full and formal commission as an Apostle. He was *called*, but not yet *sent*.

Again and again in his epistles S. Paul speaks of himself as called by God to be an Apostle, and lays great stress upon the fact that he derived his Apostleship not from men, nor through man, but from Christ alone.

He knew that Christ had called him, moreover, to be the Apostle of the Gentiles; again and again had this been impressed upon him. He knew that the work of his life was to proclaim Christ's Gospel to the Gentiles, to open their eyes, to turn them, as he himself had been turned, from darkness to light, and from the power of Satan unto God.

But he knew also that Christ had called him into His Church; and that he was to execute his Apostleship not only by a direct inward call from Christ, but also to be an Apostle under the dispensation of the Spirit. As he had received his "*call*" from Christ, so also must he receive his "*mission*" from the Holy Ghost, that is, from the Holy Ghost dwelling in the Church, speaking by the utterance of its prophets, acting through its ministry.

It is very necessary to grasp this distinction between the call and the mission of S. Paul, for there is a great deal of confusion of thought upon the subject.

No doubt also the Church at Antioch knew that S. Paul had been called to be the Apostle of the Gentiles; it was also becoming increasingly manifest to them that the time had come for a fresh and direct missionary effort. Their community was now organized, but they felt that organization was not an end in itself, but only a means to an end. If the Church was living it must move. And so again the message was being whispered in their hearts, which was sent by Moses of old, " Speak unto the children of Israel, *that they go forward!*"

But now let us read S. Luke's account of this forward movement.

Acts xiii. 1 : Now there were at Antioch in the Church that was there, prophets and teachers, Barnabas and Symeon, that was called Niger, and Lucius of Cyrene, and Manaen the foster-brother of Herod the tetrarch, and Saul. And as they ministered to the Lord and fasted, the Holy Ghost said, Separate me Barnabas and Saul for the work whereunto I have called them. Then when they had fasted and prayed, and laid their hands on them, they sent them away. So they being *sent forth by the Holy Ghost*, went down to Seleucia ; and from thence they sailed to Cyprus.

We learn from this that the prophets and teachers of the Church at Antioch, though they knew in a general way what was the mind of the Spirit in this matter, did not anticipate His action. They waited till it should please Him to manifest His will. Nor did they wait in vain. As they ministered to the Lord and fasted, the Holy Ghost said, Separate me Barnabas and Saul for the work whereunto I have called them.

Again, with united prayer and fasting the Church at Antioch besought the direction of the Holy Ghost.

Acts xiii. 3 : And then they (i.e. the prophets and teachers) laid their hands on them, and sent them away. So they went, being sent forth by the Holy Ghost.

No one can fail to notice the prominence that is here given to the presence and the action of the Holy Ghost : nor can we help seeing that the mission of Paul and Barnabas by the Holy Ghost was given, not by the direct action of the Spirit upon their minds, but by the Spirit speaking and acting through the Church. Outwardly and visibly they were sent forth by the Church, really and truly they were sent forth by the Holy Ghost.

The scope of this book does not allow us to describe this first missionary expedition on which the two Apostles were sent forth. You will notice, by the way, that they are not called Apostles before this. They were not formally Apostles until they had been *sent*. But it was no easy expedition. The two Apostles were opposed and hindered, first by a Jewish sorcerer, and afterwards by crowds of Jewish fanatics. At one city in Lycaonia S. Paul was stoned and left for dead.

On their return journey—for nothing daunted by the ill-treatment they had sustained, they went back by these same cities—they appointed elders in every Church, and with prayer and fasting commended the new converts to their Lord.

And so they returned to Antioch, which was henceforth to be the mother Church of the Churches of the Gentiles,—the second great centre of Church life and work. And when they were come, and had gathered the Church together, they rehearsed all things that God had done with them, and how that He had opened a door of faith unto the Gentiles.

CHAPTER VI.

S. PAUL AS A MISSIONARY AND EVANGELIST.

WE have already seen how S. Paul was inwardly *called*, and outwardly *sent* to be an Apostle.

It is hardly necessary to enquire in what spirit he went forth, it breathes in every word that he spoke, in every letter that he wrote. He had no choice. Necessity was laid upon him. "Woe is me," he says, "if I preach not the Gospel;" "The love of Christ constraineth me."

If we knew nothing of S. Paul's method as a missionary and evangelist, beyond what we could gather from his Epistles, we should certainly arrive at the conclusion that S. Paul's plan was to attack those strongholds of heathenism, the great cities of the empire. His Epistles were written, for the most part, to the Christians of the great cities—to Ephesus and Colossæ, in Asia; to Philippi and Thessalonica, in Macedonia; to Corinth in Greece, and above all to Rome.

S. Paul knew that if the battle were to be won, it must be fought in the great cities. He knew that the country followed the lead of the cities, not the cities of the country. Experience justified his method. Heathenism lingered on in the country long after it had disappeared from the towns; and

5. PAUL AS A MISSIONARY AND EVANGELIST. 41

so it came about that heathens were called pagans, pagani, i.e. dwellers in the village.

Next, we may notice that one secret of S. Paul's success was that he had gathered round him a devoted band of fellow-helpers; men whom he had often proved, and whom he could entirely trust.

Such were Timothy, "his own child in the faith;" Titus, a young Greek won by him to the faith; Luke, who seems to have acted the double part of a physician, and an evangelist and historian of the Church; such also were Tychicus, Aristarchus, Epaphroditus and Onesimus, and last, Mark, sister's son to Barnabas, who having once lost S. Paul's good opinion, afterwards entirely regained it.

But not only was the great Apostle thus equipped, and thus assisted, but the field of his labours had been wonderfully prepared by God's providence.

One effect of the conquests of Alexander was to spread a knowledge of the Greek tongue over the great part of Western Asia. Greek became the medium of communication between the nations of the Roman empire. It became a second mother tongue.

Into this universal language the Scriptures of the Old Testament had been translated, and the Greek Bible became the authorized version of the Jews of the Dispersion. In every considerable town in the empire there was a colony of Jews who possessed one or more synagogues. The synagogues became centres of religious influence, a nucleus round which the most hopeful elements of Gentile life were gathered. Every synagogue was a centre of attraction to the heathen world around it. Gentiles, disgusted with their own religion, sick of superstitious vanities and empty philosophies, found in the synagogues of Israel a worship both simple and rational; there they heard in Greek the simple but grand words of Moses, and the noble utterances of Prophets and Psalmists.

Thus, in these "proselytes of the Gate" as they were called, the Apostles found the pick of the heathen gathered in readiness, men who were predisposed to welcome the Gospel, and familiar with the great truths of faith and righteousness which not even Rabbinical exposition could deprive of their inherent power.

S. Paul's invariable plan was to begin at the synagogue, and this not only because he thus gained access to the Gentile proselytes, but because he understood that the Gospel must first be preached to the chosen people.

It is very necessary to understand this. If the Jews refused to receive this Gospel, it was to their own loss; little as they thought it, by rejecting it they cut themselves off from the hope of Israel, from that which was the glory of Israel, as well as the light of the Gentiles.

Those who, like S. Paul himself, accepted Christ, did not cut themselves off from the hope of Israel or the faith of their fathers: but clung all the more to that hope, and followed that faith to its proper results.

But this hope of Israel, this faith of their fathers, did not belong only to Israel. In former ages, no doubt, it had been confined to the literal Israel: but a new era had dawned, the middle wall of partition between Jew and Gentile had been thrown down: there was no difference.

And therefore when the Jews, the literal Israel, refused to accept the Gospel, then he turned to the Gentiles, as those who by faith might become the true Israel, the true seed of Abraham, the inheritors of Israel's calling, the sharers in Israel's promise.

In the narrative of S. Paul's missionary labours, in the Acts of the Apostles, S. Luke gives what seems evidently intended as a specimen of his proceedings in dealing with Jews and proselytes in the city of Antioch in Pisidia.

Acts xiii. 13 : Now Paul and his company .... came to Antioch of Pisidia ; and they went into the synagogue on the Sabbath day, and sat down. And after the reading of the law and the prophets, the rulers of the synagogue sent unto them, saying, Brethren, if ye have any word of exhortation for the people, say on. And Paul stood up, and beckoning with the hand, said, " Men of Israel (addressing the Jews), and ye that fear God (addressing the proselytes), hearken. The God of this people Israel chose our fathers, and led them out of Egypt . . . . and gave them the land of Canaan, ... and gave them judges until Samuel the prophet. And afterward for a king gave unto them Saul. And when He had removed him, He raised up David to be their king; to whom also He bare witness, and said, I have found David the son of Jesse, a man after my heart, who shall do all my will. Of this man's seed hath God according to promise brought unto Israel a Saviour, Jesus ; . . . . Brethren, children of the stock of Abraham, and those among you that fear God [i.e. the proselytes], to us is the word of this salvation sent. For they that dwell in Jerusalem and their rulers, condemning Him, asked of Pilate that He should be slain. And when they had fulfilled all things that were written of Him, they took Him down from the tree, and laid Him in a tomb. But God raised Him from the dead: and He was seen for many days of them that came up with Him from Galilee to Jerusalem, who are now His witnesses unto the people. And we bring you good tidings of the promise made unto the fathers, how that God hath fulfilled the same unto our children, in that He raised up Jesus. Be it known unto you, therefore, brethren, that through this man is proclaimed unto you remission of sins: and by Him, every one that believeth is justified from all things, from which ye could not be justified by the law of Moses."

And as they went out they besought that these words might be spoken to them the next Sabbath. Now when the synagogue broke up, many of the Jews and of the devout proselytes followed Paul and Barnabas: who, speaking to them, urged them to continue in the grace of God. And the next Sabbath almost the whole city was gathered together to hear the word of God. But when the Jews saw the multitudes, they were filled with jealousy, and contradicted the things which were spoken by Paul, and blasphemed. And Paul and Barnabas spake out boldly, and said, It was necessary that the word of God should first be spoken to you. Seeing ye thrust it from you, and judge yourselves unworthy of eternal life, lo, we turn to the Gentiles. . . . . And the word of the Lord was spread abroad throughout all the region. But the Jews . . . . stirred up a persecution against Paul and Barnabas, and cast them out of their borders . . . . and the disciples were filled with joy and with the Holy Ghost.

When the Apostle had to encounter heathenism pure and simple, he had, of course, to alter his method. It was of no use to speak about the Old Testament Scriptures to people who had never heard of them: he was obliged to get at their hearts and consciences in some other way. S. Luke gives specimens of this side of S. Paul's teaching also.

After leaving the Pisidian Antioch, as we have just read, S. Paul and his companions came to Iconium, where a like success and a like persecution followed. The two Apostles had to take refuge in the wild district of Lycaonia. At Lystra, S. Paul cured a cripple who had never walked. The multitude were so astonished that they jumped to the conclusion that

Paul and Barnabas were no other than two of the gods come down to the earth, and proceeded to offer sacrifice to them. Then followed a scene which, I dare say, is familiar to you from Raffael's famous cartoon. As soon as the Apostles grasped the idea that the sacrifices—the oxen and garlands, which they saw—were being offered to *them*,—

Acts xiv. 15: They rent their garments, and sprang forth among the multitude, crying out and saying, Sirs, why do ye these things? We also are men of like passions with you, and bring you good tidings, that ye should turn from these vain things unto the living God, who made the heaven and earth and the sea, and all that in them is: who in the generations gone by suffered all the nations to walk in their own ways. And yet He left not Himself without witness, in that He did good, and gave you from heaven rains and fruitful seasons, filling your hearts with food and gladness.

Still more striking was the preaching of S. Paul at Athens, the head-quarters of heathen religion and heathen philosophy.

Athens was not a commercial city, so that there was but a small colony of Jews resident there. As usual, S. Paul reasoned in the synagogue with such of the Jews and Gentile proselytes as resorted thither, but it does not seem to have had much effect.

He also talked with the people whom he found in the central square of the city, where he was encountered by Epicurean and Stoic philosophers, who brought him to the Areopagus, or hill of Ares, where the famous court of the Areopagites held its sessions. Standing there in the midst, S. Paul spoke as follows:—

Acts xvii. 22: Ye men of Athens, in all things I perceive that ye are somewhat superstitious,—

(or that you carry your religious observances to a somewhat excessive extent).

For as I passed along, and observed the objects of your worship, I found also an altar with this inscription, To AN UNKNOWN GOD. What therefore ye worship in ignorance, this set I forth unto you. The God that made the world, and all things therein, He, being Lord of heaven and earth, dwelleth not in temples made with hands; neither is He served by men's hands, as though He needed anything, seeing He Himself giveth to all life and breath and all things . . . . that they should seek God, if haply they might feel after Him, and find Him, though He is not far from each one of us: for in Him we live, and move, and have our being; as certain even of your own poets have said, FOR WE ARE ALSO HIS OFFSPRING. Being then THE OFFSPRING of God we ought not to think that the Godhead is like unto gold, or silver, or stone graven by art and device of man. The times of ignorance therefore God overlooked: but now He commandeth men that they should all everywhere repent, inasmuch as He hath appointed a day, in the which He will judge the world in righteousness by the man whom He hath ordained; whereof He hath given assurance unto all men, in that He hath raised Him from the dead.

In spite of the marvellous skill which the great Apostle showed in introducing his subject, and the great truths which he continued to give forth, directly he reached the special doctrines of the faith, and proclaimed the resurrection of Christ, they would hear him no further.

Thus we see how S. Paul, to use his own words, became all things to all men: to Jews he became as a Jew, that he might gain the Jews; to the Gentiles he became as a Gentile, that he might gain the Gentiles. He became all things to all men, that he might by all means save some.

But though S. Paul varied his method according to circumstances, the subject of his preaching was always the same. He preached unto them Jesus and the resurrection.

And whether this Gospel was preached by himself or by others, in sincerity or from contention, he could and did rejoice.

And though at Athens his labours did not seem crowned with success, yet he was casting the seed of life upon the waters, and would reap the harvest after many days.

CHAPTER VII.

S. PAUL'S GREAT CONTROVERSY.

S. PAUL was not only a great missionary; he was also a great controversialist. But there was this notable difference: he was a missionary by choice; he was a controversialist by necessity.

The special controversy in which the Apostle was engaged, was not of his own seeking; it was forced upon him by the exigencies of his own particular work as the Apostle of the Gentiles.

The subject of the controversy was this:—On what terms were Gentile believers to be received into the Church of Christ? were they to be received on a profession of faith by baptism, or must they also be circumcized, and become obedient to the law of Moses?

The best plan will be, I think, to enquire first of all, what was this Church of Christ into which the Gentiles were to be admitted.

To follow out this enquiry we must go back to the time when Christ began His earthly ministry.

For 400 years the Jewish people, the members of the Jewish Church, had been living, some in Judea, some scattered over the empire, without any voice from heaven. No prophet had been sent to them. Deliverers most noble and heroic they had had, but no prophet. Deprived of the keen criticism and higher teaching of the prophets, the religion of the chosen people had degenerated into an intricate ceremonialism, and a still more intricate system of casuistry and ecclesiastical hair-splitting. The living spirit had departed from their worship, and had left only a gorgeous ceremonial: the divine law was no longer a law of liberty, but was degraded into a mechanical system of rules and ceremonies.

Suddenly the whole nation was roused and startled by a prophet, who preaching in the wilderness, and baptizing with a baptism of repentance, announced that the Messiah's kingdom was at hand, and the Messiah Himself standing unknown among them. To prepare the way for the coming Christ was his special mission; to this end he summoned the whole nation to repentance, with the warning that they were not to rest in being children of Abraham, since God was able from the very stones of the desert to raise up children unto Abraham.

He proclaimed that the Kingdom of Heaven was at hand, that the Messiah had already come, whose coming would usher in the end of the age, the winding up of the old dispensation, and bring in the new age, the dispensation of the Spirit; that His winnowing fan was in His hand, and that with it He would thoroughly purge the harvest floor of the Jewish Church, and gather what was sound and good of the chosen nation into His kingdom, and leave the worthless residuum to be consumed in the fires of an impending judgement.

As John the Baptist had said, Christ was manifested.

He, too, and His disciples preached that the kingdom of heaven was at hand, and that the end of the age was near. In parable after parable He taught that His coming would be a time of separation and winnowing; that the approaching

consummation, the winding up of the Jewish age
was very near, when the wheat should be gathered
into the barn, and the tares burnt with unquenchable
fire ; that the draw-net of the gospel would be drawn
through the waters of the Jewish world, and the good
would be stored up, and the bad rejected ; that the
vineyard should be taken away from the wicked
husbandmen, and should be given to others.

This winnowing process began with the first
proclamation of the gospel of the kingdom : the
disciples were led on step by step to a clearer knowledge of Christ's person and His work: and His
enemies advanced step by step from suspicion to
hatred, and from hatred to final rejection and
judicial murder.

But the work of the Christ did not end with His
rejection and death. While on earth He had chosen
twelve men to be His witnesses and heralds. In
a few weeks after His death the Apostles were
preaching in the streets of Jerusalem, and in the
Temple courts, that Jesus was risen from the dead,
and was exalted to the right hand of God, and that
He would soon come again, in the clouds of heaven,
to judge the Church and a nation which had rejected
Him. They proclaimed, moreover, that the kingdom
which John the Baptist and their Master Himself
had said was at hand, was now set up.

But now let us ask what was the outward appearance of this kingdom? How did it show itself to
the world of the Jews?

To outward appearance it was a society of Jews,
admitted into fellowship by baptism, a society still
worshipping in the Temple, still observing the ceremonial law, undistinguishable in most respects from
other Jews. They had not ceased to be Jews. They
had not rejected their calling as Israelites. No, they

were more intensely Israelitish than before: the hope of Israel burnt more brightly than ever in their souls. They recognized the calling of Israel to be their calling, they were the seed of Abraham, in whom all the families of the earth were to be blessed; they were a chosen generation, a royal priesthood. If we could have asked them, they would have told us, that in believing in Christ they had forfeited no privilege, but had gained blessings unspeakable; they were more conscious than ever of the worth and dignity of the covenants and the promises of Israel.

And they were right. *They*, and not the unbelieving Jews, were the true Israel. *The Twelve Apostles*, and not the chief priests and scribes, were the true leaders of Israel. *They*, and not the unbelieving Jews, were the true children of Abraham. *They* were the wheat gathered into the barn of Christ's Church; the unbelieving Jews were the tares which were to be burnt, the rebellious citizens who would miserably perish in the fire which should burn up their city.

Christ had said that the Apostles would hardly have gone through the cities of Israel before His coming. But through their ministry during the forty years between the Ascension and the destruction of Jerusalem, all that was good and sound, and worth preserving in the Jewish nation, was gathered into the Church.

But we must go back to the early days of the Church in Jerusalem. As we have seen in former chapters, it increased with wonderful rapidity. By degrees little bodies of believers were gathered together in Judea and Galilee.

Then came the first persecution, of which the martyrdom of S. Stephen was the signal. The

Christians were scattered far and wide. Some wandered as far as Antioch. Here after a while the gospel was preached to the Gentiles, many of whom believed and were received by holy baptism into the One Flock under the One Shepherd.

But it was, you understand, to the already existent Church of Jewish believers that these Gentile converts were gathered. The question was—there was no help for it, it must come—on what terms they should be received into the communion of the Church.

Now the rooted belief of all, or nearly all the members of the mother Church at Jerusalem, was that if Gentiles were to be admitted into their fellowship (which you will remember involved eating together), they must be circumcised and observe the law.

From their point of view this was the obvious and natural thing. It would seem like treason and heresy to doubt it.

We hardly realize in what an imposing light the religion of their childhood appeared to the Jewish believers in Christ.

Could they forget that their great ancestor had been called and chosen by God Himself, that their great law-giver received the law from God amidst the lightnings and thunders of Sinai? Were not their sacred scriptures the utterances of Jewish prophets and of Israel's singers?

Was not the Lord Jesus the Son of David? was He not the King of Israel? Had He not declared that He had come not to destroy the law and the prophets but to fulfil them, that heaven and earth should pass before one jot or one title of the law should fail? Had not He observed their feasts, and worshipped continually in the Temple?

Was all this to go for nothing? were Gentiles to be admitted on such easy terms, not only to the special privileges of the followers of Christ, but to the hereditary honours and hopes of the covenant people? If the Gentiles indeed believed in a Jewish Messiah, must they not as a necessary preliminary be received by circumcision into the commonwealth of Israel?

The first element in the settlement of this question was the reception of the Gentile Cornelius.

You will remember how step by step, by God's providence, S. Peter was led to Joppa, and how he was divinely taught that he must no longer regard any man as common or unclean, but that in every nation, he that serveth God, and worketh righteousness, is accepted with Him. You will remember also how Cornelius, following the instruction of the angel who was sent to him, sent to Joppa for S. Peter.

Well, he came. While the Apostle was still speaking to Cornelius and his friends the Holy Ghost came down upon them in the same way, and accompanied by the same outward signs as those which had characterized His first descent at Pentecost.

None of the Jewish Christians who accompanied S. Peter could resist the Apostle's appeal—who can forbid the water, that these should not be baptized, which have received the Holy Ghost as well as we?

This, one would have thought, would have settled the question once for all; but it did not. It was probably regarded as an exceptional case; the angelic messenger, the thrice-repeated vision might all be held to mark it as an exception to the rule, not as an example of it.

Somewhere about this time certain men, emissaries from the extreme Judaistic party in the

Church at Jerusalem, came to Antioch, and threw the whole Christian community into alarm and doubt by saying, "Except ye be circumcised after the custom of Moses, ye cannot be saved."

To allay this strife it was arranged that Paul and Barnabas and others should lay the case before the apostles and elders, and brethren of the mother Church. This plan was carried out; the two Apostles of the Gentiles went up to Jerusalem, and after a private conference the general assembly of the Church was summoned. The assembly kept silence. That is, they did not actually interrupt, while Paul and Barnabas declared what things God had wrought among the Gentiles by their ministry.

They were followed by S. Peter, who gave his adhesion to the cause of Christian liberty, and protested against laying upon the Gentile believers a yoke which neither they nor their fathers had been able to bear.

Then S. James the Just, the President of the Church of Jerusalem and of the Council, "his long Nazarite locks flowing down over his white robe," rose to deliver his judgment.

It was a critical moment. Humanly speaking, the whole future of Christianity hung in the balance.

The judgment was decisive on the main point at issue. It was not necessary that Gentile converts should be circumcised, or should be obliged to observe the ceremonial law; though on their part the Gentiles were to abstain from such Gentile customs as would be abhorent to a Jew, and from the moral impurity which was only the too frequent accompaniment of idolatrous worship.

But even this deliberate judgment did not set the controversy at rest.

Again we find, some years after, these Judaizers, so far from being silenced, dogging S. Paul's steps from Church to Church.

They seem to have taught first of all that S. Paul was no real apostle, that he knew nothing of the tradition of the twelve, that his teaching, therefore, went for nothing: that even allowing that circumcision was not absolutely necessary to salvation, it was necessary to the attainment of the higher graces of the Christian life. Gentile converts might indeed be Christians without it, but not perfect Christians; baptism admitted them, as it were, only to the outer courts of the Temple, while circumcision admitted them to the inner sanctuary of Christian privilege.

It was to refute these errors that S. Paul, as we shall see presently, wrote the controversial series of his Epistles, the Second Epistle to the Corinthians, the Epistle to the Galatians, and the Epistle to the Romans.

It was not a question merely of one ordinance more or less, it was not a little matter affecting, as it were, the fringe of the Church's doctrine; but one which affected its very heart and life.

It really involved the question, "whether Christ was the Lord of man, or only the Lord of the Jews; whether He had redeemed and reconciled man, or only a certain class or men." In these Epistles S. Paul vindicated his apostolic authority; he proved that the law was only a temporary expedient, till the coming of Christ: and that by being circumcised, so far from advancing to perfection, they were brought back to the very bondage from which Christ had come to deliver them: he proved that both Jews and Gentiles had alike sinned, and must be alike saved by God's free grace.

He also laid down the proposition, which agreed with what Christ had himself taught, that Israel had not attained to righteousness; but that an elect remnant had attained to it in Christ, and the rest were blinded.

It is very noticeable that S. Paul, though so strongly opposing the Judaizers, never dissociates himself from the true Judaism, from the hope and calling of Israel. When in his Roman lodging he spoke to the Jews of the Roman synagogue, he declared that because of the hope of Israel, he was bound with that chain. In his view the religion of Christ had not divorced the past, but had absorbed it; the forms of Judaism must die, but its spirit lived in the gospel of Christ.

But it was not till Christ sent forth His armies to destroy those murderers, and to burn up their city; it was not till the end of the age was consummated, and Christ came in the clouds of heaven, and the elements of Judaism melted with fervent heat, and the heavens passed away with a great noise; it was not till the Temple and the Temple service were swept away, that the Christian Church stood out before the world as the future universal religion, the Catholic Church.

CHAPTER VIII.

S. PAUL BEFORE KINGS AND RULERS.

WHEN the Lord appeared to Ananias and bid him go and seek out Saul of Tarsus, He said of him—" He is a chosen vessel unto me to bear my name before the Gentiles, and kings, and the children of Israel."

We have already seen how he had borne his Master's name before the Gentiles, and before the children of Israel; let us now enquire how he bore that name before kings and rulers.

At the outset of his first missionary journey he stood before the Proconsul of Cyprus, and proclaimed his Master's Gospel with such effect, that this highly placed official of the Empire, Sergius Paulus, believed, even if he did not become a disciple of the Crucified.

He stood before the would-be Roman prætors at Philippi, who shamefully treated him, scourging him uncondemned in defiance of all law and justice, and casting him into an inner prison.

He stood ready to plead his cause at Corinth before Gallio the Proconsul of Achaia, when the indignant Roman drove the Apostle's accusers from his judgment-seat.

On his last visit to Jerusalem he had pleaded his cause before the Sanhedrim, of which in former years he had been a prominent member.

He pleaded before Felix the unjust judge. He spake before Felix and Drusilla, when he reasoned of righteousness, and continence, and the judgment to come. He pleaded before Festus for life and liberty; and proclaimed the faith of Christ before Festus, Agrippa, and Bernice. And finally, after an acquittal before some unknown judge at Rome, he again stood for the last time before an earthly tribunal, and pleaded his cause, it may be in the hated presence of Nero himself; and then passed from the blood-stained tribunal of Rome to the judgment-seat of Christ, from the presence of the Anti-Christ to the glorious presence of Christ his Lord.

S. Paul's last journey to Jerusalem was undertaken with full knowledge of the dangers that awaited him. To the presbyters of the Church of Ephesus, whom he had summoned to meet him at Miletus, he said,

Acts xx. 22 : And now, behold, I go bound in the Spirit unto Jerusalem, not knowing the things that shall befall me there : save that the Holy Ghost testifieth unto me in every city, saying that bonds and afflictions abide me. But I hold not my life of any account as dear unto myself, so that I may accomplish my course, and the ministry which I received from the Lord Jesus, to testify the gospel of the grace of God.

And again, when they arrived at Cæsarea, S. Luke tells us that,

Acts xxi. 10 : There came down from Judea a certain prophet named Agabus. And coming to us and taking Paul's girdle, he bound his own feet and hands, and said, Thus saith the Holy Ghost, So shall the Jews at Jerusalem bind the man that owneth this girdle, and shall deliver him into the hands of the Gentiles. And when we heard these things, both we and they of that place besought him not to go up to Jerusalem. Then Paul answered, What do ye, weeping and breaking my heart? for I am ready not to be bound only, but also to die at Jerusalem for the name of the Lord Jesus. And when he would not be persuaded, we ceased, saying, The will of the Lord be done.

S. Paul and his companions were well received by the elders and brethren of the mother Church. At their suggestion S. Paul adopted a plan to show publicly that he himself was still a loyal son of Israel. "The plan they recommended was, that S. Paul should take charge of four Jewish Christians, who had taken temporarily the vow of a Nazarite, accompany them to the Temple, and pay for them the necessary expenses attending the termination of their vow." It must have seemed at first as if the warnings of Agabus would be falsified: but the event turned out as the indications of the Holy Spirit had led him to expect. His old enemies the Jews from Asia, who had persecuted him from city to city, caught sight of him, and with piercing yells for help rushed at him, and dragged him out of the Temple. Every moment the crowd increased, yelling and shrieking and casting dust into the air, after the fashion of an oriental mob. But soon the heavy tread of the ever watchful Roman legionaries was heard, as they rushed down the steep causeway which led down from their barracks in the fortress of Antonia to the Temple court, and forced their way through the crowd to the spot where S. Paul was like to be struck down by the repeated blows that were aimed at him. Once in the hands of a Roman officer he was safe, safe at least from lawless violence, for his Roman citizenship secured him from outrage. Then battered, bleeding as he was, with torn clothes, to all appearance a care-worn, feeble-bodied Jew, with the Chief Captain's sanction he stood upon the stairs and addressed the raging multitude. They heard' him with unexpected patience, till he spoke of his mission to the Gentiles, which Christ had given him.

The mention of the Gentiles was enough, they knew what was coming, and they would not hear it. They rent the air with their cries, Away with him, away with him, it is not fit that he should live.

The next day a meeting of the Sanhedrim was held, and Paul was brought down under a guard of soldiers, and set before the council.

It must have been with strange feelings that S. Paul stood before this council, of which sixteen years before he had been a prominent member. His eye passed along the familiar benches, and scanned their occupants, recognizing one and another, and then he began,—" Brethren, I have lived before God in all good conscience until this day." This bold assertion of innocence, and the manly, uncringing form of his address, was too much for the high priest Ananias, who presided; he ordered one of the officers of the court to smite this blaspheming apostate on the mouth.

S. Paul was naturally a hot-tempered man, and such an insult, such a gross contempt for the dignity of the law, was more than he could bear with patience. The Apostle's sight was defective, but he saw opposite to him the president in his raised chair, and in his white robes; the blood rose to his face, and the words rushed to his lips—" God shall smite thee, thou whited wall: and sittest thou to judge me according to the law, and commandest me to be smitten contrary to the law?" If the words were strong, the provocation was great. This Ananias was one of the worst, if not the very worst of the worldly dissolute Sadducees, who disgraced the Jewish priesthood. "The Talmud describes him as a rapacious tyrant who reduced the inferior priests almost to starvation by defrauding them of the tithes, to glut his insatiable avarice." Though we cannot blame the Apostle for being indignant, and for thus expressing his indignation, we cannot but contrast with it the divine meekness of our Saviour, who, when he was smitten in the same way, only said, "If (in my public teaching) I have spoken evil, come forward and bear witness of the evil; but if I have spoken well, why smitest thou me?"

The high priest and the council were utterly unscrupulous men, and they did not hesitate to accept an offer made to them by forty of the cut-throats, the professional murderers that abounded in those evil days, to murder the man, whose eloquence they feared, and whose arguments they could not refute.

Happily this plot was discovered, and S. Paul was sent under the guard of a small army to Cæsarea. What an idea it gives us of the insecurity of life in Palestine, that Claudius Lysias thought it necessary to send S. Paul under an escort of nearly 500 men!

Under this escort S. Paul was brought to Cæsarea, which he had left under such different circumstances little more than a week before. After an interval of five days S. Paul was brought before Felix, on a charge, brought against him by the high priest, and a deputation from the council, of treason, heresy, and sacrilege. Felix had been Procurator of Palestine for six years. He might be described in the words of our Lord's parable, as an unjust judge, who feared not God, nor regarded man. There was hardly a redeeming point in his character: he was greedy, cruel, and treacherous, "steeped with the blood of private murder and public massacre." His private life was infamous. The Roman historian Tacitus wrote of him, that "with every sort of cruelty and lust, he exercised the power of a king in the spirit of a slave."

Felix having heard the accusation and the Apostle's defence, deferred giving a decisive judgment, in the hope that the Christian community would be willing to pay a heavy bribe to insure the deliverance of their great leader; and the Apostle accordingly remained under arrest.

Before this infamous Roman, and his high-born but dissolute wife Drusilla, who was a Jewish princess, S. Paul had the opportunity of speaking of the faith in Christ.

Acts xxiv. 24: After certain days, Felix came with Drusilla, his wife, which was a Jewess, and sent for Paul, and heard him concerning the faith in Christ Jesus. And as he reasoned of righteousness and temperance, and the judgment to come, Felix was terrified, and answered, Go thy way for this time; and when I have a convenient season, I will call thee unto me.

The conscious-stricken governor qualed before his prisoner, the unjust judge trembled as he heard of the judgment to come. He would hear no more, another time he would ask for the continuation of his Prisoner's discourse. But though the convenient season came again and again—for Felix often sent for S. Paul and talked with him—the desire to hear never came. And thus as no money was forthcoming from his friends, it came about that S. Paul remained for two years a prisoner at Cæsarea: at the end of which time Felix was succeeded by Porcius Festus.

Festus was a governor of a different stamp. As soon as he came into his province he went up to Jerusalem, and there the chief priests petitioned as a favour, that he would send Paul to Jerusalem, on the plausible ground that the charges against him being religious, it would be more suitable for him to be tried there. To this, however, Festus would not consent. He would willingly hold his court at Jerusalem, but not without the free consent of the accused. When the governor put the question to S. Paul, the Apostle saw clearly that if he were sent to Jerusalem, he would never reach it alive: and he refused, saying that he was there standing before Cæsar's judgment-seat, and rather than allow himself to be given up into the hands of his enemies, he would claim the privilege which his Roman citizenship secured to him of appealing to the supreme court of the Emperor himself, and so he concluded with the words which must have sent a thrill through the Court, *I appeal unto Cæsar.*

This appeal settled the question. Festus had only one duty, and that was to keep this Roman citizen in safety and to send him to Rome as soon as opportunity served.

A few days after S. Paul's appeal, Agrippa the titular king of Chalcis, whom the Roman authorities allowed to exercise some authority in ecclesiastical matters in Jerusalem, came with his sister Bernice, to pay his respects to Festus, on his arrival in the Province. After they had been with him many days, it occurred to Festus, knowing that Agrippa was versed in Jewish questions, that it would be a good plan to get him to give an informal opinion about the charges which the Jews brought against Paul. Accordingly Festus told him what he knew about his prisoner, and confessed his own perplexity in dealing with a case which involved matters about which he knew nothing, especially as part of the dispute was about "one Jesus, who was dead, whom Paul affirmed to be alive."

Agrippa would have consented to anything which the Procurator might suggest; so he readily fell in with what he saw Festus was leading up to.

Agrippa, though he had little or no actual power as king, was not at all averse from displaying the outward tokens of sovereignty, and at the same time publicly showing on what good terms he was with the new Procurator. Agrippa came of a bad family; but he does not appear to have been a specially bad man, though he was probably a creedless voluptuary. Agrippa was not a persecutor himself, but he "came of a line of persecutors; his great-grandfather doomed the infant Christ, his grandfather Antipas murdered John the Baptist, his father killed S. James, and intended to kill Peter also."

On the next day Agrippa and Bernice came with great pomp. The king with all the trappings of royalty, the Jewish queen blazing, no doubt, with gold and jewels, entered the hall where a distinguished company were collected. Festus took his seat in his chair of state, with his lictors and guards on either side.

When all was ready Paul was brought in, with one arm chained to a soldier who stood beside him. Festus in a few words opened the proceedings, and then called upon Paul to make his defence.

Acts xxvi. 1: Then Paul stretched forth his hand and made his defence: I think myself happy, King Agrippa, that I am to make my defence before thee this day, . . . especially because thou art expert in all customs and questions which are among the Jews; wherefore I beseech thee to hear me patiently.

After a short description of his bringing up, he went on to say:—

Acts xxvi. 6: Now I stand here to be judged for the hope of the promise made of God unto our fathers; .... And concerning this hope I am accused by the Jews, O king.

Then follows a description of his persecution of the believers in Christ, and of his wonderful conversion, after which he continues:—

Acts xxvi. 19: Wherefore, O King Agrippa, I was not disobedient unto the heavenly vision: but declared both to them of . . . . Jerusalem, and also to the Gentiles, that they should repent and turn to God, doing works worthy of repentance. . . . . Having therefore obtained the help that is from God, I stand unto this day testifying both to small and great, saying nothing but what the prophets and Moses did say should come, how that the Christ must suffer, and how that he first by the resurrection of the dead should proclaim light both to the people and to the Gentiles. . . . . King Agrippa, believest thou the prophets? I know that thou believest.

But Agrippa had no idea of being betrayed into a confession of faith which would be scorned by that brilliant assembly; he only met S. Paul's moving appeal with a sneer.

Acts xxvi. 28: And Agrippa said unto Paul, With but little persuasion thou wouldest fain make me a Christian. R. V.

Agrippa, the polished man of the world; Agrippa, with his royal crown and mantle; Agrippa to turn Christian! It was something too absurd.

But though Agrippa might put off S. Paul's appeal with a jest, the Apostle himself was serious; with lofty courtesy, refusing to take the King's answer as other than serious, he answered in words in which Christian love are mingled with princely courtesy:—

Acts xxvi. 29: And Paul said, I would to God, that whether with little or with much, not thou only, but also all that hear me this day, might become such as I am, except these bonds.

With these noble words the conference came to an end. If it had lain with Festus and Agrippa, Paul would have been at once acquitted; but they had no power, the irrevocable step had been taken, he had appealed to Cæsar and to Cæsar he must go.

F

CHAPTER IX.

THE VOYAGE TO ROME, AND THE FIRST IMPRISONMENT.

S T. PAUL'S noble defence before Festus and Agrippa, though it sounded like mere raving to the unimpressive Roman, and failed to pierce the triple armour of selfish indifference with which the Jewish prince was armed, was not thrown away; it made for him many powerful friends, if it did nothing more.

Julius, the centurion of the Augustan Cohort, to whose charge S. Paul was committed, was probably one of the distinguished audience before whom the Apostle had pleaded his Master's cause, and his own. At any rate, nothing could exceed the courtesy with which the great Apostle was treated by this Roman officer.

It was not an easy matter to find a ship bound for Italy. It was far on towards the end of June when Festus arrived in the Province, and it was now probably late in August, and the time was quickly approaching when the sea would be closed to the navigation of those days. Every day the weather became more uncertain. So as there was no vessel at Cæsarea, bound for Italy, and there was no time to lose, the centurion took passage for his prisoners in a ship of Adramyttium which was about to sail for the coast of Asia.

S. Paul's friends, Luke and Aristarchus, took their passage in the same ship, that they might be with their leader, a circumstance for which we also have reason to be thankful, or otherwise we might have known nothing of this eventful voyage. The sacred historian thus begins his account :—

Acts xxvii. 1 : And when it was determined that we should sail for Italy, they delivered Paul and certain other prisoners to a centurion named Julius, of the Augustan band. And embarking in a ship of Adramyttium, which was about to sail to the places on the coast of Asia, we put to sea, Aristarchus, a Macedonian of Thessalonica, being with us. And the next day we touched at Sidon : and Julius treated Paul kindly, and gave him leave to go unto his friends and refresh himself. And putting to sea from thence we sailed under the lee of Cyprus, because the winds were contrary. And when we had sailed across the sea which is off Cilicia and Pamphylia, we came to Myra, a city of Lycia. And there the centurion found a ship of Alexandria sailing for Italy ; and he put us therein.

It must have been a great refreshment to S. Paul to be allowed to spend even a few hours with his friends and fellow-believers at Sidon : and they too, no doubt, would gladly embrace the opportunity of providing him with necessaries for his voyage.

At Myra, as we have just read, S. Paul and his companions, and the other prisoners, were transferred to a large ship of Alexandria bound for Italy, which had been driven out of its course ; one of the numerous vessels engaged in carrying wheat from the valley of the Nile to Rome, and whose arrival at Ostia was an event of such deep interest to the Roman people, who depended upon these ships for their supplies.

The voyage began badly, the wind was still contrary, and it took them "many days" to reach Cnidus. a distance of only 120 miles. From this

Crete, but the direction of the wind made this impossible. The only course open to them was to make for Cape Salmone and to sail under lee of the island. Accordingly they crept along the coast to a little harbour, known as the Fair Havens. There they had to stop; for as long as the wind continued to blow from the N.W. it was useless to think of continuing the voyage beyond Cape Matala, as they would be driven ashore, as you will see if you look at the map.

Then came the question whether to remain at Fair Havens for the winter, or seize the first opportunity of a favourable wind, to round Cape Matala, and to reach Phœnice, a far better harbour and winter quarters, only 34 miles beyond it; the only harbour, indeed, in the whole of the island which was safe in all weathers. The master and owner of the ship were both for this latter course, and though S. Paul gave his voice against it, and warned them of the disasters that they would bring upon themselves by adopting it, the centurion naturally yielded to professional advice.

Before long the wind fell, and a gentle breeze sprang up from the South. This was exactly what they wanted, it was only a few hours run to Phœnice. They seem to have started under full sail, and had not even thought it necessary to get their boat aboard.

They had not long passed Cape Matala, when a terrible gale from E.N.E. came upon them without a moment's warning. The suddenness of the hurricane did not leave the sailors one moment to furl the great mainsail, so under full sail the heavily laden ship plunged along, till she neared the island of Clauda, or Cauda.

In modern sailing vessels the sails are distributed over the whole length of the ship, and thus the strain is divided; but in these old-world ships, there was one large sail stretched from an enormous mainyard, and the strain was consequently concentrated in the middle of the ship. It is probable, then, that already the vessel had sprung a leak.

The captain took advantage of the comparative lull which they experienced as they passed the little island of Clauda, first of all in getting the boat, now probably half filled with water, on board, which was only done with great difficulty; and secondly, to prevent the leak from increasing, and this they did by passing thick cables round and round the middle of the ship, where the strain was the greatest.

But another and that the greatest danger still remained. Directly they passed out of the comparative shelter of Clauda, the furious gale would catch them, and bear them along helplessly to the "Goodwin sands of the Mediterranean," the great Syrtis which you will see marked upon the map.

There was only one possible way of escape. To do what the authorized version of our Bibles seems to say they did, "to strike sail, and so be driven," would be to allow themselves to drift into the jaws of destruction. The revised version gives it, "they lowered the gear, and so were driven." This manœuvre was probably what sailors call " lying to."

That is, in common language, they so steered as to bring the ship's head round to the wind, and at the same time lowered the mainyard, leaving only a portion of the mainsail to catch the wind, sufficient to steady the vessel, and prevent her falling into the trough of the sea.

A ship, however, in such circumstances does not drift in the direction in which she appears to sail, but falls away to leeward.

In this case the ship would appear to be sailing

somewhere near N., but in reality would be drifting W. by N.

Now it is very singular, and shows the minute accuracy of S. Luke's account, that it has been calculated, that a ship drifting in this direction under such circumstances would move at the rate of about 36 miles in the 24 hours, and at this rate, and in this direction, would reach Malta in just about 13 days, which is the time given by S. Luke.

With these explanations we shall read with greater understanding and greater interest the narrative itself.

Acts xxvii. 13: And when the south wind blew softly, supposing that they had obtained their purpose, they weighed anchor and sailed along Crete close in shore. But after no long time there beat down from it a tempestuous wind, which is called Euraquilo: and when the ship was caught and could not face the wind, we gave way to it, and were driven. And running under the lee of a small island called Cauda, we were able with difficulty to secure the boat: and when they had hoisted it up, they used helps, undergirding the ship; and fearing lest they should be cast upon the Syrtis, they lowered the gear and so were driven.

All night the storm raged. In spite of the undergirding, the vessel still leaked. The next day they had to throw out everything that could be spared to lighten the ship. On the third day they were still in such imminent danger that it was necessary to take a still more decisive step. In a modern vessel this would be to cut down the masts: in an ancient vessel what would have to be done would be to heave overboard the huge mainyard. This they did, though it took the whole available force of the crew and passengers to do it.

This would relieve the vessel, though she would

still be swept from stem to stern by the dashing spray.

The passengers and crew seem to have given themselves up for lost. We can fancy them, 276 in number, huddled together on the deck, clinging to the bulwarks or any available spot. The sky was dark above them, neither sun nor stars appeared for many days. The fires would be put out, and there could be no food cooked. In this desperate juncture there was one who remained unmoved and calm. S. Paul stood up and spoke a few cheering words.

Acts xxvii. 22: I exhort you to be of good cheer: for there shall be no loss of life among you, but only of the ship. For there stood by me this night an angel of the God whose I am, and whom also I serve, saying, Fear not, Paul; thou must stand before Cæsar: and lo, God hath granted thee all them that sail with thee. Wherefore, sirs, be of good cheer: for I believe God, that it shall be even so as it hath been spoken unto me. Howbeit we must be cast upon a certain island.

After drifting a whole fortnight tossed up and down on the sea of Adria, that is, the sea lying between Greece, Italy, and Africa, about midnight the quick ears of the sailors caught the dreaded sound of distant breakers, and saw perhaps the white glimmer of the surf in the far distance. They sounded and found the depth of the water 20 fathoms: they sounded again, and found it 15 fathoms. There was no room for doubt, they were drifting fast upon the rocks. There was only one thing left to be done, to drop anchor. Accordingly they dropped four anchors out of the stern, through the holes through which the rudders were ordinarily worked. If they had anchored in the usual way by the prow, the ship would have swung round, and perhaps dashed against a reef.

When the day broke an attempt was made by the sailors to save themselves in the boat. They began to lower the boat under pretence of letting down anchors from the bows. If they had succeeded in their selfish attempt, it would be impossible for the soldiers and passengers to work the ship.

The attempt was frustrated by S. Paul, who said to the centurion and the soldiers, "Except these abide in the ship, ye cannot be saved." You will notice that he says, "ye," not "we." Of his own safety he was secure; theirs was conditional on their doing their duty. Such was the influence that the Apostle had acquired that they at once drew their swords and cut the ropes, and the boat fell off into the sea.

Then again S. Paul strove to encourage his despairing fellow voyagers.

Acts xxvii. 33 : And while the day was coming on, Paul besought them all to take some food, saying, This day is the fourteenth day that ye wait and continue fasting, having taken nothing. Wherefore I beseech you to take some food : for this is for your safety: for there shall not a hair perish from the head of any of you. And when he had said this, and had taken bread, he gave thanks to God in the presence of all : and he brake it and began to eat.

Being thus fortified by food, and encouraged by the cheerful words and demeanour of S. Paul, they set to work to take what steps they could for their safety. The ship you remember was laden with wheat, and in their long drifting the wheat, which was packed loose, would have got shifted over to the left side of the vessel, and made it difficult to steer. So they opened the hatchways and began to cast the wheat into the sea. The ship having righted, they cast off the anchors, and let them drop into the sea, let down the rudders, which were large spade-like paddles on each side of the stern, hoisted the foresail [not the mainsail as in the A.V.], and steered straight for the beach.

Apparently they did not succeed in reaching the creek for which they steered, but happening on a place where two seas met, they ran the ship aground, and the foreship struck and remained immoveable, but the stern began to break up by the violence of the waves.

When it was apparent that the land was near, and that there was every reason to suppose that some of the prisoners might make their escape, the soldiers, habitually indifferent to human life, urged the centurion to give orders for them to be killed. To understand this cruel counsel of the soldiers, we must remember that they were responsible with their own lives for the safe custody of their prisoners. However the centurion, anxious to save Paul, kept them from their purpose, and gave orders that those who could swim should first cast themselves overboard, and get first to the land, and the rest, some on planks, and some on other things from the ship. "And so it came to pass"—S. Luke gratefully recounts—"that they all escaped safe to land."

The shipwrecked crew were kindly received by the inhabitants of Malta, and after a three months' stay in the island, they set sail in the good ship "The Twin Brothers," which had wintered in the island, and without further adventure disembarked at Puteoli. After a week's rest they continued their journey towards Rome, which was 140 miles distant. When they arrived at the market of Appius they were met by a party of Roman Christians, who had come to greet the Apostle; and ten miles further on, at the Three Taverns, another band of the brethren met them, "whom, when Paul saw, he thanked God, and took courage."

In company with these welcome visitors they journeyed on towards the great city along the Appian Way, with its marble tombs and statues lining it on either side; its rows of villas and ever-thickening crowds, till they arrived at the Prætorian barracks. Here the Centurion's charge concluded, when he had formally handed over his prisoners to the Captain of the Guard.

It was no doubt owing to his favourable representations, as well as to the favourable despatch from Festus, that the Apostle was allowed as much liberty as the Roman law permitted.

For thus the sacred historian concludes his narrative:—

Acts xxviii. 16-30: And when we entered into Rome, Paul was suffered to abide by himself with the soldier that guarded him. . . . . . . And he abode two whole years in his own hired dwelling, and received all that went in unto him, preaching the kingdom of God, and teaching the things concerning the Lord Jesus Christ with all boldness, none forbidding him.

CHAPTER X.

S. PAUL'S SECOND IMPRISONMENT AND MARTYRDOM.

THE abrupt close of the Acts of the Apostles leaves us without any further direct information as to the remainder of the Apostle's life.

S. Luke enables us to follow every incident in this last journey to Rome. Then suddenly the darkness closes in upon us. We see dimly the great Apostle, dwelling in his own hired lodging, chained first to one soldier, then to another, as they relieved guard. We see him receiving visitors, deputations from the Roman synagogues, messengers from distant Churches.

It was a period of rest rather than of hardship. He had his friends about him: Luke, the beloved physician, who remained with him to the last; Aristarchus, who had shared the perils of the voyage, and whose attendance was now so constant that S. Paul describes him as his fellow-prisoner; and Timothy his special friend, his own child in the faith.

We see also in this dim light, Tychicus bringing to the imprisoned Apostle news from Ephesus; we see Epaphroditus the envoy, perhaps the Chief Pastor of the Church at Philippi, bringing substantial aid, as well as the assurance of sympathy, from his beloved Philippians; we see Epaphras, who has come to consult his spiritual commander-in-chief about the heresies which were beginning to show themselves in the Churches of Colossæ, Laodicea, and Hierapolis. From Colossæ also we see a strange visitor to S. Paul, a runaway slave named Onesimus, whom S. Paul sends back to his master Philemon, bearing the most touching and graceful letter on his behalf.

The two years of enforced quiet were thus by no means years of inactivity. In fact S. Paul did more for the cause of Christ and His Church in his Roman lodging, than if he had been carrying on his labours in Ephesus or Corinth, or had been planting the Standard of the Cross in yet unvisited countries.

For besides the watchful guidance with which he directed the affairs of the Gentile Churches, besides spreading a knowledge of the truth through the Pretorian guard, to hundreds of whom he was chained in turn for hours together; we owe to this period the group of letters, which, as we shall see when we come to them, were written at this time, letters which have been the delight and comfort of the Church through eighteen centuries, and the divine treasures of which are not exhausted yet. If S. Paul had been at liberty he would doubtless have visited the Churches of Philippi, Ephesus, and Colossæ, instead of writing letters to them. They might have gained, but we should have lost unspeakably.

From allusions scattered through the Epistles to Timothy and Titus, it would appear that the two years' confinement of which S. Luke speaks, was not ended by the condemnation and martyrdom of the

SECOND IMPRISONMENT AND MARTYRDOM. 77

Apostle; but that he was set at liberty, and continued his apostolical labours till he was again taken into custody and condemned to death.

From the letters which S. Paul wrote in his first imprisonment, it is clear that he himself expected to be released.

In the Epistle to the Philippians he says:—

Phil. ii. 19–24: I hope . . . to send Timothy shortly unto you . . . . so soon as I shall see how it will go with me; but I trust in the Lord that I myself also shall come shortly.

Writing much about the same time to Philemon at Colossæ, he says:—

Philem. 22: But withal prepare me also a lodging; for I hope that through your prayers I shall be granted unto you.

Of course, it is conceivable that S. Paul was mistaken, and that from this imprisonment he was only released by death.

But in this case we must suppose that the Pastoral Epistles, as we call them, that is, the Epistles to Timothy and Titus, if they were written by S. Paul, must refer to some period before his apprehension at Jerusalem and his voyage to Rome.

But " it is now admitted by nearly all those who are competent to decide on such a question, first, that the historical facts mentioned in the Epistles to Timothy and Titus cannot be placed in any portion of S. Paul's life before or during his first imprisonment in Rome; and, secondly, that the style in which these Epistles are written, and the condition of the Church described therein, forbids the supposition of such a date. Consequently we must allow that after S. Paul's first imprisonment he was travelling at liberty in Ephesus, Crete, Macedonia, Miletus, and Nicopolis, and that he was afterwards a second time in prison in Rome."

This is confirmed by Eusebius, the historian of the Church, who says: "After defending himself successfully, it is currently reported that the Apostle again went forth to proclaim the Gospel, and afterwards came to Rome a second time, and was martyred under Nero."

In fact, the all but unanimous testimony of the early Church points in this direction.

Several reasons conduce to the belief that S. Paul's martyrdom occurred in the last year of Nero's reign. If this be so, there remains a period of five years between A.D. 63, the end of the first imprisonment, and A.D. 68, the year of Nero's death.

But we must now go back to the point at which the history of the Acts leaves us.

The course of Roman law was not much more speedy than that of more recent times. It might be a long time before S. Paul's appeal would be heard; witnesses would have to be brought both for the prosecution and for the defence; and all this would take time.

At last the eventful day arrived. Nero heard appeals in the imperial palace. "Here at one end of a splendid hall, lined with precious marbles, sat the Emperor and his assessors, twenty in number, and men of the highest rank."

The charges brought against him were those of heresy and sacrilege against one of the recognized religions of the Empire; and, what was of far more practical importance, of conspiring to disturb the public peace. We can easily understand that the charge which was brought against him at Philippi might be repeated at Rome, that he had proclaimed "another king, one Jesus."

SECOND IMPRISONMENT AND MARTYRDOM. 79

When both parties had been heard, and the witnesses examined and cross-examined, the judgment of the court was given. "Each of the assessors gave his opinion in writing; the Emperor, having read the opinions, gave sentence as it pleased him quite irrespective of the verdict of the assessors." We may suppose that the evidence against S. Paul broke down; at any rate, the trial resulted in his acquittal.

Immediately on his liberation it may be reasonably supposed that he carried out his intention of travelling eastward through Macedonia to visit Colossæ and other Churches of Asia Minor. The great Egnatian road by which he would travel would lead him through Philippi, where he would enjoy the society of his ever-faithful friends and disciples of that Church. But he would probably hasten on to Ephesus, and from thence to the Churches of the Valley of the Lycus. We may imagine him as the guest of Philemon, for we may be sure that this good man would provide for the Apostle no other lodging than his own house. Here he would renew his acquaintance with Onesimus, of which we shall hear when we come to read the Epistle to Philemon.

If S. Paul ever fulfilled his intention of visiting Spain, we must suppose that visit to have taken place somewhere about this time.

If this be so, S. Paul seems to have returned to Ephesus in company with Timothy.

From Ephesus S. Paul seems to have gone to Macedonia, leaving Timothy in charge of the Church at Ephesus (1 Tim. i. 3). Possibly finding that his presence would be required there longer than he expected, and feeling that Timothy would require more explicit instructions as well as more ample credentials, he wrote the First Epistle to Timothy.

His mission over in Macedonia, he would probably return to Ephesus. From Ephesus he would seem to have made a voyage to Crete, accompanied by Titus. Leaving Titus to organize the Cretan Churches, S. Paul returned to Ephesus, where he remained long enough to write the Epistle to Titus.

This last letter gives some indication of the Apostle's movements.

Titus was desired, after his work in Crete was finished, to join the Apostle at Nicopolis.

From an incidental notice in the Second Epistle to Timothy (ch. iv. 20), it appears that the route he pursued was from Ephesus to Miletus, where Trophimus was taken ill, and had to be left; thence to Corinth, where he left Erastus; and thence to Nicopolis, where he intended to spend the winter.

It is uncertain whether S. Paul was apprehended at Nicopolis, or whether, as it has been conjectured, he paid another visit to Thessalonica and Philippi, and so to Troas, perhaps on his way to Ephesus, and that at Troas he was seized. In almost the last words that he wrote, he referred to a visit to Troas: "The cloke that I left at Troas with Carpus, bring with thee; and the books, especially the parchments."

But either at Nicopolis, or Troas, or elsewhere, S. Paul was again brought before the authorities.

Times had greatly changed; S. Paul no longer found the Roman authorities ready to protect him. In the interval a great part of Rome had been burnt down, and the crime had been laid to the charge of the Christians.

If S. Paul were apprehended, as would be likely, on the charge of having with others conspired to destroy the city, he would be sent to Rome, as otherwise he would have been dealt with by the local authorities.

On this last sad journey he had but few friends to cheer him, but the faithful Luke, at any rate, was with him. No Christian brethren came to meet him as he neared Rome. He was a marked man, and was treated as a malefactor (2 Tim. ii. 9). His imprisonment was far more severe than before. He was no longer permitted to live in his own hired lodging. It was difficult and dangerous to visit him in prison (2 Tim. i. 16): so perilous to show any sympathy with him, that no one ventured to stand by his side in his last trial (2 Tim. iv. 16).

It would certainly seem that he was brought before the Emperor, in person, from his saying, that he was delivered "out of the mouth of the lion." Though S. Clement of Rome says that "he suffered martyrdom under the prefects."

S. Paul alludes to his trial in his Second Epistle to Timothy. We may imagine a lofty spacious basilica, consisting of a nave and two aisles divided by rows of pillars. At the far end of the nave was a raised platform called the tribunal, in the centre of which was placed the ivory chair of the presiding magistrate, with other chairs for the assessors, and seats for other distinguished persons along its sides. Fronting the presiding magistrate stood the prisoner, with his accusers and advocates. The public were admitted into the remainder of the aisles and nave. There were also galleries along the whole length of the aisles, on one side for men and on the other for women.—(*Conybeare and Howson.*)

Before such a tribunal and such an audience S. Paul was called upon to make his defence, to plead his own and his Master's cause. He stood friendless and alone.

2 *Tim.* iv. 16 : At my first defence no one took my part, but all forsook me: may it not be laid to their account. But the Lord stood by me and strengthened me; that through me the message might be fully proclaimed, and that all the Gentiles might hear: and I was delivered out of the mouth of the lion.

He was not acquitted, but he was not condemned. The verdict probably amounted to "Not proven." He was thus delivered from the immediate peril, and saved from an ignominious and painful death, which might have been his fate if convicted on the charge of incendiarism.

He was remanded to prison, there to wait till his cause should be brought on again. It was then that he wrote his Second Epistle to Timothy, which is so doubly precious as telling us how he thought and felt while he was waiting for his crown.

2 *Tim.* iv. 7: I am already being offered, and the time of my departure is come. I have fought the good fight, I have finished the course, I have kept the faith : henceforth there is laid up for me the crown of righteousness, which the Lord, the righteous Judge, shall give to me at that day, and not only to me, but also to all them that have loved His appearing.

S. Luke, the ever-faithful friend, was with him, and remained with him to the last, but none of his other friends. Demas had forsaken him. Crescens had been sent, we may conclude, on a mission to Galatia, Titus on another mission to Dalmatia. There was one friend, however, whom the Apostle had a yearning desire to see; this was Timothy, his child in the faith. To him, therefore, he writes an urgent appeal to come to him:—

2 *Tim.* iv. 10, 21: Do thy diligence to come shortly unto me. Do thy diligence to come before winter.

SECOND IMPRISONMENT AND MARTYRDOM. 83

We cannot tell for certain whether Timothy reached Rome in time to see his beloved father in the faith before he suffered. It might seem from an allusion in the Epistle to the Hebrews that he did come, and shared his master's imprisonment, but was afterwards released. The writer of that Epistle announces to the Hebrew Christians that their brother Timothy had been set at liberty (Heb. xiii. 23).

At last the fatal day came. Again S. Paul stood before the tribunal of the Emperor. This time he was brought in guilty, and sentence was pronounced against him.

His Roman citizenship saved him from torture and an ignominious death. He was led out to execution beyond the city walls, on the road to Ostia; and there the sword of the executioner closed the earthly life of one of the greatest and noblest of men.

"So passed his strong heroic soul away."

"His weeping friends took up his corpse, and carried it for burial to those subterranean labyrinths in which the persecuted Church found a refuge for its living members, and sepulchres for its dead." Near the spot where S. Paul was martyred, on the road to Ostia, outside the walls of Rome, now stands a noble Basilica, on the site of one built by the Emperor Constantine, and dedicated to his memory.

But the great Apostle needs no monument to recount his worth, or to describe his work. The constitution of the Catholic Church, the theology of the Catholic faith, this is the monument of S. Paul!

Who would not wish to visit the place where this great Apostle won the martyr's crown?

But there is one thing which we can do better than

making offerings at his tomb, and that is to imitate his life, to follow at however great a distance his noble devotion, his glorious hopefulness, his dauntless courage, his sublime endurance ; for across the gulf of eighteen centuries comes to us an echo of the voice of the great Apostle, the voice of his dying message to us:—

"Be ye imitators of me, even as I was of Christ."

CHAPTER XI.

THE EPISTLES OF S. PAUL TO THE THESSALONIANS.

THE subject for our readings, you remember, was not only the life of S. Paul, but also his letters.

In this chapter and in the remaining portion of the book I propose to choose out for our consideration the most characteristic and distinctive portions of each Epistle, such portions as contain the main drift of the Apostle's argument. I hope by this means, when you have grasped the main issue of the Apostle's argument in each Epistle, you will be able, with more profit and greater intelligence, to read the Epistles as a whole.

We have now the great advantage of being able to read S. Paul's Epistles in the Revised Version, which more than any other portions of the New Testament have gained in force and clearness by the new translation.

Now of all the Epistles which S. Paul wrote, or at least of all which have come down to us, the two Epistles to the Thessalonians are the earliest. Indeed they are probably the oldest books of the New Testament. Before, however, we begin to consider the Epistle, it will be necessary to recall the circumstances of S. Paul's visit to Thessalonica, and also the circumstances under which this Epistle was written.

It was on S. Paul's second missionary journey that

he first visited Thessalonica. He was accompanied by Silas (a shortened form of Silvanus) and Timothy, who joined them at Lystra. Thessalonica was one of the principal cities in Macedonia, and was a busy thriving town when S. Paul visited it. It is a busy thriving town now, under its modern name of Saloniki, as thriving as any town can be under Turkish misrule.

The sister of Alexander the Great was named Thessalonica; and this Macedonian city was called after her.

There was a large colony of Jews in Thessalonica, as there was sure to be in a city of commercial importance; and consequently there was a synagogue.

Now it was through the synagogue that the Apostle used to commence his operations. His habitual practice was to go to the synagogue, and, availing himself of the privilege which was usually accorded to any learned Jew to address the congregation, there proclaim the Gospel, and prove from the scriptures that Jesus was the Christ, with what success he might. By this means he not only got a hearing from the Jews, but had the opportunity of putting the truth before the numerous class of Gentile proselytes which was attached to every synagogue. These proselytes, "devout men" as S. Luke usually calls them, formed the nucleus of the Apostle's converts, and afterwards the backbone of the growing Church.

Let us now read S. Luke's account of it:—

Acts xvii. 1, &c.: Now when they had passed through Amphipolis and Apollonia, they came to Thessalonica, where was a synagogue of the Jews: and Paul, as his custom was, went in unto them, and for three sabbath days reasoned with them from the scriptures, opening and alleging that it behoved the Christ to suffer, and to rise again from the dead; and that this Jesus, whom, said he, I proclaim unto you, is the Christ. And some of them were persuaded, and consorted with Paul and Silas; and of the devout Greeks a great multitude, and of the chief women not a few. But the Jews, being moved with jealousy, took unto them certain vile fellows of the rabble, and gathering a crowd, set the city on an uproar; and assaulting the house of Jason, they sought to bring them forth to the people. And when they found them not, they dragged Jason and certain brethren before the rulers of the city, crying, These that have turned the world upside down are come hither also; whom Jason hath received; and these all act contrary to the decrees of Cæsar, saying that there is another king, one Jesus. And they troubled the multitude and the rulers of the city, when they heard these things. And when they had taken security from Jason and the rest, they let them go. And the brethren immediately sent away Paul and Silas by night unto Berœa.'—But here again the Jews from Thessalonica stirred up the people against them, so that 'the brethren sent forth Paul to go as far as to the sea; and Silas and Timothy abode there still. But they that conducted Paul brought him as far as Athens: and receiving a commandment unto Silas and Timothy that they should come to him with all speed, they departed. . . . . After a short stay he departed from Athens and came to Corinth. And he reasoned in the synagogue every sabbath, and persuaded Jews and Greeks. But when Silas and Timothy came down from Macedonia, Paul was constrained by the word, testifying to the Jews that Jesus was the Christ. And when they opposed themselves, and blasphemed, he shook out his raiment, and said unto them, Your blood be upon your own heads; I am clean: from henceforth I will go unto the Gentiles. And he departed thence (i. e. from the synagogue), and went into the house of a certain man named Titus Justus . . . and many of the Corinthians hearing believed, and were baptized. And he dwelt there a year and six months, teaching the word of God among them.

It was some time during these eighteen months that S. Paul wrote the two Epistles to the Thessalonians.

Timothy would seem to have re-visited Thessalonica in this interval, and brought tidings to the Apostle of how his converts were getting on. S. Paul could not spare either of his companions to return to Thessalonica, for there was much to be done at Corinth, where the Lord told him, in a vision, that He had much people, so he resolved to write a letter to the Thessalonians.

In dealing with this Epistle, I think our best plan will be to pick out those parts which illustrate the history of the Apostle, and of the Thessalonian Christians. The opening words are:—

Ch. i. 1: Paul and Silvanus and Timothy, unto the Church of the Thessalonians in God the Father and the Lord Jesus Christ. Grace to you and peace.

You notice that though the Epistle was altogether the Apostle's own letter, he associates with himself Silas and Timothy, not merely because they happened to be with him at the time, but because they had been his companions and fellow-labourers at Thessalonica. Notice also that S. Paul does not address them as isolated believers in Christ in Thessalonica; but as the *Church* of the Thessalonians: and not that only, but as a Church whose existence and life depended not upon its members, but upon *God and Christ*. "*Grace be to you and peace.*" This was S. Paul's habitual salutation. The word "grace" corresponds with the ordinary salutation of the nations of the West; "peace" was the salutation of the nations of the East. S. Paul addressing himself to a community consisting of both Gentiles and Jews adopts the salutation of both, grace and peace.

He begins his letter, as he always does where thankfulness and praise were possible, with thanking God for the work of His grace in these beloved converts, and commending them for their faith and patience.

Ch. i. 2: We give thanks always for you all, remembering your work of faith, and labour of love, and patience of hope ... and how ye turned unto God from idols to serve a living and true God.

He then reminds them how he had preached the word, and they received it in much affliction.

And then in a very beautiful passage, he gives an account of his own manner of life and pastoral work among them.

Ch. ii. 7: We were gentle in the midst of you, as when a nurse cherisheth her own children, being ..... well pleased to impart unto you, not the Gospel of God only, but also our own souls, because ye were become very dear to us. For ye remember our labour and travail, working night and day that we might not burden any of you, as ye know how we dealt with each one of you, as a father with his own children, exhorting you and encouraging you to the end that ye should walk worthily of God who calleth you into His own kingdom and glory.

Then he goes on to tell them what a longing he had to see them again, how he would have liked once and again to come unto them, had not Satan, acting through his Jewish emissaries, hindered him. But when he could no longer endure without tidings of them, though it involved his being left alone at Athens, he sent Timothy to them, to establish and comfort them, and to bring him news of them. What Timothy's report was and how S. Paul received it we see in the following words.

Ch. iii. 6: But when Timothy came even now unto us

from you, and brought us glad tidings of your faith and love, and that ye have good remembrance of us always, longing to see us, even as we also to see you; we were comforted over you, for now we live if ye stand fast in the Lord.

And then he finishes this part of his letter with an earnest prayer for their spiritual welfare; and that he himself might be allowed to come and see them again.

Ch. iii. 11: Now may our God and Father Himself, and our Lord Jesus, direct our way unto you: and the Lord make you to increase and abound in love one toward another, and toward all men, to the end that He may stablish your hearts unblameable in holiness before our God and Father, at the coming of our Lord Jesus with all His saints.

CHAPTER XII.

THE EPISTLES TO THE THESSALONIANS
(*continued*).

IT was only to be expected that in his letter to the Church of the Thessalonians, S. Paul would carry on the same line of instruction that he had begun during his brief ministry among them.

One point that S. Paul had evidently laid great stress upon in his preaching was that Jesus was the Christ, the true King, the King of Israel, the King of men. And this was the reason that the Jews at Thessalonica instigated the special charge against S. Paul, that he had proclaimed another, a different King, one Jesus.

S. Paul had comforted his converts by telling them that their King would soon come, that His coming would be the crown and completion of their faith, and would bring about a terrible punishment upon those who had been hindering His work and persecuting His truth.

The speedy coming of the King and Judge, to judge and to save, was the point S. Paul had most insisted upon in his preaching; and you cannot read these two Epistles without seeing that this speedy coming is their great subject.

The Thessalonian Christians were thus firmly impressed with the belief that the day of the Lord was at hand. But this belief showed itself in ways which their great teacher could not approve of.

They seemed to have argued, If the day of the Lord is indeed so near, what occasion is there for us to toil and labour? Why should we sow fields that will never be reaped? What need to prune our vines and dig round our olives, when the vintage of the world is at hand? What need to attend to business in the shop, or at the wharf, when the end of all things is at hand? How can we be expected to trouble about domestic duties in such a time as this, must we not devote every moment to prayer and watching? In the First Epistle, S. Paul in very gentle terms censures this overwrought exaggeration of feeling. Nothing can be more admirable than the way in which S. Paul calms the excitement of the Thessalonians. It reminds us of the story told of S. Carlo Borromeo. The saintly bishop was one day playing at chess, when the conversation of the company turned upon the Day of Judgment. One of those present asked the rest what they should do if it were suddenly announced that Christ was at hand. "I should begin to pray" said one. "I should go to confession" said another. At last they asked the Saint what he should do. "I should go on with my game of chess," was his reply, "for I began it to the glory of God, and should continue it for the same end." Without telling them in so many words that they were *not* labouring with their own hands, *not* walking wisely toward their heathen neighbours, S. Paul contrived to imply as much.

Ch. iv. 11: We exhort you, brethren, that ye study to be quiet, and to do your own business, and to work with your hands, even as we charged you, that ye may walk honestly toward them that are without, and may have need of nothing.

In the Second Epistle, when he found that this evil

had increased instead of diminished, the Apostle speaks more plainly and more sharply.

2 *Ep.* iii. 11: We hear of some that walk among you disorderly, that work not at all, but are busybodies. Now them that are such we command and exhort that with quietness they work and eat their own bread. . . . If any will not work, neither let him eat.

But there was another cause for anxiety which seemed to spring from the very expectation which the Apostle had encouraged them to entertain.

Since his leaving Thessalonica some deaths had occurred in the Christian community, and "these deaths had been regarded by some of the survivors with a peculiar despondency. They had been taught again and again to hope for, to look unto, the coming of Christ, as the solution of all difficulties, the righting of all wrongs, the consolation of all sufferings."

What then was to be said about those who had died without seeing the day of Christ's coming? To this solemn question S. Paul addresses himself in the well-known passage which has comforted so many Christian mourners from that time to this.

Ch. iv. 13: But we would not have you ignorant, brethren, concerning them that fall asleep; that ye sorrow not, even as the rest, which have no hope. For if we believe that Jesus died and rose again, even so them also that are fallen asleep in Jesus will God bring with Him (i. e. with Christ). For this we say unto you by the word of the Lord, that we that are alive, that are left unto the coming of the Lord, shall in no wise precede them that are fallen asleep. For the Lord Himself shall descend from heaven, with a shout, with the voice of the archangel, and with the trump of God: and the dead in Christ shall rise first: then we that are alive, that are left, shall together with them be caught up in the clouds to meet the

Lord in the air, and so shall we ever be with the Lord. Wherefore comfort one another with these words.

However *we* may understand these words, there can be no question that the Thessalonian Christians would understand them as speaking of events which would come to pass in their own days. There can hardly be a doubt that at this time, at any rate, S. Paul expected the Day of the Lord in his own time. Indeed Christ Himself had said that the existing generation should not pass away till all should be fulfilled. He had told His Apostles that they would hardly have gone through the cities of Israel before His coming. He had said of S. John that he should tarry till He came. The question is, were the Apostles mistaken in thinking that the Day of the Lord was very near, that it might come in their own day? Or were they right in so thinking? Did the Lord come? Did S. John tarry on earth long enough to see his Lord's coming? Did the Lord descend from heaven with a shout, with the voice of the archangel, and the trump of God?

This is much too weighty a question to be lightly dismissed. I will ask you to read very carefully the following words of one of the foremost of our living divines, the occupant of the Chair of Theology at one of our Universities:—

"No one can study the New Testament without feeling that the thought of Christ's Return was everywhere present and powerful in the first age. ... And more than this: it was instant. The dawn of an endless day was held to be already breaking after a weary night . . . The Apostles looked for Christ, and Christ came in the life-time of S. John. He founded His immoveable kingdom. He gathered before Him the nations of the earth, old and new, and passed sentence upon them. He judged, in that shaking of earth and heaven, most truly and most decisively the living and the dead. He established fresh foundations for society, and a fresh standard of worth. The fall of Jerusalem was for the religious history of the world an end as complete as death. The establishment of a spiritual Church was a beginning as glorious as the Resurrection. The Apostles, I repeat, looked for Christ's coming in their own generation, and Christ came. The form of His coming, His coming to judgment, then, is a lesson for all time. As we study it we can learn part at least of the meaning of our present faith that He shall come again . . . that Christ has not yet revealed the fulness of His power, or uttered the last voice of His judgment. For beyond all these preparatory comings there is a day when 'every eye shall see Him, and they also which pierced Him.' . . . When His Presence shall be made clear, clear in the world at large, clear in our own souls, clear with the manifestation of perfect righteousness, and with the consequence of inevitable retribution." (Dr. Westcott, Historic Faith.)

The great matter for us is to prepare ourselves for the coming of Christ, and for the Day of His judgment, whatever shape that coming may take, and in whatever way that judgment may be manifested. And no lessons of preparation can be better than those which S. Paul enforces in these Epistles to the Thessalonians. As when he says,—

Ch. v. 4: Ye, brethren, are not in darkness that that day should overtake you as a thief: for ye are all sons of light, and sons of the day. . . . . So then let us not sleep as do the rest, but let us watch and be sober;—

or when he says in the Second Epistle,—

2 *Ep.* ii. 1: Now we beseech you, brethren, . . . that ye be not quickly shaken from your mind, nor yet be

troubled, either by spirit, or by word, or by epistle as from us, as that the day of the Lord is now present.

It is often asserted that S. Paul wrote the Second Epistle to the Thessalonians to disabuse their minds of the idea with which his First Epistle had possessed them, that the day of the Lord was at hand, or, as in the Revised Version, " the day of the Lord is now present."

But this was not the case; the Second Epistle, no less than the First, is full of the nearness of the Lord's coming. S. Paul wrote it to tell them that the day of the Lord, though near, was not actually come, and that there were some things which would happen first, which had not yet happened.

If he had meant to tell them that the Lord was not at hand, and that they had misunderstood him, in thinking so, he could easily have done so.

But as a matter of fact he tells them nothing of the sort; what he does tell them is that the Day of the Lord was not actually present, that the Lord would not come that day or the next day; but that the things which must happen first would very soon happen, and that then the Lord would come veiled in the clouds of heaven to take vengeance upon the evil and apostate race which had rejected Him, and in rejecting Him had filled up the measure of their iniquities.

The Second Epistle closes with a solemn warning against those who thought they were preparing for the Lord's coming by neglecting the ordinary duties of life, and going about like chattering busybodies, idle themselves and infecting others with their idle fancies. "If any will not work," he says, "neither let him eat." But let them rather, he says, work their work with quietness, and eat their own bread.

Then follows a short prayer on their behalf—

Now the Lord of peace Himself give you peace at all times, in all ways. The Lord be with you all.

At this point we may imagine the Apostle taking the pen or style from the hand of the secretary, and in large, straggling characters writing down with his own hand the Apostolic benediction, which was henceforth to be the token whereby genuine epistles were to be known from forgeries:—

Ch. iii. 17: The salutation of me, Paul, with my own hand, which is the token in every epistle; so I write. The grace of our Lord Jesus Christ be with you all.

One thing more I wish to say before we close this chapter. We none of us know what will happen to us. We none of us know under what circumstances we may at some time be placed. We may have to live, as the early Christians did, in the time of a grave religious crisis. The coming, the presence of Christ may be manifested in some unexpected way. It may be even that the supreme crisis, the Daylight of Judgment, the winding up this present Dispensation, the final coming of the Lord may overtake us. We may have to pass through some fiery trial; we may be placed amidst scenes in which we might easily lose our heads, as we say; lose our mental balance; be in danger of falling into some strange fanaticism, or of deserting our posts in the great army. Some terrible plague or cholera visitation may come, and will judge us, show what stuff we are made of; show whether we should run away like cowards, or stay and do our duty like men. In such a time we could have no better guide than these two earliest Epistles of S. Paul. They would teach us that quiet courage, that calm confidence in God, that simple persistence in plain duty, which are things most valuable at all times, but especially in times of great peril and excitement.

CHAPTER XIII.

THE FIRST EPISTLE TO THE CORINTHIANS.

YOU will remember that it was from Corinth that S. Paul wrote his two letters to the Thessalonians, and that he remained there for a considerable time, more than eighteen months. But the time came when he had to leave that city in which the Lord had told him that He had much people. Accordingly S. Paul set sail for Syria, paying a hurried visit on the way to Ephesus. After having visited Jerusalem, he went through the region of Galatia and Phrygia in order, stablishing all the Churches, and at last arrived at Ephesus, according to the promise made on his previous visit.

We can hardly fail to overlook the fact which I have already pointed out, that the victory of the Faith was won in the great cities of the Empire. S. Paul and his companions did not begin in the villages and country places, but unfurled the Standard of the Cross in the great cities. Antioch, Thessalonica, Corinth had heard the Gospel: now Ephesus was to hear it also. Next to Rome, Ephesus was the most important scene of the Apostle's labours. If Antioch was the cradle of the Church, Ephesus was its nursery. There the Christian Church planted by S. Paul, watched over by Timothy, was at last placed under the care of S. John, the theologian, the great teacher of the Church.

Ephesus was the most magnificent of the magnificent cities of Asia. The Great Temple of Artemis (Diana) was reckoned one of the wonders of the world. The Ephesians had no higher boast than that their city was the caretaker or sacristan of the Temple. It was a gay, busy, luxurious and wicked city, the "Vanity Fair" of Asia. It was a very religious city; but a religion of luxury and vice and superstition. No story was too improbable, no imposture too gross to be believed at Ephesus. It was the congenial home of impostors, magicians, soothsayers, and quacks of all descriptions.

To S. Paul, however, it presented itself as a great and effectual door opened to him, by which he might gain access to the surrounding district.

For three months the Apostle carried on his usual work in the synagogue, till the opposition of the Jews grew too strong, and then he separated the disciples, and reasoned daily in the school of an Ephesian sophist named Tyrannus. This continued for two years, so that not only the people of Ephesus itself, but the inhabitants of the whole Province of Proconsular Asia, heard the word of God. Though this two years seems to have been a good time for the Gospel, it was a very hard time for S. Paul; for he speaks of himself at this time as suffering from hunger, and thirst, and nakedness; as having no certain dwelling-place; as being buffeted, reviled, persecuted; as being doomed to death, and made a spectacle unto the world, and to angels and to men.

Small wonder then that he was, as he said he was, pressed on every side, perplexed, smitten down; though upheld then as ever by the mighty hand of God. So terrible, indeed, and so perilous was his position, that he speaks of himself as having fought with wild beasts at Ephesus.

Nor was this all. It was bad enough to have his work opposed and himself persecuted; but it was still worse to hear that one of his Churches was falling away from the Faith, and that another was falling into licentiousness of life, and heretical doctrine.

And this was what he had to hear. During his absence from Corinth the Church of the Corinthians had been visited by Apollos, a very eloquent and learned Alexandrian. He preached in a very different style from S. Paul—with much greater eloquence and learning; and seems to have fascinated many of the more intellectual of the Corinthians, who were disposed, not at all with his consent, to make him the head of a distinct party in the Church. Then there were others who professed to be followers of S. Peter, and who disparaged S. Paul's claim to be an Apostle; there were others who, disclaiming all parties, were the most sectarian of all, and ventured to style themselves as special disciples of Christ Himself.

Apollos returned to Ephesus, and brought back still more deplorable tidings. Many of the members of the Church were falling back into the licentiousness and impurity which were almost universally prevalent in Corinth, which indeed was a bye-word among the heathen for its vice. Like the Israelites in the wilderness, they had began to lust after the flesh-pots of Egypt, and to loath the light bread of Christ's pure doctrine.

S. Paul had also received a letter from the Corinthians, most self-complacent in its tone, asking for advice on some practical points, such as marriage and divorce, the eating of things offered to idols, and other matters relating to the regulation of their assemblies for worship and discipline, but totally silent on their scandalous conduct in conniving at a gross moral offence committed by one of their members, an offence so gross as even to scandalize the loose morals of Corinth, and ignoring the fact that factions, jealousies, back-biting, tumults were rife amongst them.

It was then with this letter before him, and his heart burning with indignation, and yet overflowing with affection, at these terrible disorders and scandalous immoralities, that we may imagine S. Paul in his Ephesian lodgings dictating, perhaps to his companion Sosthenes, the famous letter known as the First Epistle to the Corinthians.

All that I can hope to do, in dealing with this long and deeply interesting Epistle, will be to give you a general idea of the whole, and to dwell upon some of its most important parts.

1 *Cor.* i. 1 : Paul, called to be an apostle of Jesus Christ through the will of God, and Sosthenes our brother, unto the Church of God which is at Corinth, even them that are sanctified in Christ Jesus, called to be saints. . . . Grace to you, and peace, from God our Father and the Lord Jesus Christ. I thank my God always concerning you, for the grace of God which was given you in Christ Jesus, that in everything ye were enriched in Him, in all utterance and all knowledge, so that ye come behind in no gift, waiting for the revelation of our Lord Jesus Christ.

This is a strange beginning, is it not, to a letter addressed to a Church so torn with faction, so disgraced with vice, as we have seen the Church of Corinth to have been? Yet so it is. S. Paul addresses them as sanctified in Christ Jesus, called to be saints. He thanks God for their possession of the only gifts which even his charity can attribute to them, the gift of utterance and the gift of knowledge; he even says that in no gift do they come behind.

How can we explain this? The Epistle is written to *all*; not to some.

It was because S. Paul considered their baptismal incorporation into Christ a fact and a reality. He speaks of them as they were in God's purpose, as what God intended them to be. He does not tell them that they are not real Christians, and bid them become so. He does not tell them, baptized, though falling Christians, to be born again; but he accepts their position as Christians, and then with alternate stern rebuke and loving appeal endeavours to win them to peace and holiness.

After this opening the Apostle proceeds to deal with their factions and party spirit.

Ch. i. 10: Now I beseech you, brethren, through the name of our Lord Jesus Christ, that ye all speak the same thing, and that there be no divisions among you. For it hath been signified unto me concerning you, my brethren, that there are contentions among you. Now this I mean, that each one of you saith, I am of Paul; and I of Apollos; and I of Cephas; and I of Christ. Is Christ divided? was Paul crucified for you? or were ye baptized in the name of Paul? . . . .

Ch. iii. 1: And I, brethren, could not speak unto you as unto spiritual, but as unto carnal . . . . for whereas there is among you jealousy and strife, are ye not carnal, and walk after the manner of men? For when one saith, I am of Paul; and another, I am of Apollos; are ye not men? What then is Apollos? and what is Paul? Ministers through whom ye believed. I planted, Apollos watered; but God gave the increase. . . . . Wherefore let no one glory in men. For all things are yours; whether Paul, or Apollos, or Cephas, or the world, or life, or death, or things present, or things to come; all are yours; and ye are Christ's, and Christ is God's. Let a man so account of us as of ministers of Christ, and stewards of the mysteries of God.

Of the various parties into which the Corinthian Church was divided, the most important was the party which called themselves after the name of the eloquent Apollos.

They seem to have laid great stress upon the mysterious side of the Truth; they talked a great deal about the hidden wisdom of God, hidden from the many, revealed to the chosen few; they dwelt much upon the action of the Divine Word upon the soul of man.

Now, how did S. Paul deal with these people? Did he tell them that there was no mystery about religion; that there was no hidden wisdom; that there was no Divine Word or Voice that spoke to the hearts and consciences of men? Far from it. He speaks of proclaiming to them "the mystery" of God, of speaking God's wisdom "in a mystery." He declares that he speaks wisdom among the perfect, among the initiated.

In what, then, did his teaching differ from theirs? Why, in this. They spoke of a mystic voice speaking only to a few elect spirits; S. Paul spoke of a voice sounding in the ears of all. They spoke of a hidden wisdom; and so did he. But the hidden wisdom of which S. Paul spoke was the wisdom which was hidden from the wise and prudent, and was revealed unto babes.

God had spoken to men from the Cross of Christ, the WORD of God was not a metaphysical abstraction, but an Incarnate Word, a living Word, nay, a dying Word; revealing in that death the essential character of God, His essential love and holiness, as well as His essential power and wisdom. But let us hear the Apostle speak for himself.

Ch. i. 17: For Christ sent me . . . to preach the Gospel: not in wisdom of words, lest the Cross of Christ should be made void. For the word of the Cross is to them that are perishing foolishness; but unto us which are being saved it is the power of God. For . . . . we preach Christ crucified, unto Jews a stumbling-block, and unto Gentiles foolishness; but unto them that are called, both Jews and Greeks, Christ the power of God, and the wisdom of God. . . . .

Ch. ii. 1: And I, brethren, when I came unto you came not with excellency of speech or of wisdom, proclaiming to you the mystery of God. For I determined not to know anything among you, save Jesus Christ, and Him crucified. . . . . Howbeit we speak wisdom among the perfect, (even) God's wisdom in a mystery, even the wisdom that hath been hidden, which God foreordained before the worlds to our glory, and revealed it unto us through the Spirit.

The chapters that follow the passages which we have already read are taken up with keen but loving rebukes of the Corinthians for their immorality and unbrotherliness. Then follow answers to the questions which they had put to the Apostle in their letter. This brings us to the 10th chapter.

It is plain that what S. Paul had in his mind when he thought of the Corinthians, was that he was writing to people who had a great notion of their calling as Christians, of their blessings and privileges, but who were slipping into practical idolatry, and into the gross immorality with which idolatry was mostly accompanied. Theirs was just the case of the Israelites, who, having been delivered out of Egypt, redeemed from bondage, brought very near to God, made a kingdom of priests, a holy nation, were yet provoking God by their murmurings, their idolatries, their impurity, loathing the bread of angels, and hankering after the flesh-pots of Egypt, so that God sware in His wrath that they should not enter into His rest.

So the Apostle reminds them of this sad history, as a wholesome warning against similar conduct.

You will notice in the passage that we are about to read, that the emphasis is upon the word *all*. *All* were partakers in the redemption, *all* sharers in privilege, *all*, or nearly all, overthrown in the wilderness.

Ch. x. 1: For I would not, brethren, have you ignorant, how that our fathers were all under the cloud, and all passed through the sea; and were all baptized unto Moses in the cloud, and in the sea; and did all eat the same spiritual meat; and did all drink the same spiritual drink: for they drank of a spiritual rock that followed them; and the rock was Christ. Howbeit with most of them God was not well pleased: for they were overthrown in the wilderness. Now these things were our examples, to the intent we should not lust after evil things as they also lusted. Neither be ye idolaters as were some of them; as it is written, The people sat down to eat and drink, and rose up to play. Neither let us commit fornication, as some of them committed, and fell in one day three and twenty thousand. Neither let us tempt the Lord, as some of them tempted, and perished by the serpents. Neither murmur ye, as some of them murmured, and perished by the destroyer. Now these things happened unto them by way of example; and they were written for our admonition, upon whom the ends of the ages are come. Wherefore let him that thinketh he standeth take heed lest he fall.

CHAPTER XIV.

THE FIRST EPISTLE TO THE CORINTHIANS
(*continued*).

YOU will remember that the Church of Corinth had written a letter to S. Paul, to consult him upon many questions that they were troubled about. This letter was brought by three members of the Church of Corinth, Stephanas, Fortunatus, and Achaicus.

S. Paul would no doubt have many conversations with these representatives of the Church, representatives perhaps even of different parties in the Church, and would ask them many searching questions about what was going on in the Christian community at Corinth.

They had to tell him a sad and shameful story, not only of gross immorality and faction of the bitterest sort, but of the rivalry, and love of display, and the general disorder of their religious assemblies.

Sad to say, the religious assemblies of the Corinthian Church, even the solemn meetings for "the Breaking of the Bread," were characterized by selfishness, faction, and excess. The things that should have been for their wealth, had become to them an occasion of falling. The Sacrament of love and unity had become the occasion of selfishness and envy; the Sacrament of holiness had become an occasion of drunkenness and excess.

In the first fervour of Christian love and unity, the Christians of Jerusalem had all things common; among other things they had a common meal, to which each contributed according to his ability, which became known as the Agapé or Love-feast. This was succeeded by the celebration of the Holy Eucharist, the true Lord's Supper.

The Christians who first organized these love-feasts were men whose whole souls were possessed with the spirit of brotherhood; they had what has been called "the enthusiasm of humanity;" with them it answered perfectly well, and the Agapé became a not unworthy introduction to the Holy Supper itself.

But when this practice was transplanted to other countries, and introduced, as in some cases it seems to have been, into foreign Churches, made up of Jews and Gentiles; and in times when the first love of Christians had cooled down; when the spirit of faction and selfishness had tainted, if not destroyed, the feeling of brotherhood in the community, the Feast of Love became a contradiction and an absurdity, and could lead to no good results.

We do not know to what results the Agapé led in other Churches; but we do know what it came to be at Corinth.

Of all the Churches which S. Paul planted, the Church at Corinth seems to have been the most immoral, the most disorderly, and the most divided.

The divisions and factions which prevailed among them, instead of being extinguished and lost in the Feast of Brotherhood and in the Sacrament of Love, were only emphasized and made more revolting.

Let us endeavour to picture to ourselves, as S. Paul's description enables us to do, the sort of scene that went on every Sunday night at Corinth.

The assembly would be held in the evening, for it had not yet become necessary for the Christians, for safety's sake, to meet at the dead of night or before daybreak. The place of assembly would be merely a large room, with nothing church-like about it to our notions.

Presently—if we may venture to imagine what must have occurred—a party of well-dressed, well-to-do looking people would come in, and take their places at one of the tables, and spread out the provisions which they had brought, consisting of costly viands and choice wine, and instead of waiting for the rest of the brethren to take their places, they would begin upon their supper, till, by the time the Agapé was over, they were noisy, or perhaps merely heavy and stupid with drink. Another, and a very different party would next come, and take their places as far as possible from the previous comers, and would, with ostentatious simplicity, spread their part of the table with bread, vegetables, and fruit, with plain water for their drink. Then a larger party would come in, consisting of poor people, and would take places where they could find them. Most of them had brought but little, some, perhaps, had brought none at all, and the result would be that their scanty provision was done long before their appetites were half satisfied. There they would sit watching the richer members—it would be too absurd to call them brethren—while they finished their luxurious repast, with feelings not far removed from envy and hatred.

Then the signal would be given, the Bread and Wine would be placed before the celebrant, and the service of the Holy Communion would begin; and so it would come to pass that the Body and Blood of Christ would be partaken of by a congregation, some of whom were hungry, and some were drunken.

Can we be surprised that S. Paul, in dealing with such profanation as this, should use strong language of rebuke? Indeed, the surprise is all the other way, that he should have rebuked them as mildly as he did.

With this explanation, and with the great advantage of having a revised translation of this passage, which more perhaps than any other has suffered by the change of meaning in the words used, and which it is to be feared has kept numbers of God's children from the Table of their Lord, I think you will be able to understand without much difficulty, and perhaps with a new insight, this famous passage.

Ch. xi. 17: But in giving you this charge, I praise you not, that ye come together not for the better, but for the worse. For first of all when ye come together in the Church [i.e. the congregation, not of course the building], I hear that divisions exist among you, and I partly believe it. . . . . When, therefore, ye assemble yourselves together, it is not possible to eat the Lord's Supper: for in your eating, each one taketh before the other his own supper; and one is hungry, and another is drunken. What? have ye not houses to eat and to drink in? or despise ye the Church of God, and put them to shame that have not? What shall I say to you? shall I praise you in this? I praise you not. For I received of the Lord, that which also I delivered unto you, how that the Lord Jesus in the night in which He was betrayed took bread; and when He had given thanks He brake it, and said, This is my body, which is for you: this do in remembrance of me. In like manner also the cup, after supper, saying, This cup is the new covenant in my blood: this do, as oft as ye drink it, in remembrance of me. For as often as ye eat this bread and drink the cup, ye proclaim the Lord's death till He come. Wherefore whosoever shall eat the bread or drink the cup of the Lord unworthily, shall be guilty of the body and the blood of the Lord. But let a man prove himself, and so let him eat of the bread, and drink of the cup. For he that eateth and drinketh, eateth and drinketh judgment to himself, if he discern not the body. For this cause many among you are weak and sickly, and not a few sleep. But if we discerned ourselves we should not be judged. But when we are judged we are chastened of the Lord, that we may not be condemned with the world. Wherefore, my brethren, when ye come together to eat, wait one for another. If any man is hungry let him eat at home; that your coming together be not unto judgment. And the rest will I set in order whensoever I come.

The next section of the Epistle has to do with the nature and regulation of the spiritual gifts and ministries with which the Church of Christ was enriched.

Now at Corinth, which seems to have been the most disorderly of the Christian societies, the exercise of these spiritual gifts ran to complete riot, and by no means tended to edification.

We have very slight means of knowing what was the nature of the religious services in which, in these early times, the Christian community engaged.

It seems probable that the ordinary service of the Church was constituted on the lines of the synagogue service. People seldom invent altogether new forms, but alter and adapt existing ones. The service of the synagogue seems to have consisted of stated prayers, and readings of the Holy Scriptures, with a sermon or address, which might be given by any Jew who might wish to address the assembly. Whether this service was connected with the one act of worship which our Lord instituted, viz. the celebration of the Eucharist, the Christian Sacrifice, or whether it was held at a different time, we do not know. But the language which S. Paul uses in this Epistle enables us to realize to some extent what sort of service it was.

Let us try and picture it to ourselves as well as we can.

We imagine ourselves, then, in Corinth. We find the place where the Christians assemble, not far it would appear from the Jewish synagogue. The service begins with prayers formed on the model of the prayers of the synagogue; this is followed by a reading from the Greek Bible of the Septuagint. The Lesson, as we should call it, being ended, one of the recognized teachers of the Church begins an address or instruction; he has not got far, when strange sounds are heard from another part of the room; they are presently seen to arise from a man who, standing in his place, and with a rapt expression on his face, is giving utterance to what appears to the hearers mere gibberish, full of sound and fury, but signifying nothing; he, in his turn, is overpowered by some one else; who in yet more piercing tones pours out in some unknown tongue what sounds like mere raving. Presently another breaks in with a psalm of his own composing; or a woman with uncovered head, and her frame quivering with apparent inspiration, looking more like a heathen priestess than a Christian woman, begins to address the assembly. After a while one of the prophets of the Church rises and pours forth some impassioned utterance, prefacing his words with the prophetic formula, Thus saith the Holy Ghost.

This sounds very strange and irreverent to us, accustomed as we are to the solemn and orderly worship of our own branch of the Church; but there was a brighter side to it, and we must not forget that the Corinthians were excitable, keen-witted

Greeks. It might happen at a Christian assembly for worship, that one gifted Christian would rise after another to prophesy, that is to preach, and that some stranger brought there by curiosity would feel as he listened that the secrets of his heart were made manifest, and thus convicted by all, judged by all, he would fall down and worship God, and declare that God was indeed among them.

But it was clear that this disorderly conduct of divine service needed regulation, these exuberant shoots of religious enthusiasm needed to be pruned with no sparing hand; and it is to this regulation of spiritual gifts that, as I have said, S. Paul addresses himself in this section of his Epistle. With reference to the exercise of these gifts in the assemblies of the Church, the Apostle writes:—

Ch. xiv. 26: What is it, then, brethren? When ye come together each one hath a psalm, hath a teaching, hath a revelation, hath a tongue, hath an interpretation. Let all things be done unto edifying. If any man speaketh in a tongue, let it be by two or at the most three, and that in turn; and let one interpret. But if there be no interpreter, let him keep silence in the Church. . . . . And let the prophets speak by two or three, and let the others discern. For ye all can prophesy one by one, that all may learn, and all may be comforted. . . . . Wherefore, my brethren, desire earnestly to prophesy, and forbid not to speak with tongues. But let all things be done decently, and in order.

After this the Apostle passes on to the general question of the various gifts and ministries which were exercised in the Church, and lays down various rules as to how they were to be regarded and exercised.

The Corinthians regarded spiritual gifts as things which one had, and another had not, as things which glorified their possessors.

S. Paul taught them that spiritual gifts were only desirable, only valuable just so far as they tended to the common good, to the building up of the body of Christ.

In the very nature of things these gifts could only be possessed by few, whereas there were other gifts, and they the highest, which were open to all alike. And so in the 13th Chapter he goes on to show the Corinthians, and shows us, a more excellent way.

This way was one which all could find, a method which all could practise; it was a divine way, for it was the way of love, and "God is love."

Beautiful as is the description of love or "charity" to use the more familiar rendering of our ordinary Bibles in the famous passage which we are going to read, it becomes even more interesting and intelligible when we remember S. Paul's teaching about spiritual gifts.

The Corinthians, remember, prided themselves on their possession of the gift of tongues, on their knowledge, on their faith; the Apostle shows them that without love all these are valueless.

Ch. xiii. 1: If I speak with the tongues of men and of angels, but have not Love, I am become sounding brass, or a clanging cymbal. And if I have the gift of prophecy, and know all mysteries, and all knowledge; and if I have all faith, so as to remove mountains, but have not Love, I am nothing. And if I bestow all my goods to feed the poor, and if I give my body to be burned, but have not Love, it profiteth me nothing. Love suffereth long and is kind; Love envieth not; Love vaunteth not itself, is not puffed up, doth not behave itself unseemly, seeketh not its own, is not provoked, taketh not account of evil; rejoiceth not in unrighteousness, but rejoiceth with the truth; beareth all things, believeth all things, hopeth all things, endureth all things. Love never faileth: but whether there be prophecies, they shall be done away; whether there be tongues, they shall cease; whether there be knowledge, it shall be done away. For we know in part, and we prophesy in part: but when that which is perfect is come, that which is in part shall be done away. When I was a child, I spake as a child, I felt as a child, I thought as a child: but now that I am become a man I have put away childish things. For now we see in a mirror, darkly; but then face to face: now I know in part, but then shall I know even as also I have been known. But now abideth faith, hope, love, these three; but the greatest of these is Love.

The last verse has often been misunderstood. The Apostle has been supposed to mean, that love is greater than faith and hope, because *they* will come to an end, while love abideth for ever. But this is not so: what the Apostle says is, that while all three alike abide, still love is the best and highest. There is no special intellectual difficulty in this marvellous eulogy of love. The difficulty is not to understand what the Apostle means, but to put in practice what he teaches. In fact, it needs not a commentary but a prayer; and such a prayer we have not far to look for.

"O Lord, who hast taught us that all our doings without charity are nothing worth; Send thy Holy Ghost, and pour into our hearts that most excellent gift of charity, the very bond of peace, and of all virtues, without which whosoever liveth is counted dead before thee: Grant this for thine only Son Jesus Christ's sake. *Amen.*

CHAPTER XV.

THE FIRST EPISTLE TO THE CORINTHIANS
(continued).

WE come now to the famous 15th Chapter of our Epistle, which is so familiar to most people, and associated with the saddest periods of their lives; for it is the Chapter which is read in the service for the Burial of the Dead.

The same state of mind which led the Corinthians to value the individual Christian more than the body, to set "tongues" and prophecy above love, led many of them to substitute for the truth of the resurrection of the body, the doctrine that the Resurrection meant only the rising to a higher spiritual state; and that as they, the gifted, the spiritual, had reached this state, the resurrection, as far as they were concerned, was passed already. The Corinthians were Greeks, and deeply rooted in the Greek mind was reverence for the soul and contempt of the body. That the soul of man might live on after his body had crumbled in the dust, they could believe readily enough, but that the body should rise again, that seemed too absurd. When S. Paul preached at Athens and spoke of the resurrection of the body, some mocked, and would listen no more.

This deeply rooted feeling led the Corinthian Christians, or some of them, to think that whatever was common and simply human was despicable because it was common; and that whatever was peculiar and distinguishing was glorious, just because it was peculiar.

It is very striking to see how S. Paul deals with men who advocated views so subversive of Christian hope and Christian purity. He deals very gently with them, though in his gentleness there is a strong dash of ironical pity.

S. Paul calmly reasons with them; he treats these men, full of conceit of their spiritual perfection, as carnal, fleshly-minded men, as mere babes, whose little tempers must be borne with, and who must be fed with milk, not with strong meat. He begins by declaring the simple common gospel, which he had taught them long ago, the plain facts of the creed which they had professed at their baptism, that Christ had died for their sins, and risen again the third day from the dead. These were facts. If there were no such facts, if these acts had not been accomplished, if no such victories over death and the grave had been won, they were still in their old slavery, they were not redeemed at all.

Ch. xv. 1: Now I make known unto you, brethren, the Gospel which I preached unto you, which also ye received, wherein also ye stand, by which also ye are saved, ... except ye believed in vain. For I delivered unto you first of all that which also I received, how that Christ died for our sins according to the scriptures; and that He was buried; and that He hath been raised on the third day, according to the scriptures; and that he appeared to Cephas; then to the twelve; then He appeared to above five hundred brethren at once, of whom the greater part remain until now, but some are fallen asleep; then He appeared to James; then to all the Apostles; and last of all He appeared unto me also.

Now if Christ is preached that He hath been raised

from the dead, how say some among you that there is no resurrection of the dead?

You will understand that it was not the Resurrection of Christ that these Corinthians denied, but the resurrection of Christians. That Christ died and rose again, this they believed: but they looked upon it as the grand exception to the rule, not as the rule itself. They did not understand that Christ was the Head and Root of Humanity, and could not separate Himself from it; that His death affected not only Himself, but humanity; that His Resurrection was not His own personal triumph, but the triumph of humanity. You will see that what S. Paul asserts is not that if Christ did not rise, there was no resurrection for them; but—and what an astounding assertion it is—if there is no resurrection for us, there was no resurrection for Him. If we do not rise, then Christ is not risen. Either He did not rise from the dead at all, or in that rising He exhibited the law of the race with which He was united.

Ch. xv. 13: But if there is no resurrection of the dead, neither hath Christ been raised: and if Christ hath not been raised, then is our preaching vain, your faith also is vain . . . . For if the dead are not raised, neither hath Christ been raised: and if Christ hath not been raised, your faith is vain; ye are yet in your sins. Then they also which are fallen asleep in Christ have perished. If in this life only we have hoped in Christ, we are of all men most pitiable. But now hath Christ been raised from the dead, the first fruits of them that are asleep. For since by man came death, by man came also the resurrection of the dead. For as in Adam all die, so also in Christ shall all be made alive. But each in his own order: Christ the first fruits; then they that are Christ's at His coming (or presence).

Then cometh the end, when He shall deliver up the

kingdom to God, even the Father; when He shall have abolished all rule and all authority and power. For He must reign, till He hath put all His enemies under His feet. The last enemy that shall be abolished is death. For, He put all things in subjection under His feet . . . . that God may be all in all.

These are most wonderful words; we can hardly open our minds wide enough to take them in. We have need to remind ourselves that God's thoughts are not as our thoughts, that as the heaven is higher than the earth so are His ways higher than our ways, and His thoughts than our thoughts. What S. Paul was able to express in words fell short of what God had enabled him to feel and believe, and falls infinitely short of the full truth as it stands in the mind and purpose of God.

The resurrection to a higher spiritual attainment in which these Corinthians boasted, was a narrow restricted thing; they delighted in it just because it was narrow and restricted. But the resurrection of which S. Paul speaks, how wide, how universal it is! *As in Adam all die, so also in Christ shall all be made alive.*

We have here an assertion as broad as that which we shall find in the Epistle to the Romans, and exactly corresponding with it. There it is said,

Rom. v. 18: As through one trespass, the judgment came unto all men to condemnation; even so through one act of righteousness the free gift came unto all men to justification of life.

What do such words mean?

They must mean that the law of death for the race is manifested in Adam, and the law of life for the race in Christ: and that the resurrection has proved that the law of life is stronger than the law of death.

And in this triumph of the law of life, there is seen to be an orderly sequence: first Christ; then those who are Christ's in His Presence; then the end, the fulfilment, the completion of Christ's mediatorial work—God all in all.

Then follows a section in which the question is dealt with, How are the dead raised? and with what body do they come? How? By the power by which the seed is quickened in the furrow. With what body? Why, each man with his own proper body, his real body, not the husk which crumbles in the earth and sees corruption. They say that the matter of a man's body is changed once in seven years. If a man, then, lives 70 years he has had ten bodies, and why should the last set of particles be raised more than any previous set of particles? It is quite time that we got rid of such gross and carnal notions. The resurrection body is a glorious body, a spiritual body. By the glorious resurrection we do not mean the revivification of a handful of dust.

Let me quote the words of a great living divine whom I have quoted before :—

"In shaping for ourselves this belief—i.e. the resurrection of the flesh—we need to use more than common care lest we allow gross, earthly thoughts to intrude into a realm where they have no place. The 'flesh' of which we speak as destined to a resurrection, is not that substance which we can see and handle, measured by properties of sense. It represents as far as we now see, ourselves in our actual weakness, but essentially ourselves. We in our whole being, this is our belief, shall rise again. And we are not these changing bodies which we bear. They alter, as we know, with every step we take, and every breath we draw.... When, therefore, the laws of our existence are hereafter modified, then we, because we are unchanged, shall find some other expression [i.e. our own proper body], truly the same in relation to that new order, because it is not the same as that to which it corresponds in this." (Dr. Westcott's Historic Faith.)

There will be a continuity between the body of our humiliation and the body of our glory, but it will be the continuity not of fleshly particles, but the continuity of the spiritual life. For it follows:—

Ch. xv. 50: Now this I say, brethren, that flesh and blood cannot inherit the kingdom of God; neither doth corruption inherit incorruption. Behold, I tell you a mystery: We shall not all sleep, but we shall all be changed, in a moment, in the twinkling of an eye, at the last trump: for the trumpet shall sound, and the dead shall be raised incorruptible, and we shall be changed. For this corruptible must put on incorruption, and this mortal must put on immortality. But when this corruptible shall have put on incorruption, and this mortal shall have put on immortality, then shall come to pass the saying that is written, Death is swallowed up in victory. O death, where is thy victory? O death, where is thy sting? The sting of death is sin, and the power of sin is the law: but thanks be to God, which giveth us the victory through our Lord Jesus Christ.

Then follows an exhortation about a collection that was to be made for the poverty-stricken Christians at Jerusalem:—

Ch. xvi. 2: Upon the first day of the week let each one of you lay by him in store, as he may prosper, that no collections be made when I come . . . and I will send to carry your bounty unto Jerusalem.

This passage is important as giving us a warrant for "the Offertory." We gather from it that the best way of collecting money for various Church purposes is not to trust to special appeals and spasmodic efforts, but to make the laying by of our substance a regular and systematic thing, an integral part not only of Christian duty, but of Christian worship.

It is not enough to have a fixed day for making our offerings; this should be done on the Sunday, the Lord's Day, and in the time of Divine Service.

And then, having summed up his advice to them in the words—

Ch. xvi. 13: Watch ye, stand fast in the faith, quit you like men, be strong. Let all that ye do be done in love;—

he concludes:—

Ch. xvi. 21: The salutation of me Paul with mine own hand. If any man loveth not the Lord, let him be anathema. Maran-atha (our Lord cometh). The grace of the Lord Jesus Christ be with you. My love be with you all in Christ Jesus. Amen.

CHAPTER XVI.

THE SECOND EPISTLE TO THE CORINTHIANS.

THIS second letter to the Corinthian Church was written very shortly after the first. The first, you remember, was written from Ephesus, and sent by the same messengers that had brought the letter to which it was an answer. That first letter was written, so the Apostle tells us, in a time of " much affliction and anguish of heart, and with many tears."

He dictated it with a heavy heart, and with sad misgivings as to how it would be received.

So much did these misgivings disquiet him that he sent Titus to Corinth to see what was going on, and to bring word to him at Troas.

Just as we might expect, S. Paul reached Troas too soon. Titus had not yet come, and though a great opening for evangelistic work presented itself, the Apostle could not rest there, but crossed the sea to Macedonia. In one of the cities of Macedonia, perhaps in Philippi, he met Titus, and also it would seem Timothy and S. Luke. Titus brought him on the whole good tidings, or what S. Paul with his intense hopefulness contrived to consider good tidings. Titus had been well received; indeed, so great was the belief of the majority of the Church (however much they might listen to the disparaging comments of his enemies) in the power of the great Apostle, that his envoy was received with fear and trembling. The offender who had caused such great scandal had been severely dealt with, at any rate by the majority of the Church; and had been brought to a sense of his sin, and was in danger of being swallowed up—being perhaps a weak rather than a high-handed sinner—with over-much sorrow.

But the report of Titus was by no means altogether satisfactory.

The Jewish party in the Church had apparently been reinforced by men from Jerusalem, and especially by one man who took the lead in their opposition to S. Paul. They showed letters of commendation from the Church of Jerusalem, perhaps even from S. James himself. They boasted of having had a personal knowledge of Christ. These men made a dead-set at S. Paul's authority. He was no real Apostle. He had not seen the Lord. He could produce no authority from the Twelve. He could be very bold, no doubt, at a distance; he could write letters weighty and powerful, but he was afraid to come himself. He had said he was coming, but he was always shuffling with his promises, and would not really come. Indeed, bold as he was, he had not the face to come, for he knew that he had been found out, that his hidden deeds of shame were known, that the Church would not endure any longer to be cheated and led astray by him. It was all very well for him to boast that he had taken nothing from them. What was this pretended zeal about the collection for the poor? It was part of his slyness and cunning; what he would not do openly he did in an underhand way; being crafty, he was trying to catch them with guile. Indeed, his refusal of a maintenance from the Church, which was always claimed by real Apostles, showed that he had no confidence in his own claims. Such were the sort of things that were being said of S. Paul at Corinth.

Can we wonder that his indignation was roused? Can we wonder at what seems like a fierce vindication of his authority?

We must remember that though nominally an attack upon himself, it was in reality a determined reaction against the truth. In vindicating his apostolic authority he was really fighting his Master's battle, and contending earnestly for the faith.

If he was not an Apostle, if Jesus had not sent him, what was he, what authority did he possess?

So you see he was forced into this controversy, he was compelled to assert his apostolic claims, he was compelled to speak of what he had done and suffered, though he did so under protest, as it were, and with a half apology for the apparent folly of doing so.

With these thoughts in his mind he dictated (probably to Timothy, his child in the faith) this second letter, which " of all his Epistles is the one which enables us to look deepest into his heart."

2 *Cor.* i. 1: Paul, an apostle of Christ Jesus through the will of God, and Timothy our brother, unto the Church of God which is at Corinth, with all the saints which are in the whole of Achaia: Grace to you and peace from God our Father and the Lord Jesus Christ.

Blessed be the God and Father of · our Lord Jesus Christ, the Father of mercies, and the God of all comfort; who comforteth us in all our affliction, that we may be able to comfort them that are in any affliction, through the comfort wherewith we ourselves are comforted of God. For as the sufferings of Christ abound unto us, even so our comfort also aboundeth through Christ. But whether we be afflicted, it is for your comfort and salvation; or whether we be comforted, it is for your comfort. . . . For we would not have you ignorant, brethren, concerning our affliction which befell us in Asia, that we were weighed down exceedingly, beyond our power, insomuch that we despaired even of life.

You will notice in this opening of the Epistle how the Apostle rings the changes upon the two thoughts of affliction and comfort. Indeed, this is one distinct characteristic of the Epistle.

S. Paul then goes on to meet the charge that had been made against him, that he had shown fickleness in changing his plans, and that he was afraid to show himself at Corinth.

Ch. i. 15 : In this confidence—that is in the rectitude of his intentions—I was minded to come before unto you . . . . but I call God for a witness upon my soul, that to spare you I forbare to come to Corinth.

Then referring to the letters of commendation which his opponents made so much of, and taunted him with not possessing, he continues :—

Ch. iii. 1: Are we beginning again to commend ourselves? or need we, as do some, epistles of commendation to you or from you? Ye are our epistle, written in our hearts known and read of all men; being made manifest that ye are an epistle of Christ, ministered by us, written not with ink, but with the Spirit of the living God; not in tables of stone, but in tables that are hearts of flesh . . . .

Ch. iv. 1 : . . . . Therefore seeing we have this ministry we faint not . . . . for we preach not ourselves, but Christ Jesus as Lord, and ourselves as your servants for Jesus' sake . . . .

Ch. iv. 8 : But we have this treasure in earthen vessels, that the exceeding greatness of the power may be of God, and not from ourselves.

When S. Paul speaks of having the treasure in earthen vessels, it would seem as if he had in his mind the story of Gideon. You remember how Gideon equipped his men, not with sword and spear, but with trumpets and torches concealed in pitchers; and then at the critical moment the trumpets were blown, the pitchers broken, and the torches brandished.

So S. Paul felt it to be with himself. To him was committed the *light* of the knowledge of the glory of God. But this light was hidden in the earthen vessel of his weakness: and the very sufferings which he endured, were but the breaking of the pitcher by which the light was manifested. And so he continues:—

Ch. iv. 8: We are pressed on every side, yet not straitened; perplexed, yet not unto despair; pursued, yet not forsaken; smitten down, yet not destroyed; always bearing about in the body the dying of Jesus, that the life also of Jesus may be manifested in our body. For we which live are alway delivered unto death for Jesus' sake, that the life also of Jesus may be manifested in our mortal flesh.... Wherefore we faint not; but though our outward man is decaying, yet our inward man is renewed day by day. For our light affliction, which is for the moment, worketh for us more and more exceedingly an eternal weight of glory; while we look not at the things which are seen, but at the things which are not seen: for the things which are seen are temporal; but the things which are not seen are eternal.

It is interesting to notice how, in this passage, the Apostle's expressions of faith and hope are pressed out of him by affliction: just as some aromatic plants whose sweet odour is latent until their leaves are bruised. We should notice also how readily the expression of personal weakness, weariness, and pain, passes into the thought of Christ's sufferings. They were the tokens of communion with Christ's sufferings, the nails by which he was crucified with Christ. He speaks of Christ's dying being manifested in him, of being always delivered unto death for his sake: and yet of this death being overcome by life, by the life of Jesus also manifested in him. Thus he was able to speak of his affliction, heavy as it was in itself, as but a light affliction, and as enduring but for a moment.

If we ask how he was able to reach this eminence of hope, this triumph of faith, it was because he lived in eternity, because the new life in him was an eternal life; and that he measured things with an eternal standard, looking not at the things which are seen, but at the things which are not seen, knowing that what was seen was temporal, what was not seen was eternal. And so he continues in the same strain:—

Ch. v. 1: For we know that if the earthly house of our tabernacle be dissolved, we have a building from God, a house not made with hands, eternal, in the heavens. For verily in this we groan, longing to be clothed upon with our habitation which is from heaven: if so be that being clothed we shall not be found naked. For indeed we that are in this tabernacle do groan, being burdened; not for that we would be unclothed, but that we should be clothed upon, that what is mortal may be swallowed up of life. Now He that wrought us for this very thing is God, who gave unto us the earnest of the Spirit.

In the light of eternity in which S. Paul was walking, his frail body, through which the troubles of life reached him, was felt to be no permanent abode for his spirit; it was decaying day by day, it would soon be dissolved, soon turned to its kindred dust; but he believed that he should not pass away altogether unclothed, but that God would provide for him a fitting body; no temporary dwelling, but a house, and that an eternal one, when what was mortal was swallowed up of life. And this hope of immortality he regarded not as an exceptional privilege belonging to himself, but one in which his brethren had a share. He believed that for this very purpose, and for nothing short of this, God had redeemed them by His Son, and sanctified them by His Spirit.

And this gift of the Spirit which they had already received, was, he tells them, an earnest of their ultimate redemption.

In the purchase of an estate a certain sum was paid down as an assurance that the whole purchase money would be paid in due time, and this was called the earnest-money. So the gift of the Spirit to us now is a pledge that the promised redemption shall be made good.

When we are young we look upon youth and strength as a treasure practically inexhaustible :-but as we get older we see how small the treasure is becoming. But if we try to live in the light of eternity, we shall see that there is laid up for us a better treasure than this. If we cherish the presence of the Holy Spirit within us, if we yield up ourselves to His moulding influence, we shall find that though the outward man is decaying, our inward man is being renewed day by day, that beneath the outer robe of this mortal body the garments of immortality are being woven; and when we put off this earthly tabernacle, we shall find that God has given us a house not made with hands, eternal, in the heavens.

CHAPTER XVII.

THE SECOND EPISTLE TO THE CORINTHIANS
(*continued*).

THE life of S. Paul was so far above the experience of ordinary Christians, he regarded things from such a different standpoint, that in reading such a passage as we had before us in our last chapter, we can only follow him at a humble distance; as an Alpine traveller follows in the footsteps of an experienced guide, and wonders to see him find a sure footing on what seems an inaccessible height.

What made him so superior to us, what gave him such strange views of life and death, was that he habitually looked not at the things which are seen, but at the things which are not seen. He lived in a world of realities, not in a world of appearances. It was this that made his unexampled affliction seem light, and a life-long sorrow to last only for a moment. It was this that made him look forward not only calmly but gladly to death. He knew that his spirit had a better and a more enduring home than this perishable tabernacle of flesh, a house not made with hands, eternal, and of heavenly origin; that what was only mortal in him would be swallowed up of life. He knew that to this end God had been leading him, that for this God had created him, Christ had redeemed him, the Holy Ghost was sanctifying him. The gift of the Spirit was not only a present possession, a very present help in trouble, but a pledge and assurance of an eternal weight of glory to be hereafter manifested. And in the same strain he continues:—

Ch. v. 6: Being therefore always of good courage, and knowing that, whilst we are at home in the body, we are absent from the Lord (for we walk by faith, not by sight); we are of good courage, I say, and are willing rather to be absent from the body, and to be at home with the Lord. Wherefore also we make it our aim, whether at home or absent, to be well-pleasing unto Him. For we must all be made manifest before the judgment-seat of Christ; that each one may receive the things done in the body, according to what he hath done, whether it be good or bad.

It is perhaps not very easy to trace the connection of thought in this passage. This reference to the great judgment, at which not only he but all would be made manifest, would be seen to be what they really were, and receive exactly what they had done, is hardly what we should have expected from what has gone before.

The Apostle had just said that he would rather be absent from the body, because to put off "this mortal coil" was to be at home with the Lord. What a contrast that home would be to his present life! *Here* he was misunderstood, misrepresented; here his character was systematically blackened, his motives slandered, his conduct maligned; *there* he would be at home, in the light of the judgment through which he would pass, what he really was would be shown, his character and actions would be fairly judged.

The fact is that S. Paul regarded the great judgment as an object of faith and hope. He was so unfairly judged, so unscrupulously condemned, that he longed for a *fair* judgment and a *just* sentence.

And this was what he felt sure that he and every one else would get. He believed in the *justice* of his Judge, and in the absolute *fairness* of His judgment.

This perfect confidence in the fairness and justice of his Judge, S. Paul had learnt from the Bible. Nothing is more striking than the way in which the Prophets and Psalmists of Israel thought of God's jugdment with thankfulness and joy.

"The Lord shall judge the people; judge me, O Lord, according to my righteousness, and according to my integrity that is in me."

"O let the wickedness of the wicked come to an end, but stablish the just: for the righteous God trieth the hearts and reins."

"Let the heavens rejoice, and let the earth be glad, for He cometh, He cometh to judge the world with righteousness, and the people with His truth."

"Unto Thee, O Lord, belongeth mercy, *for* Thou renderest to every man according to his work."

This subject is so important, that before we pass on I wish you to notice the manner in which the judgment to come presents itself to the Apostle's mind. "We shall all *be made manifest.*" Not merely we shall all appear, as our Authorised Version has it, but we shall all *be made manifest* before the tribunal of Christ. "The judgment of Christ," says the great divine I have so often quoted, "is the revelation of things as they are. His judgment does not change the judged, it simply shows them. It is not, as far as we can conceive, a conclusion drawn from the balancing of conflicting elements, or a verdict upon a general issue. The judgment of God is the perfect manifestation of truth. The punishment of God is the necessary action of the awakened conscience. The judgment is pronounced by the sinner himself, and he inflicts inexorably his own sentence. . . . In the perfect light of Christ's Presence everything will be made clear in its essential nature: the opportunity which we threw away, and knew that we threw away, . . . the temptation which we courted in the waywardness of selfish strength, the stream of consequence which has flowed from our example, the harvest which others have gathered from our sowing. We know our own hearts imperfectly; but is there one of us whom the thought of this revelation does not fill with contrition? Our imaginations are dull; but is there one of us who can imagine keener suffering than to see the glory for which we were made, and feel that we have sacrificed our birthright?" (Dr. Westcott's Historic Faith.)

We cannot wonder, then, at what the Apostle goes on to say.

Ch. v. 11: Knowing therefore the fear of the Lord, we persuade men, but we are made manifest unto God; and I hope that we are made manifest also in your consciences . . . . . For whether we are beside ourselves, it is unto God; or whether we are of sober mind, it is unto you. For the love of Christ constraineth us; because we thus judge, that One died for all, therefore all died; and He died for all, that they which live should no longer live unto themselves, but unto Him who for their sakes died and rose again. Wherefore we henceforth know no man after the flesh: even though we have known Christ after the flesh, yet now we know Him so no more. Wherefore if any man is in Christ, he is a new creature (or there is a new creation): the old things are passed away; behold, they are become new.

The Apostle had in his mind the thought of the

great judgment, when the secrets of all hearts should be disclosed, when every man should be shown exactly as he was, not as he seemed.

Living constantly in the light of God's judgment, knowing as an abiding principle the fear (not the *terror* as the A. V.) of the Lord, he endeavoured to persuade men of his rectitude and honesty of purpose. He tried to persuade *men* of this; he had no need to persuade *God*, for to God he was already made manifest. His enemies at Corinth said he was mad. Well, if he were beside himself, if at times he saw visions and heard unspeakable words; if he poured out his soul in his gift of tongues, a gift which he possessed in greater abundance than any, it was to God. And when, as was generally the case, he was in the ordinary condition of sober self-restraint, it was still unto them, that by teaching and exhortation he might do them good. "For," he continues, in words which let us into the secret of his spiritual life, which show what was the root and ground of this entire devotion to the glory of God and the good of men, "the love of Christ constraineth us."

The word which S. Paul here uses was used by Christ Himself when He said, " I have a baptism to be baptized with; and how I am *straitened* till it be accomplished." What constrained S. Paul, what held him in on every side and concentrated his energies upon his work, was the love of Christ; not the love which he bore to Christ, but the love of Christ for man.

But what is this that he goes on to say? "Because we thus judge, that One died for all, therefore all died."

He means that Christ was so indentified with the race of man, whose nature He took, that when He died, the whole race died in Him: here was the actual consequence of Christ's death. He died for all, that they which live should no longer live unto themselves, but unto Him who for their sakes died and rose again: here was the purpose of Christ's death.

Then he goes on somewhat in this track of thought. To know Christ in this way, to know Him and the power of His resurrection, to share His life, and in the power of that life to walk even as He walked, was far better than to have known Jesus in the flesh. This was what the false teachers at Corinth boasted of; and because he himself had not known Jesus in the flesh, they disparaged his authority and derided his claim to be an Apostle.

In answer to this, S. Paul had naturally laid great stress upon Christ's appearance to him. But this he says he will do no longer. Though I have known Christ after the flesh, yet now I know him so no more, for I know Him in a better way, as the Lord of my spirit.

And this was true not of him alone, but of every man. "Wherefore if any man is in Christ, he is a new creature, he enters upon a new creation,—new heavens and a new earth; the old things are passed away; behold they are become new." "But," he continues:—

Ch. v. 18: All things are of God, who reconciled us to Himself through Christ, and gave unto us the ministry of reconciliation; to wit, that God was in Christ reconciling the world unto Himself, not reckoning unto them their trespasses, and having committed unto us the word of reconciliation. We are ambassadors therefore on behalf of Christ, as though God were intreating by us: we beseech you on behalf of Christ, be ye reconciled to God. Him who knew no sin He made to be sin on our behalf; that we might become the righteousness of God in Him.

And working together with Him we entreat also that ye receive not the grace of God in vain.

This passage is one of the most important in the New Testament, as showing us the true nature of the Atonement.

The whole work of man's salvation is declared to spring from God. The whole Deity was in Christ reconciling the world. The reconciliation and pardon were not forced from an unwilling Father: God loved the world, not because He sent His Son, but sent His Son because He loved the world.

On God's part the reconciliation is effected; on God's side all barriers are broken down, all obstacles removed. We have no need to attempt to reconcile God to us. He *is* reconciled; what we have to do is to be reconciled to Him. We have no obstacles to surmount except such as we put in the way ourselves. The real obstacles that stand in the way of a full reconciliation with God, are our own pride and selfishness; these must be put away, or, terrible to think of, we may receive the grace of God in vain.

CHAPTER XVIII.

THE SECOND EPISTLE TO THE CORINTHIANS
(*continued*).

WE come now to another section of S. Paul's second letter to the Corinthians. It is a section that often troubles people a good deal, because it seems to breathe a spirit of boasting and self-assertion.

We are apt to forget that it is impossible to form a fair judgment unless we are in possession of the circumstances that called it forth. A man may be brought to such a pass, that self-assertion becomes a positive duty to him, and what sounds like boasting and vainglory, is found to be the best means of self-assertion, and that not for his own sake, but for the sake of others, and for the truth's sake.

There is many a man who, if he followed his own inclinations, would never emerge from private life, yet who is forced to enter upon a life of controversy and strife, and to be, like Jeremiah, a man of contention when he would fain be a man of peace.

It was so with S. Paul. Controversy and self-assertion were forced upon him. A man who is suddenly attacked cannot afford to be over nice in the choice of weapons, he must take what comes first to hand. Here were these Judaizers at Corinth leaving no stone unturned to undermine his character, to injure his reputation, to disparage his authority, and to spoil his work. If he had not been first of all the servant and Apostle of Jesus Christ, if he had not been a witness for God's truth, he might have remained silent and allowed them to do their worst.

But feeling as he did the importance of the truth for which he witnessed, feeling that the purity of the Gospel of the grace of God would be sullied, its power limited, its embrace narrowed, unless he earnestly contended for it, S. Paul put aside his own personal feelings, and vindicated his authority as an Apostle of Christ. And was not such vindication necessary?

How could he hope to be believed, how could he give force to his convictions, if his enemies were allowed unopposed, and unanswered, to deny his claim to be the Apostle of Jesus Christ?

If he was not an Apostle, what was he? If Jesus Christ had not sent him, had not taught him, how could he enforce the truth? If he were not free from every human authority; if he were not absolutely independent of the very chiefest Apostles; if he were not inspired by the Holy Ghost; what claim had he to be listened to, if it could be made to seem that what he taught was not in perfect harmony with the received doctrine of the Church of Jerusalem, and the alleged teaching of the Twelve?

It was necessary therefore to show that he was an Apostle, and that his Apostleship was not derived from any human source, and was of equal authority with that of the original Apostles.

You will remember that one of the things which the Apostle's enemies said of him was, that however bold he might be in his letters when he was absent, he was feeble and timid at close quarters, and that because he did not feel any confidence in his own position or authority.

It was to meet this charge in the first place that he wrote as follows:—

Ch. x. 1: Now I Paul myself intreat you by the meekness and gentleness of Christ, I who in your presence am lowly among you, but being absent am of good courage toward you: yea, I beseech you, that I may not when present [be forced to] show courage with the confidence wherewith I count to be bold against some, which count of us as if we walked according to the flesh..... For though I should glory somewhat abundantly concerning our authority (which the Lord gave for building you up, and not for casting you down), I shall not be put to shame: that I may not seem as if I would terrify you by my letters. For, his letters, they say, are weighty and strong; but his bodily presence is weak, and his speech of no account. Let such a one reckon this, that, what we are in word by letters when we are absent, such are we also in deed when we are present.... Would that ye could bear with me in a little foolishness: nay indeed bear with me.... I say again, Let no man think me foolish; but if ye do, yet as foolish receive me, that I also may glory a little .... Seeing that many glory after the flesh, I will glory also .... Are they Hebrews? So am I. Are they Israelites? So am I. Are they the seed of Abraham? So am I. Are they ministers of Christ? (I speak as one beside himself) I more; in labours more abundantly, in prisons more abundantly, in strifes above measure, in deaths oft. Of the Jews five times received I forty stripes save one. Thrice was I beaten with rods, once was I stoned, thrice I suffered shipwreck, a night and a day have I been in the deep; in journeyings often, in perils of rivers, in perils of robbers, in perils from my countrymen, in perils from the Gentiles, in perils in the City (i.e. Jerusalem), in perils in the wilderness, in perils in the sea, in perils among false brethren; in labour and travail, in watchings often, in hunger and thirst, in fastings often, in cold and nakedness.

Beside those things that are without, there is that which presseth upon me daily, anxiety for all the Churches. Who is weak, and I am not weak? Who is made to stumble, and I burn not? If I must needs glory, I will glory of the things that concern my weakness.

Is not this a wonderful description? If the great Apostle had been silent, if he had said nothing of all this, if he had not condescended to meet his adversaries on their own ground, and boast as they boasted; if he had been too great, too proud to speak of himself, as, according to his critics, he ought to have been, think what we, and the whole Church in every age, would have lost. It is very well for people who live in quiet and comfortable homes, whose Christianity has never caused them to suffer the slightest pain, has never cost them a single sigh or a single tear, it is all very well for them to say that it is unbecoming to boast of one's own doings as S. Paul did: but let them think what the solitary missionary, the pioneer of Christianity and civilization would have lost, if those miserable Judaizers at Corinth had not wrung this noble defence from the agonized heart of this great Apostle! How many men whose lives have been one long scene of poverty, loneliness, violence, persecution, and calumny, of pain and weariness, disappointment and despair, have been cheered and encouraged by reading of the sufferings of S. Paul!

What a list of sufferings, what a catalogue of perils it is!

We see that the narrative of the Acts, which extends much further into the life of S. Paul than the point at which we are now arrived, does not relate a tenth part of the labours and sufferings of S. Paul.

The shipwreck which is related with such fulness in the Acts was still in the future, and yet S. Paul tells us that already he had thrice suffered shipwreck, and had besides been a night and day in the deep, clinging perhaps to some fragment of the ship or to some floating mast.

Already he had been publicly scourged five times in the synagogues of the Jews, as a heretic and false teacher. Three times, in spite of Roman citizenship, he had been beaten with the rods of the Roman lictors; and in addition to all these perils and persecution, he had to bear the ever-increasing burden of anxiety caused by the Churches he had founded.

Passing on from this description of his apostolic labours, S. Paul deals with the visions and revelations of the Lord which had been accorded to him. If his depreciators attached great importance to visions and revelations, what were any that they could pretend to, compared with what had been made to him? Which of them had been, like S. Paul, caught up into the third heaven and heard words unspeakable, which it is not lawful for a man to utter? But breaking off from a theme so mysterious, and so personal, he continues:—

Ch. xii. 6: But I forbear, lest any man should account of me above that which he seeth me to be or heareth from me. And by reason of the exceeding greatness of the revelations—wherefore, that I should not be exalted overmuch, there was given to me a thorn in the flesh, a messenger of Satan to buffet me, that I should not be exalted overmuch. Concerning this thing I besought the Lord thrice, that it might depart from me. And He hath said unto me, My grace is sufficient for thee: for my power is made perfect in weakness. Most gladly therefore will I rather glory in my weaknesses, that the strength of Christ may rest upon me. Wherefore I take pleasure in weaknesses, in injuries, in necessities, in persecutions, in distresses, for Christ's sake: for when I am weak, then am I strong.

What special and humiliating affliction is referred to in the expression, thorn or stake in the flesh, cannot be known for certain. It has been thought that it was some affection of the eyesight, and there would seem to be some traces of such partial blindness; but as we cannot know for certain it is useless to speculate.

Whatever it was, it was something very trying, and perhaps humiliating. More important is it to notice, how his prayer for its removal was answered, for it *was* answered.

As the Lord Himself had prayed three times that the cup of suffering might pass from Him, and yet notwithstanding had to drink it to the dregs, so His tried and afflicted servant prayed three times that this thorn in the flesh might depart from him, and had still to bear it.

But in neither case was the prayer unheard or unanswered. Each time the Saviour had prayed that the cup might pass from Him, He had been careful to add the prayer, that His Father's will should be done. And that prayer was heard and answered, the Father's will was done; and as for Himself, an angel appeared and strengthened Him.

So with S. Paul, the answer came to him: "My grace is sufficient for thee, for my power is made perfect in weakness" (2 Cor. xii. 9).

How sufficient we learn from what the Apostle says,—"when I am weak, then I am strong." When I most feel my own weakness, then I am most strong, because I lean in my weakness upon Him that is mighty.

But we must now pass on to the Apostle's closing words.

Ch. xiii. 11: Finally, brethren, farewell. Be perfected, be comforted, be of the same mind, live in peace: and the God of love and peace shall be with you. Salute one another with a holy kiss.

All the saints salute you.

And then follow the words that are so familiar to us all, as the concluding prayer of our matins and evensong.

We repeat these words so often, that there is some risk of our not attaching any definite meaning to them.

It is well, perhaps, to be reminded that the communion or fellowship of the Holy Ghost is not something distinct and separate from the love of the Father and the grace of our Lord Jesus Christ; but is rather that power by which we are able to welcome the love of God, and receive the grace of our Lord Jesus Christ. It is the special work of the Holy Spirit to reveal the Father and the Son: it is His office to take of the things of Christ and show them to us. It is by Him only that we can say that Jesus is the Christ; it is He alone that can teach us to say, Abba, Father.

Ch. xiii. 14: The grace of the Lord Jesus Christ, and the love of God, and the communion [or fellowship] of the Holy Ghost, be with you all.

CHAPTER XIX.

THE EPISTLE TO THE GALATIANS.

AFTER writing the Second Epistle to the Corinthians at one of the cities of Macedonia, S. Paul, as we read in the Acts of the Apostles, came into Greece, and no doubt, though the sacred historian does not mention it, made Corinth his headquarters. S. Luke gives us no details of his visit. We should like to have heard how the Corinthian Christians received their Apostle, whether his opponents submitted at once to his authority, whether, after all, he came unto them "with a rod, or in the spirit of meekness."

When S. Paul reached Corinth, it would seem that news had been received from the Churches of Galatia, of later date than any that had yet reached the Apostle, which filled him with dismay and righteous indignation.

The Galatians were a light-hearted, fickle, and impetuous people, of the same race, and apparently of much the same character, as the Gauls of Europe. They had received the Gospel from S. Paul with great readiness. Indeed they received him, as the Apostle himself tells us, as an angel of God, nay, even as Christ Himself. They were ready, if that had been possible, to pluck out their own eyes and give them to him.

But the same restless, impulsive character which

made them so ready to receive the Gospel, made them an easy prey to the same emissaries of Judaism who had sown their tares in other fields of S. Paul's labours. These Judaizing Christians claimed, and perhaps possessed, the authority of the leaders of the Church of Jerusalem. In Corinth the Greek feeling against Judaism prevented them from having their full swing: but in Galatia, among the less civilized and fickle Gauls, they had it all their own way.

These men began as usual by undermining S. Paul's authority, blackening his character, imputing to him the worst motives. He was no real Apostle. He had never seen the Lord, except in a vision real or pretended; what knowledge of Christ's truth he had he had derived from the Twelve, and this he had perverted and adulterated. He was an unscrupulous flatterer and hypocrite, becoming all things to all men. Who was this apostate Jew, this turncoat Pharisee, to set himself against James the Just, against Peter and John? Would they rather believe this sham Apostle than Abraham, the friend of God and Moses, who saw God face to face?

Then they attacked his doctrine. What right had he to say that the Law was abrogated, when Jesus Himself had said that He came not to destroy the Law but to fulfil it? Who was he that presumed to say that circumcision was of no importance?

Baptism, it is true, they might allow, might admit Gentiles into the outer courts of Christ's true Church; but if the Galatian converts wished to gain admission into the sanctuary, the holy place of Christ's Church, they must be circumcised, even as the Lord was circumcised.

This was the key to their position: and, accordingly, S. Paul attacked it with all the fervour and concentrated passion of his fiery nature.

His keen spiritual insight, naturally keen, but now keener by the Spirit of Christ in him, saw at a glance that the real issue of this controversy was not whether he, Paul, was equal in apostolic authority to the Twelve, or whether circumcision was necessary or useless, but whether the religion and Church of Christ was to be free or enslaved; whether the fountain of the Gospel was to flow freely for all, or whether it was to be choked up with the ashes of a dead Judaism.

These Judaizers were not merely hurting his reputation, not merely substituting another *method* of teaching for his: they were preaching another, a different Gospel, which was indeed no Gospel, no good tidings at all.

It was, then, to meet this pressing need, this vital danger, that S. Paul wrote this letter. Unlike his other Epistles, he wrote it with his own hand.

Its very opening, its very style, showed that there was something wrong. There are no expressions of affection, no thanksgiving to God on their behalf. He begins thus:—

Ch. i. 1: Paul, an apostle (not from men, neither through man, but through Jesus Christ, and God the Father, who raised Him from the dead), and all the brethren which are with me, unto the Churches of Galatia: Grace to you and peace from God the Father, and our Lord Jesus Christ, who gave Himself for our sins, that He might deliver us out of this present evil world, according to the will of our God and Father: to whom be the glory for ever and ever. Amen.

After this salutation the Apostle plunges into the midst of his subject, writing in short, broken, abrupt sentences, as a man speaks in great excitement :—

Ch. i. 6: I marvel that ye are so quickly removing from Him that called you in the grace of Christ unto a different

Gospel; which is not another Gospel: only there are some that trouble you, and would pervert the Gospel of Christ.

But though we, or an angel from heaven, should preach unto you any Gospel other than that which we preached unto you, let him be anathema.

In the next sentence the Apostle repeats his assertion that the Gospel which he preached was not after man; that he did not receive it from man, was not taught it by man, but that it came to him by the immediate revelation of Jesus Christ. Then he reminds them of his own vehement attachment to Jewish tradition, and tells them how God had freed him from his bondage by the revelation of His Son in him.

As for learning of the Twelve, after his conversion he had not gone to Jerusalem at all, but went to Arabia. And when he did go to Jerusalem he only stayed fifteen days, and saw only Peter and James. Nor was it till fourteen years after that he went to Jerusalem again, and then it was by the express direction of God. The result of the conference which he had there, was that the pillars of the Church added nothing to him, imposed no new restraints, but frankly recognized his mission to the Gentiles, as distinct from, and yet parallel to, their own mission to the Jews.

So much had been made of the paramount authority of Peter and James, that plain speaking was necessary, and accordingly S. Paul goes on to relate—what he would doubtless have rather consigned to oblivion—the inconsistency which Peter had displayed, which made it necessary to withstand him. When Peter came to Antioch he fully recognized the Gentile Christians as brothers in Christ, and mixed freely with them in private, as well as in public: but when certain came from James, Peter's

Jewish prejudices revived, and he withdrew from his former free intercourse, and stood aloof from the Gentile Christians, and by the overwhelming force of his character and authority induced Barnabas to do the same. Then publicly S. Paul withstood him, and rebuked his inconsistency and forgetfulness of the true principles of the common faith.

Ch. ii. 14: I said unto Cephas before them all, If thou, being a Jew, livest as do the Gentiles, and not as do the Jews, how compellest thou the Gentiles to live as do the Jews? We yet knowing that a man is not justified by the works of the Law, save through faith in Jesus Christ, even we (Jews as we are) believed on Christ Jesus, that we (no less than the Gentiles) might be justified by faith in Christ, and not by the works of the Law: because by the works of the Law shall no flesh (whether Jew or Gentile) be justified.

Then S. Paul adopts another argument. The gift of the Holy Spirit was the special characteristic of the Gospel, it was the crowning gift of the grace of God, it was what made their profession of Christ's religion a living power. Was then, he asks of them, this Divine gift given them by the Law or by the Gospel?

Ch. iii. 1: O foolish Galatians, who did bewitch you, before whose eyes Jesus Christ was openly set forth crucified?

This only would I learn from you. Received ye the Spirit by the works of the Law, or by the hearing of faith? Are ye so foolish? having begun in the Spirit, are ye now perfected in the flesh (i.e. by Circumcision)? . . . . Now that no man is justified by the Law in the sight of God is evident: for, the righteous shall live by faith; and the Law is not of faith; but He that doeth them shall live in them.

This is the great thesis that S. Paul works out, as we shall see afterwards, in the Epistle to the Romans.

Ch. iii. 23: But before faith came, we were kept in ward under the Law, shut up unto the faith which should afterwards be revealed. So that the Law hath been our tutor to bring us unto Christ, that we might be justified [receive power to become righteous] by faith. But now that faith is come, we are no longer under a tutor. For ye are all sons of God, through faith, in Christ Jesus. For as many of you as were baptized into Christ did put on Christ ... and if ye are Christ's, then are ye Abraham's seed, heirs according to promise.

Ch. iv. 1: But I say that so long as the heir is a child, he differeth nothing from a bond-servant, though he is lord of all; but is under guardians and stewards until the term appointed of the Father. So we also, when we were children, were held in bondage under the rudiments of the world: but when the fulness of the time came, God sent forth His Son, born of a woman, born under the Law, that He might redeem them which were under the Law, that we might receive the adoption of sons. And because ye are sons, God sent forth the Spirit of His Son into our hearts, crying, "Abba, Father." So that thou art no longer a bond-servant, but a son; and if a son, then an heir through God.

Ch. iv. 28-31: For we, brethren, as Isaac was, are children of promise, ... not children of a handmaid, but of the free-woman. With freedom did Christ set us free: stand fast therefore, and be not entangled again in a yoke of bondage.

You will remember that the Judaizing false teachers tried to make the Galatians believe that baptism only made them rudimentary Christians; and that if they would advance to the full manhood of Christianity, they must be circumcized, and brought under the Law. In the passage which we have just read, S. Paul turns the tables upon them. For men who had been baptized into Christ, and who had received His Spirit, to be circumcized was to go backwards, not forwards; was to leave the completeness of spiritual privilege for a rudimentary condition; was to exchange liberty for servitude, the full free life of citizens in Christ's kingdom for the restrictions of a nursery and a school.

It was not by being children of Abraham after the flesh—whether by natural descent or by circumcision—that they became heirs of the Promise, but by being made members of Christ and partakers of His Spirit, that Spirit of adoption whereby we cry, "Abba, Father."

CHAPTER XX.

THE EPISTLE TO THE GALATIANS
(continued.)

NO one can read this Epistle without feeling that of all S. Paul's letters this is the most combative, the most controversial.

In dealing with the Judaizers at Corinth, the Apostle had contented himself with treating circumcision as a thing indifferent. He laid down in effect what was afterwards crystallized into a theological epigram: "In necessary things unity, in things doubtful liberty, in all things charity."

"Was any man called being circumcized? let him not become uncircumcized. Hath any been called in uncircumcision? let him not be circumcized. Circumcision is nothing, and uncircumcision is nothing, but the keeping of the Commandments of God."

But in dealing with the Galatians the Apostle goes much further. Circumstances alter cases, as we say. And the circumstances of the Galatians were totally different from anything that had obtained in Corinth.

In the case of the Galatian Christians, circumcision could no longer be considered a thing indifferent. For them, Gentiles by birth and education, Christians by profession, children of God by adoption and grace, for them to be circumcized was to cut themselves off from Christ, was to seek salvation in another, and that an impossible way. To be circumcized was in effect to say that Christ had not redeemed them, to put themselves under the curse of the Law from which Christ had died to deliver them. It was to lay themselves under a formal obligation to obey the whole Law, and that not merely as the rule of life, but as the ground of their acceptance with God. It was to fall from grace.

"Behold," he says, "I, Paul, say unto you, that if ye receive circumcision Christ will profit you nothing ... ye are severed from Christ ... ye are fallen from grace."

For a Christian believer to be circumcized, was like a free man voluntarily entering a prison, and with his own hands binding himself with the heavy chains of a wearisome ceremonialism. Christ had made them free, for freedom were they called, in this freedom let them stand fast.

But then comes the question, what is freedom? In renouncing the Law, in refusing circumcision, were they rebelling against the unchangeable Law of God's holy will? Was the liberty with which Christ had made them free, the liberty of fleshly licence, the liberty of each man to please himself and live for himself? No: rather was it the liberty of yielding to God's Holy Spirit, the liberty to serve one another in love. Thou shalt love thy neighbour as thyself, was indeed, as S. James himself declared, the true law of liberty.

"There were two powers," says one of the greatest thinkers of our day, speaking on this Epistle, "contending for them. The flesh was lusting against the Spirit, the Spirit against the flesh, so that they did not do all the things which they would, either all the good or all the evil which they intended. But if they submitted to be led by the Spirit, they would not fulfil the lusts of the flesh, and they would not be under the yoke of the law. For law exists to condemn the acts of the flesh; and the fruits of the Spirit are those against which there is no law. The privilege of those who belonged to Christ, is that they are crucified with Him; they have renounced the flesh and the lusts which are *their own*; they have claimed the righteousness and life which are *in Him*." (Maurice, Unity of the New Testament.)

But let us allow S. Paul to speak for himself.

Ch. v. 13: For ye, brethren, were called for freedom; only use not your freedom for an occasion to the flesh, but through love be servants one to another. For the whole law is fulfilled in one word, even in this; Thou shalt love thy neighbour as thyself. But if ye bite and devour one another, take heed that ye be not consumed one of another.

Ch. v. 16: But I say, Walk by the Spirit, and ye shall not fulfil the lusts of the flesh. For the flesh lusteth against the Spirit, and the Spirit against the flesh; for these are contrary the one to the other; that ye may not do the things that ye would. But if ye are led by the Spirit, ye are not under the law. Now the works of the flesh are manifest, which are these, fornication, uncleanness, lasciviousness, idolatry, sorcery, enmities, strife, jealousies, wraths, factions, divisions, heresies, envyings, drunkenness, revellings, and such like: of the which I forewarn you, even as I did forewarn you, that they which practise such things shall not inherit the kingdom of God.

Our Lord had said to the Jews—"If ye abide in my word, then are ye truly my disciples, and ye shall know the truth, and the truth shall make you free: and if the Son shall make you free, ye shall be free indeed."

So S. Paul said to the Galatians, " ye were called for freedom." But what sort of freedom? Freedom not to do as we like; but freedom to follow God's Holy Will. Walk by the Spirit, he says; by the Spirit which is the distinguishing gift of the Gospel, and ye shall be delivered from the only bondage that really matters, the bondage of sin reigning in our flesh.

By "*walking*" by the Spirit, the Apostle means living in the Spirit, and not only living, but moving, and not only moving, but advancing by the power of the Spirit.

"For the flesh lusteth against the Spirit and the Spirit against the flesh, that ye may not do the things that ye would."

We are subject to two antagonistic forces: the Holy Spirit of God acting upon our spirits draws us one way; the power of evil, acting through our lower nature, draws us another way. The result of this spiritual "parallelogram of forces" is that in neither direction do we proceed in the direct line of either force. The Spirit prevents our living to the flesh; the flesh hinders us in walking by the Spirit; so that, on the one hand, we are kept from doing the things to which our sinful nature prompts us; while on the other hand we are also prevented from perfectly fulfilling the things to which the Holy Spirit leads us.

Then follows a terrible catalogue of the works of the flesh, from which, if the Galatians thought circumcision would deliver them, they were very much mistaken.

"*Lasciviousness*;" rather, perhaps, wantonness, petulance, wanton insolence.

"*Sorcery*;" either sorcery as we understand it, or poisonings, the giving of potions and philters and the like.

"*Wraths*;" passionate outbreaks of temper.

The catalogue is followed by a warning that they

who practise such things shall not inherit the kingdom of God, whether they are circumcized or uncircumcized.

Notice the force of the word "*practise.*" It is not, as in our Authorized Version, such as *do* these things, but such as *practise* them. By a sudden outbreak of passion, under violent temptation, a man may be betrayed into one or other of them—as indeed S. Paul says himself a few verses further on: " Brethren, even if a man be overtaken in a trespass, ye that are spiritual restore such an one in a spirit of meekness." But that is a very different thing from *practising* them. The Apostle draws a similar distinction in the Epistle to the Romans, where he says, " Let not sin *reign* in your bodies." We cannot help sin *being* in us; but we can help sin *reigning* in us.

Then in beautiful contrast to the catalogue of the works of the flesh, the Apostle gives us a list of the fruit of the Spirit.

Notice the change in the word; he does not call them the *works* of the Spirit, though they might be so called; but he calls them the *fruit* of the Spirit. The expression "fruit" denotes the living, organic connection between these Christian graces and the Holy Spirit from which they grow. Works do not necessarily correspond with the characters of the people who do them. A man who is essentially a coward may do a brave action; a cruel man may subscribe to the Society for the Prevention of Cruelty to Animals: but such are works, not fruits, they do not grow naturally from the character of the man who does them.

We may notice also that the singular, not the plural, is used. It appears so, at least, in the Revised Version. It is not the fruits, but the fruit of the Spirit. As God is One, as the whole law is fulfilled in love; so Christian perfection is one. Just as the light is one, till it passes through a prism, and then appears in many colours, so the many-coloured virtues of the Christian life are resolvable into the one pure heavenly light of the Christ-life.

Ch. v. 22: But the fruit of the Spirit is love, joy, peace, long-suffering, kindness, goodness, faithfulness, meekness, self-control (margin): against such there is no law. And they that are of Christ Jesus have crucified the flesh with the passions and the lusts thereof.

If we live by the Spirit, by the Spirit let us also walk. Let us not be vain-glorious, provoking one another, envying one another.... [But] bear ye one another's burdens, and so fulfil the law of Christ.

Then follows a passage which contains a great principle, which we should all do well to lay to heart. This great principle is the law of the spiritual harvest: *Whatsoever a man soweth, that shall he also reap.*

The results of sin and righteousness, the results of living to the flesh and living by the Spirit, do not follow by chance or caprice, but by an inexorable law. That this law is in force in the natural world goes without saying. If a farmer sows wheat, he reaps wheat; if he sows barley, he reaps barley. If he sows his field with thistle-seed, or what comes to much the same thing, if he allows it to grow what it will, he has no right to expect to reap wheat at harvest.

So in the spiritual world we shall reap what we have sown. If we sow love, we shall reap love; we shall become loving: if we sow hatred, we shall reap hatred; we shall become hateful: if we sow impurity, we shall reap impurity; we shall become steeped in defilement.

Ch. vi. 6: Let him that is taught in the word communicate unto him that teacheth in all good things. Be not deceived; God is not mocked: for whatsoever a man soweth, that shall he also reap. For he that soweth unto his own flesh, shall of the flesh reap corruption; but he that soweth unto the Spirit, shall of the Spirit reap eternal life.

And let us not be weary in well-doing: for in due season we shall reap, if we faint not.

Then in the concluding paragraph of the Epistle S. Paul calls attention to the large characters in which, with his own hand, he had written this letter; and with a final warning against the false teachers who were leading them astray, he concludes,

Ch. vi. 11: See with how large letters I have written unto you with mine own hand. As many as desire to make a fair show in the flesh, they compel you to be circumcized ... that they may glory in your flesh. But far be it from me to glory, save in the Cross of our Lord Jesus Christ, through which the world hath been crucified unto me, and I unto the world. For neither is circumcision anything, nor uncircumcision, but a new creature (or creation). And as many as shall walk by this rule, peace be upon them, and mercy, and upon the Israel of God.

From henceforth let no man trouble me: for I bear branded on my body the marks of Jesus.

The grace of our Lord Jesus Christ be with your spirit, brethren. Amen.

CHAPTER XXI.

THE EPISTLE TO THE ROMANS.

IT was during the same visit to Corinth, during which, as we have seen, S. Paul wrote his Epistle to the Galatians, that he wrote also the Epistle to the Romans. There is a strong likeness between the two. The truths which S. Paul insisted on in his letter to the Galatians, he lays down with greater breadth of treatment, and in more general terms, in his longer and more important letter to the Christians of the Imperial City.

Little is known about the Christian Church at Rome. Strangers from Rome had been present at Jerusalem on the Day of Pentecost, but as yet it had not been visited by any of the Apostles.

S. Paul seems to have felt that, as the Apostle of the Gentiles, the Christians of the metropolis of the Gentile world had a claim upon him; so as he was uncertain when he should be able to accomplish his intention of visiting them, he determined to write them an apostolic letter which might settle their faith, and clear up some of their difficulties. This apostolical letter was that which is known to us as the Epistle to the Romans.

"We must picture to ourselves in reading this profound Epistle to the Romans, a man full of thought, his hands perhaps occupied at the moment in stitching at the tent-cloth, dictating one clause at a time to the obscure Tertius beside him, stopping only to give time for the writing, never looking it over, never perhaps hearing it read over, at last taking the style into his hand to add the last few words of affectionate benediction." (Dr. Vaughan.)

Ch. i. 1: Paul, a servant of Jesus Christ, called to be an Apostle .... to all that are in Rome, beloved of God, called to be saints: Grace to you, and peace from God our Father and the Lord Jesus Christ ....

Now I would not have you ignorant, brethren, that oftentimes I purposed to come unto you, and was hindered hitherto ... So, as much as in me is, I am ready to preach the Gospel to you also that are in Rome. For I am not ashamed of the Gospel: for it is *the Power of God unto Salvation to every one that believeth;* to the Jew first, and also to the Greek. For therein is revealed a *Righteousness of God* by faith unto faith, as it is written, "But the righteous shall live by faith."

S. Paul you see describes himself as "a servant" or "slave" of Jesus Christ. From the day that, on the road to Damascus, he had cried out, "Lord, what wilt Thou have me to do?" he had never wavered in his allegiance; the greatest honour that he could have was to be the slave of Jesus Christ.

"To *all* that are in Rome," i.e. to all, both Jews and Gentiles.

"*Grace* be to you, and *peace.*"

The word "grace," as I have before pointed out, corresponds with the ordinary salutation of the nations of the West; "peace" was the salutation of the nations of the East. S. Paul adopts the salutation of both.

Having thus given them his apostolic greeting, S. Paul goes on to say that, though often prevented, he was ready to preach the Gospel in the capital of the world as well as in other places, for that he was not ashamed of the Gospel of Christ: and this brings him to describe the Gospel in words which strike the keynote of the whole Epistle, and furnish the key to its meaning. It was the Power of God, a Revelation of God's Righteousness, leading men to salvation, accepted and lived upon by faith.

S. Paul knew the Jewish world, and he knew the Gentile world, and he saw that human nature, whether Jewish or Gentile, was powerless for good. Individual Jews might walk with God, individual Gentiles might seek after God: but there was in neither any power to lift itself to a higher righteousness, still less to raise a dead and dying world to righteousness. No, the only lever by which the world could be lifted into righteousness, was the Gospel which was committed unto him.

The Religion of Jesus Christ was not so much a system of doctrine, or a code of morals, or a special worship, as a *power*, a power which could raise sinful man to righteousness, and bring salvation to a perishing race. It revealed a righteousness of God, that is, a righteousness of which God was the author and source.

This righteousness was not left to be discovered or invented by man: it was revealed by God, and was to be appropriated by *faith*. "By faith unto faith." That is, from faith "begun" to faith "finished"; from the first imperfect faith in which we say, "Lord, I believe, help thou my unbelief," to the perfect faith which can say, "I know in whom I have believed."

In the same way we go from "strength to strength," we receive "grace for grace," are changed from "glory to glory."

Having thus stated the nature and aim of the Gospel, the next point was to show the absolute need of the Gospel; to show that both Jews and

Gentiles had fallen from righteousness, and were utterly without power to regain it. This he proceeds to do in the following verses. He takes the case of the Gentiles first:—

Ch. i. 18: For the wrath of God is revealed from heaven against all ungodliness and unrighteousness of men, who hold down the truth in unrighteousness; because that which may be known of God is manifest in them; for God manifested it unto them .... even His everlasting power and divinity; that they may be without excuse: because that, knowing God, they glorified Him not as God, neither gave thanks ... And even as they refused to have God in their knowledge, God gave them up unto a reprobate mind, to do those things which are not fitting ..... [and although] knowing the ordinance of God, that they which practise such things are worthy of death, not only do the same, but also consent with them that practise them.

In these verses the Apostle declares that all men, as men, had some knowledge of God, some knowledge of the wrath of God against sin, and that they were responsible to God for this knowledge. They had some truth, but they kept it down, kept it in prison, as it were. This truth, viz. God's power and Godhead, God manifested in them. It was indeed part of the Divine image in which man was created. It was stamped upon the nature of men. But they disregarded it. And then comes the punishment—the revelation of God's wrath against sin—" He gave them up." Sin is its own punishment. God's wrath against sin was shown in the *degradation* and *dishonour* of sin. As God set a mark upon Cain, so has He stamped His judgment of man's sin upon man himself. Sin stamps its hateful character upon a man's face; so that men can read, as in a book, in a sinner's face the degradation and dishonour which sin has wrought in him.

And now having convicted the Gentile world of sin, the Apostle turns to the *Jews*.

Ch. ii. 1: Wherefore thou art without excuse, O man, whosoever thou art that judgest: for wherein thou judgest another, thou condemnest thyself; for thou that judgest dost practise the same things ...... Thou bearest the name of a Jew and restest upon the law, and gloriest in God, and knowest His will .... being instructed out of the law, and .... having in the law the form of knowledge and of the truth. Thou therefore that teachest another, teachest thou not thyself? .... Thou who gloriest in the law, dishonourest thou God? For the name of God is blasphemed among the Gentiles because of you.

Ch. iii. 10 : [Thus have we] laid to the charge both of Jews and Greeks that they are *all* under sin .... that every mouth may be stopped, and all the world may be brought under the judgment of God ....

But now apart from the Law a *Righteousness of God* hath been manifested, even the righteousness of God through faith in Jesus Christ unto all them that believe; for there is no distinction ; for all have sinned, and fall short of the glory of God; being justified (empowered for righteousness) freely by His grace through the *Redemption* that is in Christ Jesus, whom God set forth to be a propitiation, through faith, by His Blood, to shew His righteousness, ... that He might Himself be just, and the Justifier of him that hath faith in Jesus .... (Ch. iv. 25) who was delivered up for our trespasses, and was raised for our justification, (for our renewal to righteousness). (Ch. v. 1) Being therefore justified (empowered for righteousness) by faith, let us have peace with God, through our Lord Jesus Christ.

In dealing with the Jews, S. Paul had a harder task. What he had said about the heathen world would have been sadly assented to by thoughtful Gentiles ; but in dealing with the Jews, he had to combat their self-righteousness. If to condemn sin and sinners were righteousness, then the Jews were righteous enough ; but while they condemned sin in others, they lived in the practice of it themselves.

Then having shown that both Jew and Gentile were guilty before God, and without excuse, he goes on to declare that in the Gospel God had revealed a way by which all who believed in Christ might reach a real righteousness; and that this righteousness was made possible to man by the Redemption or Atonement which Christ had made by His death, for He died for our sins, and was raised to bring us to righteousness.

CHAPTER XXII.

THE EPISTLE TO THE ROMANS
(*continued*).

ST. Paul, you will remember, has been showing that what neither Jew nor Gentile could have done for themselves, God had done for them by sending His Son to live and die for them. That righteousness which they could never have attained to by themselves, was brought near to them in Christ, and could be embraced and made their own by faith.

Now he goes back again and speaks of the condition of the world before Christ came. He speaks of man as being "*weak, without strength.*"

Man was powerless for good, sensible of guilt, and not without a sense of righteousness, but *without strength*. Mankind was like the man in the parable who fell among robbers, lying by the wayside wounded and bleeding to death. Priest and Levite could do nothing, there was no chance for him till the Good Samaritan should come.

Ch. v. 6: For while we were yet weak, in due season Christ died for the ungodly. For .... God commendeth His own love toward us, in that, while we were yet sinners, Christ died for us. Much more then, being now justified (empowered for righteousness) by His Blood, shall we be saved from the wrath of God through Him. For if, while we were enemies, we were reconciled to God through the death of His Son, much more, being reconciled, shall we be saved by His Life.

Man's extremity is God's opportunity. And so we read, "In due season Christ died for the ungodly." "In due season," that is, at the proper time. So in Gal. iv. 4, "when the fulness of the time was come, God sent forth His Son."

In this way He commended His love to us. It was not that we loved God, but that He loved us, and sent His Son to be the propitiation for our sins. "God so loved the world, that He gave His only-begotten Son." "God was in Christ reconciling the world unto Himself." This truth is so mysterious and so important that S. Paul repeats it over and over again.

We are justified by Christ's *blood:* we are reconciled by His *death.*

By the shedding of Christ's blood upon the cross the whole race was justified; when Christ resigned His Spirit into His Father's hands the whole world was reconciled. We are so used to this expression, saved or reconciled by the blood of Christ, that perhaps we hardly attach any very distinct meaning to it.

"The blood of Christ"—says a living divine, whom I have often had occasion to quote—"represents Christ's life as rendered in free sacrifice to God. The blood of Christ is the Life of Christ given for man, and the Life of Christ now given to men."

And if this be so, much more, the Apostle argues, shall we be saved by His life. What are we to understand by being saved by His life? It does not mean that we are saved by Christ's life, as something apart from His death, for it is only through His death that Christ's life can be given to us. Our

Lord's own words may help us to understand this—
"Because I live, ye shall live also." We can only
live by sharing in His life. So we are saved by His
life, by drawing His life into our souls. There is
another saying in the New Testament that helps us
to understand this—"Christ ever liveth to make intercession for us; wherefore He is able to save them to
the uttermost that come unto God by Him." (Heb.
vii. 25.)

We are saved by His Life, then, will also mean
that we are saved by the present work of Christ on
our behalf, by His continual intercession.

The Apostle then goes on to say that—

Ch. v. 12 : Through one man sin entered into the
world, and death through sin; and so death passed unto
all men, for that all sinned.

Following out this argument he proceeds to say—

For if, by the trespass of the one [i.e. Adam], death
reigned through the one; much more shall they that
receive the abundance of grace and of the gift of righteousness reign in life through the one, even Jesus Christ. So
then as through one trespass the judgment came unto all
men to condemnation; even so through one act of righteousness the free gift came unto all men to justification of life.
For as through the one man's disobedience the many were
made sinners, even so through the obedience of the one
shall the many be made righteous. And .... where sin
abounded grace did abound more exceedingly, ... through
Jesus Christ our Lord.

Now we must remember that S. Paul has already
shown that all men—both Jews and Gentiles—were
under sin, and could not of themselves attain to
righteousness and salvation: but that God by sending His Son had reconciled the world unto Himself,
and had brought righteousness and salvation to man.

But now comes the question, how far does this

justification, this renewal unto righteousness, extend? Does justification reach as far as sin reached?

To this S. Paul declares that not only did the work of Christ extend as far as the work of sin, but far beyond it.

For how did sin come into the world? It came in by the transgression of one man. Adam sinned, and the whole race sinned in him.

And as sin came into the world, and death by sin, so in the same sort of way righteousness and life came in.

As by *one trespass* the condemnation came, so by *one act of righteousness* the justification came in. And again:—As by the disobedience *of one man* the many (i.e. all) were made sinners, so by the obedience of *the One* shall the many (i.e. all) be made righteous.

"If only a certain portion of the human race had partaken of the sin of Adam, then only a certain portion had partaken of the justification of Christ. But S. Paul affirms that as all were involved in the sin, all must be included in the justification." And not only so, but he also tells us that where sin abounded, grace did abound more exceedingly. S. Paul is not in the habit of qualifying his assertions. He states in the broadest, strongest possible language one side of some great truth; and does not trouble himself to make it square with another side of the truth. Here he states without reserve that Christ's Redemption covers, and more than covers, man's sin. In other places he declares with equal confidence, that we must run the race set before us; that we must work out our own salvation with fear and trembling; that we may receive the grace of God in vain.

But the very boldness of this unqualified assertion

lays the Apostle open to an objection of this sort: If the more sin, the greater triumph of grace, will it not follow that we had better continue in sin, that grace may abound?

No, says the Apostle, a thousand times no. How shall we who *died* to sin, continue to *live* in it?

Our very baptism proclaims the contrary. We have all been baptized. Well, we were baptized into Christ's death; by baptism we were buried with Him into death. But Christ did not only die, He rose again. And as we died with Him, so must we also rise with Him, rise to newness of life.

Ch. vi. 1: What shall we say then? Shall we continue in sin, that grace may abound? God forbid. We who died to sin, how shall we any longer live therein? Or are ye ignorant that all we who were baptized into Christ Jesus were baptized into His death? We were buried therefore with Him through baptism into death: that like as Christ was raised from the dead through the glory of the Father, so we also might walk in newness of life .... But if we died with Christ, we believe that we shall also live with Him; knowing that Christ being raised from the dead dieth no more; death no more hath dominion over Him. For the death that He died, He died unto sin once: but the life that He liveth, He liveth unto God. Even so reckon ye also yourselves to be dead unto sin, but alive unto God in Christ Jesus. Let not sin therefore reign in your mortal body, that ye should obey the lusts thereof: neither present your members unto sin, as instruments of unrighteousness; but present yourselves unto God, as alive from the dead, and your members as instruments of righteousness unto God .... for as ye presented your members as servants to uncleanness and to iniquity unto iniquity, even so now present your members as servants to righteousness unto sanctification .... For the wages of sin is death, but the free gift of God is eternal life in Christ Jesus our Lord.

Now in addition to what I pointed out just now, I want you to notice that not only does the Apostle meet the objection, that we might as well sin that grace may abound, by showing that our very baptism witnesses against it, and pledges us to righteousness; but also how he takes for granted the great principle of our oneness with Christ our Head.

We are so one with Him, that what is true of Him is true also of us. If He died, then we died. If He rose from the dead, we rose with Him. If when Adam sinned we also sinned in him, much more when Christ died we died with Him to sin. Christ died, and rose again, and having risen died no more, and death no more had dominion over Him; so we who died with Him, and were buried with Him by baptism, cannot live in sin: sin must not have dominion over us.

But here we must be careful to give the right meaning of the words the Apostle uses. He does not say—How shall we who died to sin, ever again fall into sin? but how shall we *live* in sin? We may, alas, fall into sin, we may always be falling short; but that is a very different thing to *living* in sin. And so he goes on to say—Let not sin *reign* in you. Let not sin be your king: do not serve sin as your master. No! God is our King, and has claimed us for Himself. We must live to Him, and if we live to Him, we cannot live to *sin*. We must yield up ourselves to God our rightful King, once for all by one supreme effort of will, and then day by day yield ourselves to Him—yield up our members as servants to righteousness, reaching forward to that holiness without which no man can see the Lord.

CHAPTER XXIII.

THE EPISTLE TO THE ROMANS
(continued).

THE Apostle had before spoken of two powers to one or other of which a man may yield obedience: one is sin, the other is Christ. There is in each man an Adam-nature and a Christ-nature. This Christ-nature, indeed, may be undeveloped, it may be overlaid, just as a beautiful carving may be overlaid, and hidden with layer upon layer of whitewash; but still there *it is*.

If we renounce sin and our Adam-nature, and claim our part in Christ as our true Lord and Head, even as He claims us; if we believe in His power to save us, and in that power yield ourselves body, soul, and spirit to Him: then we shall have peace with God, we shall *be* right, and be able to *do* right, we shall have our fruit unto holiness, and the end eternal life.

This being so, he continues:—

Ch. viii. 1: There is therefore now no condemnation to them that are in Christ Jesus. For the law of the Spirit of life in Christ Jesus made me free from the law of sin and of death. For what the law could not do, in that it was weak through the flesh, God, sending His own Son in the likeness of sinful flesh and as an offering for sin, condemned sin in the flesh: that the ordinance of the law might be fulfilled in us, who walk not after the flesh, but after the spirit ....

So then, brethren, we are debtors, not to the flesh, to

live after the flesh: for if ye live after the flesh, ye must die: but if by the spirit ye mortify the deeds of the body, ye shall live.

For as many as are led by the Spirit of God, these are sons of God. For ye received not the spirit of bondage again unto fear; but ye received the Spirit of adoption, whereby we cry, Abba, Father. The Spirit Himself beareth witness with our spirit, that we are children of God: and if children, then heirs; heirs of God, and joint-heirs with Christ; if so be that we suffer with Him, that we may be also glorified with Him.

There is *now* no condemnation to them who are in Christ Jesus.

"*Now*," i.e. now that Christ has died and is risen again.

"*For what the Law could not do.*" That which was to the Law a thing impossible, God has by the Gospel accomplished. The Law pointed to righteousness as man's true life, but it gave him no power to become righteous, to be right, and to do right. For an unfallen being, the Law might have been sufficient: but as it was, the Law was weak through the flesh,—because of man's sinful nature.

"*God sending His own Son,*" &c. But by sending His Son to take our nature, and be the sacrifice for sin, that was done which without Christ was impossible. Man was enabled to become righteous—to be right and to do right.

He came "*in the likeness of sinful flesh:*" this was His Incarnation. He came as "*an offering for sin:*" this was His Atonement. And by that Incarnation and Atonement, that which the Law required, but could not accomplish, was fulfilled in the righteous lives of those who walk not after the flesh, but after the spirit.

As I have already said, S. Paul speaks of two

possible masters, here he speaks of two possible conditions of life, the flesh and the spirit. And the two states and the two masters correspond with one another. The one master, sin, acts through the flesh; the other master, Christ, acts through the spirit. The flesh drags us down into the service of sin; the spirit draws us up to the service of Christ. If we yield to the flesh, if we live to the flesh, and walk in the flesh, "we *must* die." We *must*. There is no help for it. There is nothing arbitrary or capricious about it. It is not as if it might be one way or another, and God fixed it to be this way: but it could not, in the nature of things, be otherwise.

"But if in the Spirit we mortify the deeds of the body, we shall live."

Mortify—i.e. to put an end to by *death*. So S. Paul bids us "*Crucify* the flesh:" the meaning is the same.

The word "crucify" reminds us that this mortification, this putting to death, is a slow and gradual, and not a sudden death. The flesh takes a deal of killing: it is constantly coming to life again.

But in this terrible struggle we are not left alone. The Holy Spirit is with us to lead us, to guide us, to strengthen us. He is stronger than our strongest enemy. Sin is near to us: but the Holy Spirit is nearer still. And He will not only strengthen and fortify us, but comfort and cheer us. By Him we know God as our Father, and the inheritance of glory to which He has destined us.

"*By whom we cry, Abba, Father.* "Abba" is the Syriac word for father. So our Lord in the garden prayed, "Abba, Father."

Ch. viii. 18: For I reckon that the sufferings of this present time are not worthy to be compared with the glory which shall be revealed to us-ward. For the earnest expectation of the creation waiteth for the revealing of the sons of God. For the creation was subjected to vanity, not of its own will, but by reason of Him who subjected it, in hope that the creation itself also shall be delivered from the bondage of corruption into the liberty of the glory of the children of God. For we know that the whole creation groaneth and travaileth in pain (i.e. in birth-pangs) together until now. And not only so, but ourselves also, which have the firstfruits of the Spirit, even we ourselves groan within ourselves, waiting for our adoption, to wit, the redemption of our body.

The Apostle had just shown that "the law of the spirit of life in Christ Jesus" was the spiritual force or engine by which all who yielded themselves up to God and walked in the spirit were freed from the law of sin and death.

Now he goes on to speak of a still wider working of the same law.

It is a great truth that there is a unity of the race of man. It can be considered as a whole. But there is a still greater and more wonderful truth, and that is, that the whole creation has a unity, is *one thing*. "We cannot separate ourselves from the material world of which we form a part."

The creation shared in man's fall; it is to have a share, the Apostle says, in man's restoration.

At present the whole creation is "subject to vanity," that is, to sin: "it groaneth and travaileth" in the pains of a new birth: in other words, it is in bondage to the law of sin and death. But the same power which delivered S. Paul, the same power which delivers every faithful Christian, shall deliver the whole creation from this bondage of corruption.

The whole creation is waiting, is looking forward,

to the time of its deliverance from sin and death, to have its share in the new heavens and new earth, in which dwelleth righteousness.

This unity of creation "gives a new and most marvellous aspect to that standing marvel of self-abasement, the Incarnation of the Son of God... for thus we see Him gathering together in one, and summing up in Himself, all created life, from the lowest to the highest."

And then, having set before the mind of the Christian believer a prospect so glorious, so wide, so wonderful, that the heart aches in the effort to grasp it, and the wings of hope fall helpless at our side, the great Apostle goes on to speak of a Comforter, a Helper, who will help our infirmity, who will teach us to pray, to turn our hopes into prayers, and will Himself make intercession for us according to the will of God, interpreting the inarticulate longings of our hearts, and speaking them into the ear of God. And then, in an excess of rapture, he breaks forth into what is not part of a theological treatise, but a song of triumph:—

Ch. viii. 31: What then shall we say to these things? If God is for us, who is against us? He that spared not His own Son, but delivered Him up for us all, how shall He not also with Him freely give us all things? Who shall lay anything to the charge of God's elect? It is God that justifieth; who is he that shall condemn? It is Christ Jesus that died, yea rather, that was raised from the dead, who is at the right hand of God, who also maketh intercession for us.

Who shall separate us from the love of Christ? Shall tribulation, or anguish, or persecution,... or sword?... Nay, in all these things we are more than conquerors, through Him that loved us. For I am persuaded, that neither death nor life, nor angels, nor principalities, nor things present, nor things to come, nor powers, nor height, nor depth, nor any other creature, shall be able to separate us from the love of God, which is in Christ Jesus our Lord.

I do not know what I can say by way of explanation. The difficulty lies not in the words but in the thoughts. And that not so much that our minds are unequal to grasp the thoughts, as that our hearts are too mean, too shallow, too unloving to take them in.

I will only say in the words of a great and good man, speaking of "this song of rapture," " I apprehend those will hear it most faintly, and will join least in it, who are trying to make out for themselves the right to be God's elect, to the exclusion of others; and that those hearts will echo most clearly with it, which thank God that He has been pleased of His mere mercy and love to call them out of the pride and exclusiveness that are natural to them, to enter into those common blessings and privileges, which He has bestowed upon their kind in Him who died and rose again for it, and to have a glimpse of that infinite love which is above all, and over all, and through all, and beneath all."
—(MAURICE, *Unity of the New Testament.*)

CHAPTER XXIV.

THE EPISTLE TO THE ROMANS
(*continued*).

WE are arrived now at the section of this great Epistle which is comprised in the ninth, tenth, and eleventh chapters.

In the previous part of this Epistle, S. Paul had proclaimed the Gospel unto which he had been separated, the divine mystery which had been committed to him. Jew and Gentile he had shown to be equally guilty and equally redeemed. He had unfolded the mystery of that redemption by which alone the world could be raised to righteousness: he had shown what this redemption could do for the race and for the individual.

But while the Gentiles were receiving this Gospel, and pressing into the kingdom, it was but too plain that the Jews, the children of the kingdom, were standing aloof.

Every day it was becoming more and more certain, that the Church of the future would be mainly *a Gentile Church.*

On a previous visit to Corinth, which lasted more than eighteen months, S. Paul, being pressed in the spirit, "testified to the Jews that Jesus was the Christ. And when they opposed themselves and blasphemed, he shook his raiment, and said unto them, Your blood be upon your own heads: I am clean: from henceforth I will go unto the Gentiles."

And, again, only shortly before the writing of this Epistle, when he was at Ephesus, after three months spent in disputing with Jews, and persuading the things concerning the kingdom of God, "when divers were *hardened*, and believed not, but spake evil of the *way* before the multitude, he departed from them, and separated the disciples."

But in this case, if the chosen people thus shut themselves out, if they were going to count for nothing in God's plan for the regeneration of the world, what became of Israel's special calling, what became of their long history, what became of the testimony of the Prophets?

If they were to count for nothing, why had God chosen them? If they were to have no part in the kingdom, what became of the promises? Was the training of eighteen centuries to go for nothing?

It is to this question that S. Paul addresses himself in these three chapters.

He begins by expressing his deep sorrow, his unceasing pain that his countrymen should, as a nation, fail of the grace of God.

He shows that he is quite sensible of all the privileges which were involved in their calling as God's chosen people.

Yet in spite of these—there was no escape from the conclusion—while the Gentiles had attained unto righteousness, Israel had not attained it. They sought it, but did not find it, because they went the wrong way to work. The Gentiles attained to righteousness because they had faith; Israel did not attain to it, because they sought it by works.

The Apostle does not deny their zeal, no man could understand them better than he, for what they were, he himself had once been. They thought to find righteousness *in themselves*; they could not see that it could be found only *in Jesus Christ*. They sought for righteousness in *the law*, they would not see that Christ was the end of the law; the law fulfilled its purpose in preparing the way for Christ; when He came, its work was done, and there was no longer room for it.

But now, after this long introduction, which however, I think, is needful to enable you to understand the drift of the whole argument which I have endeavoured to compress in what follows, let us read the Apostle's own words:—

Ch. ix. 1 : I say the truth in Christ, I lie not, my conscience bearing witness with me in the Holy Ghost, that I have great sorrow and unceasing pain in my heart... for my brethren's sake, my kinsmen according to the flesh : who are Israelites ; whose is the adoption, and the glory, and the covenants, and the giving of the law, and the service of God, and the promises; whose are the fathers, and of whom is Christ as concerning the flesh, who is over all, God blessed for ever. Amen. . . . .

Ch. ix. 30 : What shall we say then ? That the Gentiles, which followed not after righteousness, attained to righteousness, even the righteousness which is of faith; but Israel, following after a law of righteousness, did not arrive at that law. Wherefore ? Because they sought it not by faith, but as it were by works . . . .

Ch. x. 1 : Brethren, my heart's desire and my supplication to God is for them, that they may be saved. For I bear them witness, that they have a zeal for God, but not according to knowledge. For being ignorant of God's righteousness, and seeking to establish their own, they did not subject themselves to the righteousness of God. For Christ is the end of the law unto righteousness to every one that believeth.

Ch. xi. 1 : I say, then, did God cast off His people ? God forbid ! . . . . God did not cast off His people which

He foreknew.... At this present time also [as well as in Elijah's days] there is a remnant according to the election of grace .... What then? That which Israel seeketh for, that he obtained not; but the election obtained it, and the rest were hardened.

God's promises had not failed nor His plans broken down, because Israel as a nation rejected Christ. The true Israel was the faithful remnant, not the unbelieving mass. As S. John saw in the Revelation, all the tribes of Israel, with but one exception, furnished their quota to the faithful remnant. This election, this chosen remnant, then, obtained the righteousness of God by faith. But the Apostle does not stop here, he goes on to say —*and the rest were hardened.* First, you see, he speaks of the faithful remnant, and then of the rejected mass.

It is of this unbelieving mass, the great mass of the Jews, that S. Paul goes on to speak about in what follows.

"'They have stumbled,' continues S. Paul. 'But is it in order that they should fall?' He answers boldly, 'By no means.' And then he proceeds with an argument which is based upon the truth he has been asserting in so many ways in this Epistle, that neither Jews nor Gentiles were holy in themselves: that they were holy only because the root was holy; that each lived only so long as it abided, by faith, in the root; that each not abiding in the root might be cut off. Israel, not abiding in the root, claiming some independent virtue for itself, has been cut off. But the like cause will produce the like effect in the case of any nation." Therefore let the Gentiles not be high-minded, but fear, lest they also should be cut off.

Ch. xi. 11: I say then, did they [these unbelieving ones] stumble that they might fall? God forbid: but by their fall salvation is come unto the Gentiles, for to provoke them to jealousy. Now if their fall is the riches of the world, and their loss the riches of the Gentiles; how much more their fulness? ... (ver. 15). For if the casting away of them is the reconciling of the world, what shall the receiving of them be, but life from the dead? ... (ver. 25). For I would not, brethren, have you ignorant of this mystery, lest ye be wise in your own conceits, that a hardening in part hath befallen Israel, until the fulness of the Gentiles be come in; and so all Israel shall be saved ..... for the gifts and calling of God are without repentance. For as ye in time past were disobedient to God, but now have obtained mercy by their disobedience, even so have these also now been disobedient, that by the mercy shown to you they also may now obtain mercy. *For God hath shut up all unto disobedience, that He might have mercy upon all.*

In this glorious passage, the great Apostle shows that "there is mercy in the Divine dealing with the millions (who seem hardened in sin), as truly as with those whom He owns as His elect."

The election obtained God's salvation, this was mercy, you will say. The rest were hardened, this is mercy also.

"It was a mercy to Israel, after they had rejected Christ, to veil the truth from their eyes. For the unprepared world at large, not less than for Israel, it was a mercy to be shut up in unbelief awhile. For to sin wholly against light is hopeless ruin. Such is the sin of devils. But to be self-blinded, and then chastised with deeper blindness, may not be inconsistent with future grace."

"Not to see a truth, not to own it, and love it, is an awful thing. But there is something darker than that. To see a truth, and suspect its certainty, and then to recoil—see it and in our heart hold back—that is a woe unutterable for any soul of man."

"But the Apostle dwells on the thought that Israel's unbelief should not be permanent." They shall come in with the fulness of the Gentiles, and all Israel shall be saved.

"And not only they, but untold millions of heathen under His eye who surveys us all, are even yet held back from deeper ruin." For "the ever-merciful Father of Spirits wills not that this world that He has made and loved—this world that has been trodden by the footsteps of His beloved Son, should so become a world of the lost."—(IRONS' *Bampton Lectures*, 1870.)

Well might the Apostle, in thus unfolding the purposes of the All-merciful, and the All-wise, break out into a fervent ascription of praise :—

Ch. xi. 33: O the depth of the riches both of the wisdom and the knowledge of God! how unsearchable are His judgments, and His ways past tracing out! . . . . For of Him, and through Him, and unto Him are all things. To Him be the glory for ever. Amen.

This ascription of praise ends the main argument of the Epistle.

In the chapters that follow, the Apostle applies the great truths which he has expounded to the practical duties of life.

The first duty of practical life is to give up ourselves in willing surrender to God. This must come first. Our first step in Christian life is to give ourselves up to God, to say, as the great Apostle did, "Lord, what wilt Thou have me to do?"

Then the Apostle exhorts to love, to humility,

to kindness and consideration for others, to diligence, to patience, and finally he thus concludes:—

Ch. xvi. 25: Now to him that is able to stablish you .... to the only wise God, through Jesus Christ, be the glory for ever. Amen.

NOTE ON THE WORD "JUSTIFY."

This word, round which so much controversy has gathered, and which, as thus translated, has introduced a totally foreign element into S. Paul's theology, is one of a set of words derived from the same root, which occupies a prominent place in certain of S. Paul's Epistles.

The noun with which this word "justify" is connected, is the word *righteousness*.

If this word could be rendered "justice," it would be possible to maintain a uniform rendering of most of these words, as just, justice, justify; but though uniform, the result would not be satisfactory, for our word "justice" does not adequately represent the purely *moral* idea of *righteousness*.

But we only introduce confusion when we render the noun by "righteousness," which carries a moral sense, and the verb by "justify," which has acquired a "forensic" sense.

It would seem, then, that the only way of reaching the Apostle's meaning, would be to make a clean sweep of the words justify and justification, and substitute words or phrases which preserve the *moral* idea of righteousness, and to translate the verb rendered "justify" by some such expression as "to strengthen, or renew, for righteousness," as for instance, in Romans iv. 25: "Who died for our sins, and rose again to renew us to righteousness." (Abridged from Irons' Bampton Lectures.)

CHAPTER XXV.

S. PAUL'S EPISTLE TO THE PHILIPPIANS.

THE Epistle to the Romans, which we concluded in our last chapter, was written by S. Paul during a three months' stay in Greece, in his third missionary journey. In that Epistle, you will remember, S. Paul spoke of the desire which he had long entertained of visiting Rome.

That desire was at last gratified, though it was brought about in a different way from what he expected; for S. Paul reached the imperial city, not as a free agent, but as a prisoner.

After leaving Corinth, which had doubtless been his head-quarters during his stay in Greece, S. Paul journeyed through Macedonia, visiting, no doubt, his beloved flocks in Thessalonica and Philippi, and then set sail for Palestine with the intention of reaching Jerusalem before the approaching Feast of Pentecost.

It was on this voyage that he summoned the elders of the Ephesian Church to Miletus, and delivered to them the memorable charge and touching farewell which S. Luke records in the 20th chapter of the Acts. The voyage ended, S. Paul, accompanied by Luke and an Ephesian Christian named Trophimus, and perhaps others, arrived at Jerusalem.

Before, however, he had been there a week, his bitter enemies the Jews of Asia, who were more fierce and fanatical even than the Jews of Jerusalem themselves, found him in the Temple, and raised the mob against him, who would have then and there murdered him, and thus have deprived the Gentiles of their Apostle, and the Christian Church of some of the most priceless of his writings. But it was not so to be: he was delivered from the furious multitude by the sudden appearance of Lysias and his soldiers. To avoid a plot which had been got up against him, he was sent off hurriedly to Cæsarea, where he remained in confinement for two years; then when the new Governor, Festus, proposed that he should be sent to Jerusalem, he was compelled to exercise the privilege which belonged to him as a Roman citizen, and to appeal to Cæsar. Accordingly, in company with other prisoners under the charge of a friendly centurion, S. Paul was despatched to Italy. S. Luke, as we have already seen, gives us a full account of this voyage, and of the shipwreck which befell them. He relates also how some of the Roman Christians came to meet the Apostle as far as the Market of Appius and The Three Taverns.

And when, he goes on to say,

Acts xxviii. 16: We entered into Rome, the centurion delivered the prisoners to the captain of the prætorian guard: but Paul was suffered to abide by himself with the soldier that guarded him .... And he abode two whole years in his own hired dwelling, and received all that went in unto him, preaching the kingdom of God, and teaching the things concerning the Lord Jesus Christ with all boldness, none forbidding him.

Here the narrative of the Acts ends, somewhat abruptly as it may appear to us, but really not so abruptly as it seems, since it leaves the Apostle of the Gentiles in the capital of the world.

It was during this two years' captivity that S. Paul wrote the set of letters which are known as " the

Epistles of the first imprisonment;" these are the Epistle to the Philippians, the Epistle to the Colossians, with the supplementary letter to Philemon, and the Epistle to the Ephesians.

If we were speaking of an ordinary writer, we should say that in these letters his genius reached its highest point: but speaking of an inspired Apostle, we may venture to say that in this group of Epistles he reached the highest level of his inspiration.

It is not certain which of these letters was written first, nor indeed is it a matter of much consequence. There seems, however, some reason for supposing that the letter to the Philippians was the first written; then the letters to Colossæ and to Philemon, and last of all, as greatest of all, the Epistle to the Ephesians.

Of all the Churches which S. Paul planted, the Church of the Philippians was the dearest to him. There seems to have been a very special affection between them. Again and again they had sent a contribution for his relief. What he would take from no other Church, he took freely from them. Theirs, too, was that most beautiful and most common of all forms of liberality, the liberality of the poor.

"The Epistle to the Philippians," says Archdeacon Farrar, "arose directly out of one of the few happy incidents which diversified the dreary uncertainties of S. Paul's captivity. This was the visit of Epaphroditus, a leading presbyter of the Church of Philippi, with the fourth pecuniary contribution by which that loving and generous Church had ministered to his necessities."

Referring to this welcome and generous gift he says—

Phil. iv. 11: I have learned, in whatsoever state I am, therein to be content. I know how to be abased, and I know also how to abound: in everything and in all things have I learned the secret both to be filled and to be hungry, both to abound and to be in want. I can do all things in Him that strengtheneth me . . . .

. . . . But I have all things, and abound: I am filled, having received from Epaphroditus the things that came from you, an odour of a sweet smell, a sacrifice acceptable, well-pleasing to God. And my God shall fulfil every need of yours according to His riches in glory in Christ Jesus.

At Rome S. Paul was unable with his fettered hands to work for his livelihood, and it is possible that he found no opening for his special trade. . . . . . Epaphroditus arrived about autumn, and succumbed to the unhealthiness of the season, and was prostrated by a dangerous and all but fatal sickness. The news of this illness had reached Philippi and caused great solicitude to the Church. We cannot doubt that Paul pleaded with God for the life of his sick friend, and God had mercy upon him. Epaphroditus recovered; and deeply as Paul would have rejoiced to keep him, he sent him back to Philippi, and with him the letter, in which he expressed his thankfulness for that constant affection which had so greatly cheered his heart.

Now to enter into the inner meaning of this letter which Epaphroditus bore back to Philippi, we must remember that the Philippian Christians clung to S. Paul with all the fervour of attached disciples, and all the tenderness of tried friends.

The news of their great Apostle's imprisonment was a terrible blow to them. The shepherd was stricken, and was himself in the power of the lion, and what would become of the flock?

Disunion seems to have been the special peril of the Philippians; but a disunion proceeding rather from despondency than from faction.

Against this despondency the whole undercurrent of the Epistle was directed. Its keynote seems to be—" I rejoice, rejoice also ye."

Why then should the Apostle's imprisonment discourage them? It did not cut him off from their sympathy, nor them from his. He was as much able to have fellowship with them in his Roman lodging, as if he had been with them in Philippi. More than that, his imprisonment was the means of making the Gospel known in the very palace of the Cæsars. Why need they be cast down, because his death might be near at hand? To him to live here in the flesh was to draw life from Christ: to die was to have the gain of a fuller, richer life. He could not himself tell which was the better. But he did not doubt that that which was most profitable to them would be granted him, and that he should be spared to meet them once more. But now let us begin the Epistle itself.

Ch. i. 1: Paul and Timothy, servants of Christ Jesus, to all the saints in Christ Jesus which are at Philippi, with the bishops and deacons: Grace to you and peace from God our Father and the Lord Jesus Christ.

I thank my God upon all my remembrance of you, always in every supplication of mine on behalf of you all making my supplication with joy, for your fellowship in furtherance of the Gospel from the first day until now. . . . And this I pray, that your love may abound yet more and more in knowledge and all discernment; . . . . that ye may be sincere and void of offence unto the day of Christ. . . . .

(v.12): Now I would have you know, brethren, that the things which happened unto me have fallen out rather unto the progress of the Gospel; so that my bonds became manifest in Christ throughout the whole prætorian guard, and to all the rest . . . . and that . . . . as always, so now also Christ shall be magnified in my body, whether by life, or by death. For to me to live is Christ, and to die is gain. . . . .

Ch. ii. 1: If there is therefore any comfort in Christ, if any consolation of love, if any fellowship of the Spirit, if any tender mercies and compassions, fulfil ye my joy, that ye be of the same mind, having the same love, being of one accord, of one mind; doing nothing through faction or through vainglory, but in lowliness of mind each counting other better than himself; not looking each of you to his own things, but each of you also to the things of others.

You will notice in the opening salutation of this letter, that S. Paul only describes himself as a servant of Christ Jesus. There was no need for him to speak of his apostleship in writing to these loyal disciples, who regarded him with the fondest love and reverence.

You will notice also that with the "saints" or faithful brethren he couples the bishops and deacons of the Church.

There have been endless controversies in connection with this designation of the ministers of the Church. In the preface to the ordination services of the Church of England, it is laid down that, "it is evident unto all men diligently reading the Holy Scripture and ancient authors, that from the Apostles' time there have been these orders of ministers in Christ's Church—bishops, priests, and deacons."

Here, however, you see, S. Paul mentions only two,—"bishops and deacons." It is clear that bishops and elders are used indifferently of the same order of ministers. Those whom we now term priests, or presbyters, were then called either elders, which expresses their dignity; or bishops, which expresses their office. It has been argued that if there had been one minister of the Church superior to these elders or bishops, he would have been addressed in the salutation of the Epistle. But in the course of this Epistle, S. Paul speaks of Epaphroditus the envoy of the Philippian Church, as their messenger, or as the word is literally, their *Apostle*. In such an embassy as this who would so naturally be selected to represent the whole body of the Church as its chief bishop or apostle. In addressing a Church, then, in a letter which was actually sent by its "bishop" or chief pastor, its salutation would naturally be addressed to the bishops (or elders) and deacons.

If this be so, then, in the Church of Philippi, as in other Churches, there were the three orders of ministers,—Epaphroditus the bishop, in our sense of the word, the bishops or elders, and the deacons.

In the passage which we last read, S. Paul had been exhorting the Philippians to unity; he had urged them to be of one mind, of one accord; he had urged upon them the duty of unselfishness, that each should esteem others better than himself, and should look not at his own things, but at the things of others. From this he passes on to what was the ground and basis of this unity. If they were all to be of one mind, it could only be by their all having the mind of Christ.

Ch. ii. 5: Have this mind in you which was also in Christ Jesus: who, being in the form of God, counted it not a prize (a thing to be grasped at) to be on an equality with God, but emptied Himself, taking the form of a servant, being made in the likeness of men; and being found in fashion as a man, He humbled Himself, becoming obedient even unto death, yea, the death of the cross. Wherefore also God highly exalted Him, and gave unto Him the name which is above every name; that in the name of Jesus every knee should bow, of things in heaven and things on earth and things under the earth, and that every tongue should confess that Jesus Christ is Lord, to the glory of God the Father.

If you are at all familiar with this passage, one of the most important in the whole New Testament, you will be struck with the different rendering which the Revisers have given in its opening words. Instead of saying, "He thought it not robbery to be equal with God," S. Paul really says, "That Christ, instead of making His oneness with the Father a matter of selfish possession, regarded it as something which He might give up for man."

Let us also be sure to notice the contrast between the two words "being" and "becoming." "Being" in the form of God. This was His essential existence. "Becoming" obedient unto death. This was his voluntary self-abasement.

The whole passage is one which needs rather thoughtful pondering and reverent meditation than any verbal explanations. One other verbal comment, however, I will make, and that is to call your attention to the word "*in*" in the words, "*in* the name of Jesus every knee shall bow." Not *at* the name of Jesus, as an *external* power, but *in* the name, in the Spirit of, in union with Jesus our Lord, shall every knee bow.

Wonderful words, too often narrowed by our exclusiveness and want of faith and love!

After various exhortations the Apostle thus concludes:—

Ch. iv. 20: Now unto our God and Father be the glory for ever and ever. Amen.

Salute every saint in Christ Jesus. The brethren which are with me salute you. All the saints salute you, especially they that are of Cæsar's household.

The grace of the Lord Jesus Christ be with your spirit. And the peace of God, which passeth all understanding, shall guard your hearts and your thoughts in Christ Jesus.

CHAPTER XXVI.

THE EPISTLE TO THE COLOSSIANS.

IF you look at the map of Asia Minor, and notice the coast-line a little south of the island of Samos, you will see the outfall of the river Mæander, a river which was so winding that its name has become a descriptive epithet of a winding, or, as we say, meandering stream. If you follow up this river to the point where the river Lycus, from the south, flows into it, you will see marked the city of Laodicea; about sixteen miles further up the valley you will see marked the splendid city of Hierapolis, and between the two, and somewhat cast into the shade by its more prosperous neighbours, stood the city of Colossæ.

Though Laodicea lay on the great road from Ephesus to the Euphrates, S. Paul does not seem ever to have visited either of the three cities. But though the great Apostle had not actually founded the Church of Colossæ, it was founded, so it would appear, under his direction.

S. Luke tells us that S. Paul remained more than two years at Ephesus, and proclaimed the Gospel with such effect that almost all that dwelt in what was technically called Asia, heard the word of the Lord. Among these converts appear to have been Epaphras, Archippus, and Philemon from Colossæ, and Nymphas from Laodicea. These, under S. Paul's direction, became the Evangelists and first teachers of the three cities. S. Paul speaks in this Epistle of Epaphras as a faithful minister of Christ *on his behalf*. Thus, though not the founder of the Church, S. Paul might be considered its father, and took in it a father's interest.

It was, then, during his imprisonment at Rome, and probably towards its conclusion, that he received a visit from Epaphras, who brought the latest news of the three sister Churches of the valley of the Lycus. It was not altogether a satisfactory account. Here, as elsewhere, the enemy had sown tares among the wheat, and a plentiful crop of heresies had sprung up in their midst. Among these false opinions that were creeping into the Church of Colossæ, and the neighbouring Churches of Laodicea and Hierapolis, was the worship of angels, accompanied by that contempt of the world and the ordinary ways of life which is known as asceticism. Side by side with this was a fanciful system of philosophy which tended to depreciate the person and work of Christ, and in conjunction with this, strange to say, a sort of hybrid Judaism, which made a great point of the observance of the Jewish sabbaths and other festivals.

Doubts were beginning to arise whether the invisible God might not be manifesting Himself through a number of different subordinate agencies, whether there was, indeed, as Epaphras had taught them, any one Person in whom they were all subjected, any one Person in whom God had fully and finally manifested Himself. It was to meet these errors that S. Paul wrote the letter which we know as his Epistle to the Colossians.

In his previous Epistles he had spoken of Christ

as the Judge, the Head and Ruler of the Church, as the Author of eternal salvation, the Bringer-in of spiritual freedom, as the Source of life and joy. In this Epistle he speaks of Christ as the Eternal, Pre-existing, yet really incarnate Word; he speaks of Him in His relation, not only to the Church, but to the universe, as containing the fulness of the Godhead, as the One only Lord, the One only Mediator, the One only Saviour.

Ch. i. 1: Paul, an apostle of Christ Jesus through the will of God, and Timothy our brother, to the saints and faithful brethren in Christ which are at Colossæ: Grace to you and peace from God our Father.

The Epistle to the Ephesians was written at the same time, and sent by the same messenger, as this Epistle to the Colossians.

There is naturally, therefore, a great likeness between them. There is the same thanksgiving for their faith and love, the same prayer for their advance in holiness, for their fuller enlightenment. There is also a very similar enunciation of the truth; but in the Epistle to the Colossians it is set forth as the refutation of actual existing error, while in the Epistle to the Ephesians it stands out in the calm majesty of absolute truth.

The main theme of the letter to the Colossians is the *Person of Christ*, in that to the Ephesians it is the life of Christ manifested in the *Church*. In the Epistle to the Colossians, Christ is the plenitude, the absolute fulness of God; in the Epistle to the Ephesians, the ideal Church is the plenitude, the recipient of His fulness, who filleth all things with all. In one word, the one sets forth Christ's *Person*; the other, Christ's *Body* (the Church).

Ch. i. 3: We give thanks to God the Father of our Lord Jesus Christ, praying always for you, having heard of your faith in Christ Jesus, and of the love which ye have toward all the saints, because of the hope which is laid up for you in the heavens.... Even as ye learned of Epaphras our beloved fellow-servant, who is a faithful minister of Christ on our behalf, who also declared unto us your love in the Spirit.

For this cause we also, since the day we heard it, do not cease to pray and make request for you, that ye may be filled with the knowledge of His will in all spiritual wisdom and understanding, to walk worthy of the Lord unto all pleasing, bearing fruit in every good work, and increasing in the knowledge of God; strengthened with all power, according to the might of His glory, unto all patience and long-suffering with joy; giving thanks unto the Father, who made us meet to be partakers of the inheritance of the saints in light; who delivered us out of the power of darkness, and translated us into the kingdom of the Son of His love; in whom we have our redemption, the forgiveness of our sins: who is the Image of the invisible God, the First-born of all Creation.

I think you will have no difficulty in understanding this passage, at least up to the last clause. Yet there are one or two things which might escape your attention, about which I will say a word or two.

In verse 12 the Apostle thanks God that He made them meet or fit for the inheritance of the saints. We should rather expect to have read, who *hath made*, or who *is making* us meet: but no, the tense of the verb shows that he is speaking of a definite moment of time in the past—who *made* us meet. That definite moment was the moment of their baptism: for in baptism the whole efficacy of the work of Christ is made over to us. In baptism Christ claims us to be what He intended us to be, and thus makes us potentially meet for the glorious inheritance of His saints; for if He is in us, the hope of glory is also in us. Of course the meetness or fitness which is in us *potentially*, must be wrought in us *actually*, but this can only be by the gradual working of the Holy Spirit.

In verse 14 the Apostle asserts that "in Christ we have our redemption, the forgiveness of our sins;" or, transposing the clauses, the forgiveness of our sins is our redemption. This suggests to us that forgiveness is something more than our sins being passed over by God; forgiveness is besides our redemption from bondage, our being made free from the bondage of sin.

In the passage which we have just read, you will see how, step by step, the Apostle advances from the contemplation of one spiritual privilege after another, till he arrives at the stupendous declaration of who He is, who is the Source and Author of them all: that He is the Image of God, or, as the writer of the Epistle to the Hebrews expresses it, "the effulgence of the Father's glory, and the very image of His substance;" He is, the Apostle declares, the Ground and Pattern of the visible and invisible creation; the Head of all powers and governments in the unseen world; the Head of His Church. The universal Head, because the fulness of the Divine nature was actually stored up in Him; its Head, because He had brought about an actual reunion and reconciliation of the torn fragments of humanity in Himself, and because He had reconciled all things to God, and enabled all men to resume their place in God's ordered Universe.

In the passage which follows, Christ is first spoken of in His relation to God and to the Universe, and then in His relation to the Church.

Ch. i. 15: Who is the Image of the invisible God, the First-born of all creation; for in Him were all things created, in the heavens and upon the earth, things visible and things invisible, whether thrones, or dominions, or principalities, or powers; all things have been created through Him, and unto Him; and He is before all things, and in Him all things consist.

Here is set forth the relation of Christ to God, and to the Universe.

Who *is* the Image of God. This is His essential Being. He *is* before all things. "Before creation was," He might say, "*I am.*" Contrast with this the use of the word "become" in ver. 18: "That in all things He might have the pre-eminence," or more literally, that he might "*become*" pre-eminent. He *is* the Image of God: He only *became* pre-eminent. One refers to His *Divine* essence: the other to his glorification as *man*. The First-born of all creation, that is, the first in order of time, and in order of dignity: for *in* Him were all things created.

The creation existed as an idea or thought before it was actually called into being, and this ideal creation was in Christ. In Him were *all things* created. By all things are meant, not the sum of individual things, but "*the* all things," the totality of things, the Universe. And in Him all things consist, in Him the totality of things hold together in one order. Christ not only is the Maker, but the Upholder of all things.

From this the Apostle passes on to His relation to the Church, which is His new creation. He is the Beginning, the Source of life and growth to the Church; the First-born from amongst the dead, that He might become in all things pre-eminent.

Ch. i. 18: And He is the Head of the body, the Church: who is the Beginning, the first-born from the dead, that in all things He might have the pre-eminence. For it was the good pleasure of the Father that in Him should all the fulness dwell; and through Him to reconcile all things (the totality of things) unto Himself, having made peace through the blood of His Cross : through Him, I say, whether things upon the earth, or things in the heavens.

This wonderful passage, one of the most wonderful in the whole New Testament, takes us straight to the very heart and purpose of God in sending His Son into the world;—it was that in Him, in His human nature, all the fulness, the fulness of God, the fulness of the Universe, should dwell : and that through Him He might reconcile all things—here, again, "*the* all things," the totality of things—unto Himself. And, lest any should presume to put limits to what was illimitable, he expands the all things into—whether things upon earth, and things in the heavens.

How the whole Universe can be said to be reconciled to God in Christ, we cannot know for certain. But it would seem that not only the world of humanity which had dropped out of its place, in the Great Order, was restored; but that the worlds of the unfallen were also, in some sort, reconciled, brought nearer to God, made partakers of some new, and to us inconceivable, blessing.

This enables us to see that the Atonement is, indeed, the at-one-ment, the reconciliation of all things to God through the Cross of Christ.

And in this reconciliation the Colossian Christians, as well as all others, had their share.

They, too, who had shared in the alienation of mankind from God, shared also in their reconciliation.

Notice that the Apostle speaks of them not as

aliens, but as alienated. To be alienated, estranged from God, was not man's natural and proper condition, but a condition into which he had fallen. Sin is not man's nature, but, as our Ninth Article has it, "a fault and corruption of man's nature."

Ch. i. 21: And you, being in time past alienated and enemies in your mind in your evil works, yet now hath He reconciled in the body of His flesh through death, to present you [either as a sacrifice, or as a bride to her husband] holy and without blemish, and unreproveable before Him: if so be that ye continue in the faith grounded and stedfast, and not moved away from the hope of the Gospel .... whereof I, Paul, was made a minister.

CHAPTER XXVII.

THE EPISTLE TO THE COLOSSIANS (*continued*).

IN the section of this Epistle which we last read, S. Paul had been setting forth the supreme dignity of Christ's Person, and the perfection and completion of His work.

He, into whose kingdom all Christians had been translated, was the Image of the invisible God, the Lord, and Supreme Head of the universe; the Lord, and Supreme Head of the Church.

The Reconciliation which by His death, by the blood of His Cross, He made, was no partial, incomplete work, it included all things, it reached to each man. His Colossian brethren were also reconciled, and would, if they remained faithful and steadfast, be presented to God in the full perfection of their nature, in the perfectly restored image of their Lord.

Then follows a passage which has caused great difficulty, and which has been quoted to justify many practical abuses in the Church; a passage which certainly, as we first read it, seems to approach dangerously near the very errors which the Epistle was written to condemn.

We have already seen in other of S. Paul's Epistles how bold and fearless he is in the declaration of truth. He lays down with firm, unfaltering hand, one side of some great truth, without thinking it necessary to qualify it by nicely-balanced assertions on the other side. Then, too, in dealing with error, he seizes fearlessly upon some point which contains an element of truth, disengages the truth from the errors which cling to it, and claims it as a stolen jewel from the treasure-house of the Divine Wisdom.

Something of this sort he seems to do in the passage which we are about to read.

The false teachers seem to have taught the Colossians that Christ's Person was not so supremely pre-eminent, nor His work so absolutely perfect, but that there remained something to be supplied from other sources, that there still remained something for them to do to complete that which Christ had left undone.

Now in dealing with such an error as this, the Apostle, before he denounces the false teachers and warns the faithful against their false doctrine, boldly asserts that, dangerous and dishonouring to Christ as this error was, there was a truth underlying it, there was a sense in which the afflictions of Christ were incomplete, and needed to be supplemented by other afflictions. But let us see what this hard saying really is.

Ch. i. 24: Now I rejoice in my sufferings for your sake, and fill up on my part that which is lacking of the afflictions of Christ in my flesh for His body's sake, which is the Church.

Now we cannot suppose for a moment that in an Epistle which was specially intended to set forth the perfection and completeness of Christ, and the perfection and completeness of His work, S. Paul could really mean to say anything to lessen the finished completeness of Christ's Person or His Work.

How then are the Apostle's words to be understood?

Well, it must be remembered that the afflictions which Christ bore on earth, were not the only afflictions that He had to endure. S. Paul had himself heard Him say, "Why persecutest thou me?" In all His people's afflictions He was Himself afflicted. The sufferings, then, which S. Paul endured were not so much his own, as *Christ's* borne in him. Christ once in His own proper person suffered for our sins: but He suffered also, and still suffers, in His Body, the Church; and it is these last afflictions of Christ that S. Paul has in view, when he speaks of filling up what was lacking in them. Christ was made perfect by the things which He suffered. His Church must also be made perfect in suffering, and every affliction endured by the members of Christ's Body goes to fill up the appointed measure of suffering which the Church must endure to reach perfection. If we can only see it, the Apostle's words, which sound so strange, unfold the most blessed truth that the sufferings which are endured for Christ's sake, and in His name, are not lost, are not wasted, but help forward the blessed consummation, "The one far-off divine event to which the whole creation moves."

> "That nothing walks with aimless feet,
>   That not one life shall be destroyed,
>   Or cast as rubbish to the void,
> When God hath made the pile complete;
> That not a worm is cloven in vain;
>   That not a moth with vain desire
>   Is shrivelled in a fruitless fire,
> Or but subserves another's gain."

But we must pass on to what the Apostle proceeds to unfold.

The false teachers at Colossæ probably discoursed a great deal of a mystery, a divine fulness; of a perfect initiation into this mystery, of an initiated few, who had shaken themselves free from the sensuality of the crowd, and soared far above the childish wisdom of their first belief.

The Apostle says, Yes, there is a mystery, a mystery deeper and more glorious than your new teachers conceive of: a mystery, once concealed indeed, but now made manifest, not to a few specially gifted souls, but to all who will receive it with humility and faith. And my mission, the work of my Apostleship, is not to teach a select few, but every man, and to present to the Lord as the fruit of my labours, not picked, chosen individuals, but every man perfect in Christ.

Ch. i. 24: Now I rejoice in my sufferings for your sake, and fill up on my part that which is lacking of the afflictions of Christ in my flesh for His body's sake, which is the Church; whereof I was made a minister, according to the dispensation of God which was given me to you-ward, to fulfil the word of God, even the mystery which hath been hid from all ages and generations: but now hath it been manifested to His saints, to whom God was pleased to make known what is the riches of the glory of this mystery among the Gentiles, which is Christ in you, the hope of glory: whom we proclaim, admonishing every man and teaching every man in all wisdom, that we may present every man perfect in Christ; whereunto I labour also, striving according to His working, which worketh in me mightily.

Imbedded in this difficult passage is one of those crystallized gems of Divine Wisdom which are so easy to repeat, and so difficult to grasp, "Christ in you, the hope of Glory."

The hope of glory, the hope of partaking of the

inheritance of the saints in light, on what does it depend? Not on our own goodness, or intelligence, or faith, but on the presence of Christ in us. Christ is the Alpha and the Omega; if He is in us as the Alpha, He will, if we are faithful, be in us as the Omega also.

How great was the Apostle's longing for the Christian believers in Colossæ and Laodicea that they might attain to a full knowledge of this mystery, and how great his jealousy over them, lest their grasp of the truth should be weakened, and their faith corrupted, appears from what follows.

Ch. ii. 1: For I would have you know how greatly I strive for you, and for them at Laodicea, and for as many as have not seen my face in the flesh; that their hearts may be comforted, they being knit together in love, and unto all riches of the full assurance of understanding, that they may know the mystery of God, even Christ, in whom are all the treasures of wisdom and knowledge hidden ... As therefore ye received Christ Jesus the Lord, so walk in Him, rooted and builded up in Him, and stablished in your faith, even as ye were taught, abounding in thanksgiving.

The false teachers promised to lead their followers to a fulness of understanding of the mystery, which would raise them above the level of the common herd. S. Paul taught that it could only be attained by love and unity, by their "being knit together in love."

Further, the Apostle cautioned them, as Jeremiah did the Jews of his day, to stand in the old paths, and not, by love of novelty, to be led into error. Then he seems to point out some particular person as the source and origin of this false teaching, and earnestly warns the Colossian Christians against his delusions.

As was pointed out in the last chapter, with these philosophical fancies was mixed up a sort of hybrid Judaism. The false teacher of this hybrid Judaism laid, it would seem, great stress upon circumcision. He would tell the Gentile Christian that baptism alone might serve as a purification from outward defilements, might admit him into an outer circle of knowledge and spirituality: but that if he wished to attain to a perfect knowledge, and to be admitted into the inner circle of truth, and be brought at last into the fulness of the Godhead, he must be circumcized.

The Apostle assures them, in contrast to all this, that the fulness of the Godhead dwells bodily in Christ; that by their baptism they were made members of Christ, and that having Him, they had all things. In fact, that what the false teachers promised them was already theirs, and was the indefeasible privilege of the humblest believer in Christ.

Ch. ii. 8 : Take heed lest there shall be any one that maketh spoil of you through his philosophy and vain deceit, after the tradition of men . . . and not after Christ: for in Him dwelleth all the fulness of the Godhead bodily, and in Him ye are made full, who is the head of all principality and power : in whom ye were also circumcized with a circumcision not made with hands . . . in the circumcision of Christ; having been buried with Him in baptism, wherein ye were also raised with Him through faith in the working of God, who raised Him from the dead.

You will have noticed that S. Paul here speaks of baptism as the Circumcision of Christ. The false teachers wanted them to be circumcized; S. Paul teaches them that they have been already circumcized with a higher and better circumcision.

Then having shown that their baptism which

brought them into relation with Christ, not only admitted them into the fulness of the wisdom and knowledge which were hidden in Him, but also freed them from the yoke of Jewish observances, for that Christ had blotted out the written law by which those observances were enforced, and nailed it to His Cross. The Apostle continues:—

Ch. ii. 16: Let no man therefore judge you in meat, or in drink, or in respect of a feast-day, or a new moon, or a sabbath day: which are a shadow of the things to come; but the body is Christ's. Let no man rob you of your prize by a voluntary humility, and worshipping of the angels ... and not holding fast the Head, from whom all the body, being supplied and knit together through the joints and bands, increaseth with the increase of God.

This passage is a sort of charter of emancipation from the ceremonial observances of the Jewish Law. Christians were not to be bound by Jewish distinctions of clean and unclean sorts of food. They were not to be bound to observe the weekly, monthly, and yearly feasts. You will notice that among these festivals which the Apostle declares were not binding upon Christians, stands the Sabbath day. The obligation of the Sabbath, no less than the obligation of the Passover, has passed away.

CHAPTER XXVIII.

THE EPISTLE TO THE COLOSSIANS
(continued).

S T. Paul was a very practical theologian; he first lays down the foundation of a sublime theology, and then builds upon it the superstructure of practical teaching and morals.

There are two ways in which a system of morals may be enforced. One way is to set it up, or attempt to set it up on its own foundation, to make it stand alone. But when this plan is adopted, it is generally found that the system of morals is very easily toppled over. The moral duties laid down may be very good and necessary, but they have no force in them. This way of setting to work is like loading a cannon with a shot or shell of the most approved construction, but with no powder. The mere moralist may hold the match to the touch-hole till he is tired, but the cannon shot remains in the cannon, the morals remain shut up in their system.

We all know how the possession of a strong motive acts upon work which we have to do. What in itself may be dull drudgery, may become noble and interesting under the influence of a high motive: while, on the other hand, the most congenial employment without adequate motive loses its zest, and has no life in it, whereby a man can live.

But S. Paul, as has been said, though the most practical of teachers, does not begin with morals.

He first lays the foundation of the all sufficiency of Christ, of the Christian being complete in Him, of his baptismal incorporation into Christ; he first assures the faithful that they died with Christ unto sin, and were quickened by His life, and rose in His resurrection; and then upon this foundation builds up the structure of the practical duties of life.

Thus in the passage which we are about to read, having already told the Colossian Christians that they had died with Christ, had been buried with Him by baptism, had risen with Him, he bids them make all this a reality.

Ch. iii. 1: If then ye were raised together with Christ, seek the things that are above, where Christ is, seated on the right hand of God. Set your mind on the things that are above, not on the things that are upon the earth. For ye died, and your life is hid with Christ in God. When Christ, who is our life, shall be manifested, then shall ye also with Him be manifested in glory.

" If then ye were raised with Christ." The " if " does not raise a doubt. It means if, as is the case, ye died and were raised. You should notice the tense in which these verbs are put; it is the tense that marks the action of the verb, as taking place at a definite moment of past time, as having been done once for all. It is not, ye are dead, ye are risen: but, ye died, ye were raised. This points of course to our baptism, as the moment in which we potentially died and were raised. We have in this passage another instance of the melting down of a theological statement into a perfect crystal of Divine truth; the Apostle says, "your life is hid with Christ in God." This is indeed a wonderful saying. All life is hidden. Of all mysterious things, life is the most mysterious. Our bodily life is hidden; the most learned biologist cannot tell you what life is; the most skilful anatomist cannot tell you where it dwells, or whence it came. And if our bodily life is a hidden life, much more should we expect our spiritual life to be a hidden life. Indeed, the only question is, *where* it is hidden. And this the Apostle tells us. It is hid with Christ in God. The utmost that science can tell us of what life is, is that it is a perfect correspondence of the living organism with its environment, i.e. with its conditions of life. God is our environment, for in Him we live and move, and have our being; spiritual life, then, eternal life, is a perfect correspondence between the living soul and God. In other words, our life is hid in God. But S. Paul does not merely say, " your life is hid in God," but " your life is hid *with Christ* in God." Our life is bound up with His. As He said Himself, " Because I live, ye shall live also."

But if our life is perfect conformity to God, this must needs be a gradual development, and so S. John says in words which throw great light upon this passage. "Now are we the children of God, and it is not made manifest what we shall be. We know that, if He shall be manifested, we shall be like Him; for we shall see Him as He is." (1 S. John iii. 2).

From this the Apostle goes on to argue, Because ye are one with Christ, because your true life is hid with Him in God, therefore mortify your members which are upon earth. This would sound to the Colossians very much like what their would-be teachers taught them; but the likeness was only in the sound, not in the reality. The false teachers, no doubt, were constantly insisting on the need of mortifying the flesh, the actual members of the body, as the only means of reaching the higher life of which they talked so much. S. Paul also taught that the earthly members must be mortified; but these were members of a very different sort.

Ch. iii. 5 : Mortify therefore your members which are upon the earth; fornication, uncleanness, passion, evil desire, and covetousness, the which is idolatry ; for which things' sake cometh the wrath of God upon the sons of disobedience; in the which ye also walked aforetime, when ye lived in these things.

To mortify is to kill, to put to death. The tense in which the verb is placed shows that S. Paul had in his mind a sudden death, death inflicted by a single death-blow. Elsewhere he speaks of crucifying the flesh. Now crucifixion was a slow, lingering death, and by applying the word to the putting to death these evil members of our sinful flesh, he implies that it can only be done gradually, as indeed our own experience tells us only too plainly.

But there is no contradiction. This putting our evil members to death is both sudden and gradual.

The actual crucifixion, the nailing to the Cross, is a thing done at a definite moment of time, though the death of the sufferer might be long delayed. So the flesh is to be nailed to the Cross by a definite act of the will, though it will die hard, and will live on while our earthly life continues.

Ch. iii. 8 : But now put ye also away all these; anger, wrath, malice, railing, shameful (or abusive) speaking out of your mouth: lie not one to another; seeing that ye have put off the old man with his doings, and have put on the new man, which is being renewed unto knowledge after the image of Him that created Him: where there cannot be Greek and Jew, circumcision and uncircumcision, Barbarian, Scythian, bondman, freeman: but Christ is all, and in all.

In this passage the Apostle speaks of putting off

and putting on; of putting off the old man, the Adam-nature, and putting on the new man, the Christ-nature. There must be a putting off before there can be a putting on. We must be emptied before we can be filled; we must be emptied of the sour wine of our old nature, before we can be filled with the good wine of Christ's nature.

To those who are one in Christ, all distinctions are banished: the distinctions that divide men are on the surface, but essentially and fundamentally they are one, one in Christ. Strongly marked as were the lives which divided men into Jews and Gentiles, free men and slaves, Roman citizens and foreigners, they were all blotted out in Christ, for Christ is all and in all.

It is to be feared that people often use the expression, Christ is all in all, without attaching any definite meaning to the words, or if they do put any distinct meaning, it is a selfish one. For what do the words really mean? They mean that mankind is not divided, but one in Christ. Christ is all, and in all. All humanity is in Christ: Christ is in all humanity.

Ch. iii. 12: Put on therefore, as God's elect, holy and beloved, a heart of compassion, kindness, humility, meekness, long-suffering; forbearing one another, and forgiving each other, if any man have a complaint against any; even as the Lord forgave you, so also do ye: and above all these things put on love, which is the bond of perfectness. And let the peace of Christ rule in your hearts, to the which also ye were called in one body; and be ye thankful. Let the word of Christ dwell in you richly in all wisdom; teaching and admonishing one another with psalms and hymns and spiritual songs, singing with grace in your hearts unto God. And whatsoever ye do, in word or in deed, do all in the name of the Lord Jesus, giving thanks to God the Father through Him.

The Apostle says, "Above all these things put on love, which is the bond of perfectness." He seems to regard the graces of which he is speaking as a robe in which the Christian is arrayed; over this robe he counsels them to place the girdle of love, which will keep it tight round the body, and keep everything in its proper place.

From this he passes on to speak of the various relationships of life, of husbands and wives, parents and children, masters and slaves. We ought to notice the fairness which the Apostle displays in treating this subject. He does not allow husbands, parents, and masters to claim obedience from their wives, their children, and their slaves, without reminding them that they also have a corresponding duty to fulfil.

If the wife is to be in subjection to her husband, the husband is to love his wife; if the children are to obey their parents, the parents are not to provoke their children; if slaves are to obey their masters, the masters must render to their slaves that which is just and equal, knowing that they, too, have a Master in heaven.

Then follows a passage in which S. Paul urges upon the Colossians the duty of prayer, both for themselves and for him, and this leads him to give them advice as to their intercourse with their non-Christian neighbours.

Ch. iv. 2: Continue steadfastly in prayer, watching therein with thanksgiving; withal praying for us also, that God may open unto us a door for the word, to speak the mystery of Christ.... Walk in wisdom toward them that are without, redeeming the time (buying up the opportunity). Let your speech be always with grace, seasoned with salt, that ye may know how ye ought to answer each one.

Then follows the customary salutations.

Ch. iv. 10: Aristarchus my fellow-prisoner saluteth you, and Mark, the cousin of Barnabas .... Epaphras, who is one of you, a servant of Christ Jesus, saluteth you, always striving for you in his prayers, that ye may stand perfect and fully assured in all the will of God. For I bear him witness, that he hath much labour for you, and for them in Laodicea, and for them in Hierapolis. Luke the beloved physician, and Demas, salute you. Salute the brethren that are in Laodicea, and Nymphas, and the Church that is in their house.

And when this epistle hath been read among you, cause that it be read also in the Church of the Laodiceans; and that ye also read the epistle from Laodicea. And say to Archippus, Take heed to the ministry which thou hast received in the Lord, that thou fulfil it.

The salutation of me Paul with mine own hand. Remember my bonds. Grace be with you.

There are two familiar names in these salutations: Mark, who had formerly accompanied Paul and Barnabas, and Luke the Evangelist and historian of the Church. Archippus, to whom a special charge is sent, is considered to have been of the chief presbyters to whom, in the absence of Epaphras, the rule of the Colossian Church had been committed.

We see throughout how close were the relations between the three Phrygian Churches. This Epistle to Colossæ was to be read in the Church of Laodicea: while the Colossians were to read an Epistle which would be passed on to them from Laodicea. There is reason to think that this Epistle was no other than the Epistle to the Ephesians, which partook of the nature of a circular letter, and was intended for other Churches, as well as for the Christians at Ephesus. And as Laodicea was on the high road from Ephesus, the Colossians would naturally receive that Epistle from Laodicea. If this be so, there is no ground for the supposition that an Epistle of S. Paul to the Laodiceans has been lost, for no such letter was written.

CHAPTER XXIX.

THE EPISTLE TO PHILEMON.

CLOSELY connected with the Epistle to the Colossians is the short private letter which S. Paul wrote to Philemon, an influential member of the Church at Colossæ.

How close this connection was you can see at a glance by comparing the opening sentences and the closing salutations of the two Epistles:—

To the Colossians.	*To Philemon.*
Paul, an apostle of Christ Jesus, and Timothy our brother, to the Saints and faithful brethren in Christ which are at Colossæ: grace to you, and peace from God our Father . . . Say to Archippus, Take heed to the ministry which thou hast received.	Paul, a prisoner of Christ Jesus, and Timothy our brother, to Philemon our beloved and fellow-worker, . . . and to Archippus our fellow-soldier, and to the church in thy house: Grace to you and peace from God our Father and the Lord Jesus Christ.
Aristarchus my fellow-prisoner saluteth you, and Mark. Epaphras, who is one of you, saluteth you. Luke the beloved physician, and Demas, salute you.	Epaphras, my fellow-prisoner in Christ Jesus, saluteth thee; and so do Mark, Aristarchus, Demas, Luke, my fellow-workers.

Philemon seems to have been a man of considerable means, and to have shown himself ready to share his wealth with others. In a room in his house the Colossian Christians met for worship and instruction. It seems probable that Philemon had been in Ephesus during the time that S. Paul was there, and that by the Apostle's preaching and influence he had embraced the faith of Christ, and afterwards, in conjunction with Epaphras, gathered together a Christian community at Colossæ.

With him is associated a Christian lady, Apphia, who was probably his wife. Archippus, who is mentioned in close connection with Philemon and Apphia, may have been their son, and at any rate was the presbyter next in authority in the Colossian Church to Epaphras.

Among the slaves in the household was one named Onesimus. We may be sure that under such a master as Philemon Onesimus must have been kindly treated. It is possible that he may have resented the change that would have passed over the household of Philemon at his conversion to the new faith, and rebelled against the strictness and soberness of a house so different from the free and easy, not to say reckless and prodigal ways of ordinary heathen families. However this may have been, Onesimus robbed his master, and made his way to Rome. How at Rome he came under S. Paul's influence we cannot know for certain. He may have been found by Epaphras in the streets of Rome, having, like the prodigal in the Gospel, spent all and begun to be in want. At any rate he was brought under the influence of S. Paul, which led to his conversion to God, and his reception into the kingdom of Christ by baptism. A Phrygian slave, a thief and a run-a-way, would not seem very promising material. But the keen insight of the Apostle recognized in this run-a-way slave qualities and powers which might render him of conspicuous service to the Christian cause.

S. Paul would gladly have retained Onesimus to be his companion, and trained him for some special work in the Church; but to do so would not, he felt, have been fair to his master.

Accordingly he sent him back to Philemon at Colossæ in company with Tychicus, bearing a letter to his master from the Apostle himself.

In this incident S. Paul was brought face to face with one of the great problems of social life with which the Christian Church had to deal, the terrible institution of slavery.

The facts of this system of slavery are horrible and revolting in the extreme.

The Roman Empire is calculated to have contained no less than sixty millions of slaves. The number of slaves said to have been retained in a single family is well nigh incredible. A Roman writer, quoted by Gibbon, asserts that as many as ten, or even twenty, thousand slaves were possessed by a single owner. The condition of these untold millions was pitiable in the extreme. Dr. Farrar describes them as "without family, without religion, without possessions, men who had no recognized rights, and towards whom none had any recognized duties, passing ordinarily from a childhood of degradation to a manhood of hardship, and an old age of unpitied neglect." Less than two years before S. Paul wrote to Philemon, a Prefect of the City had been murdered by a slave. In spite of the pity of the people, the Senate had decided that the old ruthless law should be carried out, and the entire *familia* of slaves be put to death. Regardless of the menaces of the populace, Nero ordered the sentence to be executed by military force, and four hundred human beings, of every age and of both sexes, had been led to slaughter, in spite of the indubitable innocence of the vast majority.

There is a fearful story told of a wretch named Vedius Pollio, who fed the lampreys in his fish-ponds with the flesh of his slaves.

It has been objected against Christianity that neither Christ nor His Apostles denounced slavery, but acquiesced in it with all its abominations.

Such objectors ought to remember what would have been the consequence if the Christian Church had denounced slavery, and the Apostles had preached a crusade against it. The consequence would have been a rising of the slaves, which, though it would probably have been put down by the gigantic power of Rome, would have yet deluged the Empire with blood, and with it might have perished the Christian Church itself.

S. Paul, following the leading of the Spirit of God, did not denounce slavery, or agitate for the political rights of man: for he knew that the Gospel, which declared God's love for every man and commanded all men to love one another, a Gospel which was based upon the fact that Christ had taken the nature of all men and had tasted death for every man, would sooner or later work its way, and accomplish the abolition of slavery.

In this episode of Onesimus we have a type of the influence of Christianity upon slavery. Onesimus was sent back to his master; but sent back not as a slave, but as a brother in Christ.

The emancipation of the slaves in our West Indian Colonies; the emancipation of the serfs by the late Emperor of Russia; the abolition of slavery, after a long and bloody war, in the United States of America, were brought about by the gradual working out of the principles of Christianity, in the Spirit of Christ.

We may be very thankful for the conversion of Onesimus, not only for his own sake, but that his return to his master was the occasion of the writing this letter, which is not only valuable for its practical illustration of the working of Christianity, but also for the light that it throws upon the character of S. Paul.

But it is time that we should turn to the letter itself.

Philemon i. 1: Paul, a prisoner of Christ Jesus, and Timothy our brother, to Philemon our beloved, and fellow-worker, and to Apphia our sister, and to Archippus our fellow-soldier, and to the Church in thy house: Grace to you and peace from God our Father and the Lord Jesus Christ.

I thank my God always, making mention of thee in my prayers, hearing of thy love, and of the faith which thou hast toward the Lord Jesus, and toward all the saints . . . For I had much joy and comfort in thy love, because the hearts of the saints have been refreshed through thee, brother.

Wherefore, though I have all boldness in Christ to enjoin thee that which is befitting, yet for love's sake I rather beseech, being such a one as Paul the aged, and now a prisoner also of Christ Jesus: I beseech thee for my child Onesimus, who was aforetime unprofitable to thee, but now is profitable to thee and to me: whom I have sent back to thee in his own person, that is, my very heart: whom I would fain have kept with me, that in thy behalf he might minister unto me in the bonds of the Gospel: but without thy mind I would do nothing; that thy goodness should not be as of necessity, but of free will. For perhaps he was therefore parted from thee for a season, that thou shouldest have him for ever; no longer as a servant, but more than a servant, a brother beloved, specially to me, but how much rather to thee, both in the flesh and in the Lord.

Nothing can be more beautiful, more refined, more touching, than this letter. Nothing can be more admirable than the skill, and all the more from its being so utterly unconscious, with which he introduces the subject of his letter. How delicately he pleads his own age, and his sufferings in the cause of Christ. In what a tender fashion he speaks of this run-a-way slave; he calls him his child, the child of his old age, the child of his imprisonment! With gracious pleasantry he plays upon the name Onesimus, which means "*helpful*," and speaks of him as once unprofitable, but now profitable, a true Onesimus. S. Paul takes for granted also, that Philemon will receive him, no longer as a slave, but as a brother beloved; he feels confident also that he would do even more than he was asked.

Then, as Onesimus had robbed his master, and had no opportunity of earning anything to repay it, the Apostle undertakes to make good any loss that Philemon had sustained by his servant's dishonesty, so he continues:—

Ch. i. 17: If then thou countest me a partner, receive him as myself. But if he hath wronged thee at all, or oweth thee aught, put that to mine account; I Paul write it with mine own hand, I will repay it: that I say not unto thee (lest I should be driven to remind thee) how that thou owest to me even thine own self besides.

Yea, brother, let me have joy of thee in the Lord: refresh my heart in Christ. Having confidence in thine obedience I write unto thee, knowing that thou wilt do even beyond what I say. But withal prepare me also a lodging: for I hope that through your prayers I shall be granted unto you. Epaphras, my fellow-prisoner in Christ

THE EPISTLE TO PHILEMON.

Jesus, saluteth thee; and so do Mark, Aristarchus, Demas, Luke, my fellow-workers.

The Grace of our Lord Jesus Christ be with your spirit. Amen.

Thus concludes this most beautiful specimen of the private letter of a Christian Apostle.

We have no means of knowing how it was received, and how Onesimus himself was received; but we cannot doubt that the Apostle's request concerning him was fulfilled, and more than fulfilled; that the former slave was received as a brother beloved.

Nor can we doubt that when, after his liberation, S. Paul fulfilled his intention of visiting Colossæ, and was received, as he doubtless was, under the hospitable roof of Philemon and Apphia, he would find his child Onesimus in some position of trust in the household, and holding an honourable and honoured place in the Christian community of Colossæ.

CHAPTER XXX.

THE EPISTLE TO THE EPHESIANS.

E come now to the Epistle to the Ephesians, the last and greatest of the group of S. Paul's Epistles, which are usually called the Epistles of the first imprisonment.

Why S. Paul should have written this most important Epistle at this particular time, and why he addressed it to the Church at Ephesus, it is not hard to discover.

Epaphras had brought him a sad account of the inroads of various false teachers into the Churches of Colossæ and its sister cities. If this teaching had not yet reached Ephesus and the other Churches of Asia, it might very soon appear there; and so having written the Epistle to the Colossians, in which he declared those special truths, which he considered most needful to meet the errors which had been introduced among them, S. Paul would very naturally think that the same truths, stated in a somewhat less controversial manner and in a more general form, would arm the Christians of Ephesus and of the other Churches of Asia against the same dangers, and build them up in their most holy faith.

You will remember that S. Paul lived and laboured in Ephesus for more than two years, and with such effect, that the word of the Lord grew mightily and prevailed.

It was here that idolatry first woke up to the fact that in the religion which Paul preached it had to do with a mortal foe. The heathen recognized no such mortal enemy in Judaism: and they were quite right; the Jews were haters of idols and idolatry, but idolaters had nothing to fear from them.

The Jews kept to themselves, and let the idolaters alone. The Christians welcomed to their society Jews and Gentiles alike. Demetrius and his fellow craftsmen were keen-sighted enough to see that if a society of Jews and Gentiles, worshipping one God, and recognizing no divisions, setting up no barriers, was possible, idolatry was hasting to its end.

In an Epistle written to the Christian society in this city of Ephesus, if anywhere we should expect to find laid down the ground of a spiritual society which has a deeper foundation than the Jewish calling or covenant; which has its foundations in the nature of God Himself; which explains and supports all human relationships; and which has all spiritual enemies to fight with.

And this is what we do find, as we shall presently see.

Ch. i. 1: Paul, an apostle of Christ Jesus through the will of God, to the saints which are at Ephesus, and the faithful in Christ Jesus: Grace to you and peace from God our Father and the Lord Jesus Christ.

This Epistle has been described as instruction passing into prayer, a creed soaring into song.

Accordingly, instead of a thankful remembrance of the truth and patience of the Christian believers to whom he is writing, with which the Apostle usually begins his letters, in this Epistle he breaks out at once into a fervent Thanksgiving.

Then he goes on to speak of an election, or choosing out, of a predestination or fore-ordaining.

It must be confessed that we meet these words, "election" and "predestination," with a certain amount of alarm and suspicion. They are generally taken to represent doctrines which, if true, are very terrible: terrible as effecting the destinies of mankind, terrible as affecting the character of God.

The first of the Lambeth Articles, which were vainly sought to be imposed upon the Church of England, lays down this doctrine in all its naked hideousness. "God from all eternity has predestined certain men to life; and certain men he has reprobated to death." No wonder then that these words, when they occur, should cause us to start back in alarm: but if by a vigorous effort we shake ourselves free from the hateful, God-dishonouring doctrines which have been connected with them, we shall see that these words, as S. Paul used them, describe an all-righteous, all-merciful, all-loving purpose to which we can safely trust ourselves, and the race to which we belong.

There can be no question that in the passage which we are now going to read, the Apostle asserts a Divine purpose, a purpose which, though to be carried out in time, was not formed in time, but in eternity; a purpose which can be affected by no accident, and suffer no change, and experience no break-down. And what is this purpose, this Divine plan? It is, that they who are the objects of this eternal purpose may be holy, and without blemish before Him in love.

"Our danger does not lie in thinking that God has predestinated us to this perfect holiness, but in thinking that He has *not* so predestinated us.

"But if we so believe in this our predestination as

to give ourselves credit as belonging to a class in which we do not include others, or in which we have tempted others not to include themselves, we have put our election upon *a new ground*.

"It is no longer that God, being holy, necessarily wishes the creatures He has made in His image to be like Him, but that, being Almighty, He has been able to decree that certain persons, among whom we reckon ourselves, shall have certain spiritual and divine blessings; and that certain other persons should be excluded from them. Thus God is represented not as One whose only will is a good will, who only aims at what is good, good for all; but as a great Potentate who can do what He likes, who can give blessings or withhold them as he chooses."

Very different is the Heavenly Father with whom we have to do! Very different is the election wherewith He has chosen us!

The Heavenly Father chose us in Christ, in His Son, from eternity, not that we might *have* something, but that we might *be* something—that we might be holy and without blemish; having foreordained us—to what? To *the adoption of sons*. Our original, our essential calling is to be *sons*. We are sons in God's purpose and calling, before we are actually admitted as sons into the family of His Church.

Now if God thus chose us to be holy, it would follow that when man sinned, God would make a way for forgiveness, would ordain a means whereby His Divine forgiveness might flow to man; if God fore-ordained as to the adoption of sons, it would follow that God would provide for the removal of that which would prevent our living as sons.

And thus having spoken of the work of the Father, the Apostle passes on to the work of the

Son; viz., that in Him, and through His sacrifice, we have our redemption, even the forgiveness of our sins. But the Apostle does not linger even among such vital truths as these; but hurries on to show how they are all to be referred to one ground,—the good pleasure of God's Will; and to one end,—the gathering up of all things in Christ.

Ch. i. 3: Blessed be the God and Father of our Lord Jesus Christ, who hath blessed us with every spiritual blessing in the heavenly places (literally in the heavenlies) in Christ: even as He chose us in Him before the foundation of the world, that we should be holy and without blemish before Him in love: having foreordained us unto adoption as sons through Jesus Christ unto Himself, according to the good pleasure of His will, to the praise of the glory of His grace, which He freely bestowed on us in the Beloved: in whom we have our redemption through His Blood, the forgiveness of our trespasses . . . . . having made known unto us the mystery of His will . . . . to sum up all things in Christ, the things in the heavens, and the things upon the earth. . . . . . . In whom ye (Gentiles) also, having heard the word of the truth, the Gospel of your salvation,—in whom, having also believed, ye were sealed with the Holy Spirit of promise, which is an earnest of our inheritance, unto the redemption of God's own possession, unto the praise of His glory.

In this passage we see the Three Persons of the Holy and Undivided Trinity uniting in the work of man's salvation. First they are spoken of together as included in the work of blessing, then "the threefold cord, so to speak, is unwrapped, and the part of each Divine Person separately described."

The Father in His eternal love has chosen us to holiness, ordained us to sonship, bestowed grace on us in the Beloved.

In the Son we have redemption in His blood,

knowledge of the mystery of His will, inheritance under Him the One Head.

Through the Spirit we are sealed; by hearing the word of our salvation, by receiving the earnest of our inheritance, we may hope to be brought to the inheritance of the purchased possession.

In reading this whole passage we can hardly help asking, who are the "we" of whom the Apostle speaks? who are the elect? who are the chosen?

If we remember *to what* it is that the elect are chosen, that they are chosen to be *holy*, to be God's *sons*, how shall we dare to say of any, how shall any one dare to say of himself, they are not, I am not?

If we insist upon a definite answer to the question, Who are the elect? we may say, All men in Christ. Christ, the Second Man, is really and truly God's only Elect; we are elect in Him. If it be asked Who, then, is not elect? we may say, That man is not elect whose nature Christ did not take!

Is there then, it may be said, no difference between the world and the Church, between believers and non-believers?

Yes, surely a great difference indeed. The little band of Christians in Ephesus were called out of the unbelieving mass of Jews and heathens, to show what God intended all His human children to be. The Church was the advanced guard of humanity, claiming God's election not for itself alone, but as the representative of mankind, in the sure conviction that neither Adam's sin, nor all the sin of the world, has been able to defeat the design of the Creator. And what is that design? It is to sum up all things in Christ; or, as he had before said to the Colossians, " to reconcile all things unto Himself."

Now as this glorious purpose passes before our minds, ought it not to be a relief to be told that this is no hand-to-mouth scheme, changing according to circumstances, but a purpose fixed from all eternity? Do we think it an evidence of wisdom in earthly matters to have no forethought, to live from hand to mouth, with no settled purpose, on no definite plan?

And shall we, in our little schemes, exercise forethought, and make plans, and work on system; and shall we think that God will work at loose ends as it were, that He should exercise no forethought, that He should have no plan?

God is love, His forethought in loving is our election: God is Wisdom, and the plan according to which He works is His predestination.

May we be so rooted and grounded in love, that we may be able to comprehend with all the saints, what is the breadth and height and depth, and to know the love of Christ which passeth knowledge, that we may be filled with all the fulness of God!

CHAPTER XXXI.

THE EPISTLE TO THE EPHESIANS
(*continued*).

IN this Epistle, as we have seen, instead of beginning, as was his usual practice, with an expression of thankfulness for the faith and love of those whom he is addressing, S. Paul bursts forth at once into a fervent thanksgiving to God for the wonder and greatness of His grace; a thanksgiving which not only forms the opening of the Epistle, but strikes its keynote, and declares the mystery of redeeming love which it is the purpose of the Epistle to unfold.

Then, having traced the work of redemption from its first beginning in the love of the Father before the world was, to its final completion in that divine far-off event to which the whole creation moves, the Apostle thanks God that his fellow-believers in the Church of Ephesus had responded to their high calling, and were walking in faith and love. But even here there is no finality; the thanksgiving quickly passes into prayer for their still further illumination, for their advancement in knowledge, and growth in grace. He prays that they may know what their calling means, what the hope of it is, what the wealth of the glory of God's inheritance in the saints is, what the surpassing magnitude of His power is towards those who are believing in it. But how shall he measure the greatness of that power which is at work within them; how make them understand the sort of power which the Holy Spirit is in them? He declares that the power which is working in them is the same power that worked in Christ; that the power which was bursting the bands of evil in which they had been held, was the same power that had raised Christ from the dead; that the power which was lifting them up from earthly things to spiritual, was the same power that exalted Christ to the right hand of God.

Thus the victory of Christ was their victory, His triumph was the pledge of theirs.

"Only the believer must not fancy that the Spirit of God was his own individual possession; that his faith and holiness was his own. No, he must understand that he was only faithful, only holy when he was lifted out of himself, when he counted himself the member of a living body, united to a living Head, that body being the fulness of him that filleth all in all, of Him to whom every power in this age, and in the age to come, is subjected."

Ch. i. 15: For this cause I also, having heard of the faith in the Lord Jesus which is among you, and which ye shew toward all the saints, cease not to give thanks for you, making mention of you in my prayers; that the God of our Lord Jesus Christ, the Father of glory, may give unto you a spirit of wisdom and revelation in the knowledge of Him; having the eyes of your heart enlightened, that ye may know what is the hope of His calling, what the riches of the glory of His inheritance in the saints, and what the exceeding greatness of His power to us-ward who believe, according to that working of the strength of His might which He wrought in Christ, when He raised Him from the dead, and made Him to sit at His right hand in the heavenly places, far above all rule, and authority, and power, and dominion, and every name that is named, not only in this world, but also in that which is to come: and

He put all things in subjection under His feet, and gave Him to be head over all things to the Church, which is HIS BODY, the fulness of Him that filleth all in all.

After this magnificent description of the destiny of man in Christ, and of the Church as His fulness, the Apostle goes on to show, that not only was the power which worked in Christ the same power that worked in them, but that it had already been exercised in them. They *were* quickened; they *were* raised; they *were* made to sit in the heavenlies: and this not by any action of their own; they were quickened when *Christ* revived, they were raised when *He* rose, they were made to sit with Him when *He* took His seat at the right hand of God.

Ch. ii. 4: But God, being rich in mercy, for His great love wherewith He loved us even [when ye (Gentiles) were dead through your trespasses]; and we (Jews) were dead through our trespasses, quickened us (both Jews and Gentiles) together with Christ, and raised us up with Him, and made us to sit with Him in the heavenly places, in Christ Jesus: that in the ages to come He might show the exceeding riches of His grace in kindness toward us in Christ Jesus: for by grace have ye been saved through faith; and that not of yourselves: it is the gift of God: not of works, that no man should glory. For we are His workmanship, created in Christ Jesus for good works, which God afore, prepared that we should walk in them.

Now let us go back to the passage which we read just now, to the prayer of the Apostle for the Ephesian Christians.

That prayer is addressed (i. 17) to "the God of our Lord Jesus Christ, the Father of Glory." S. Paul is speaking of Christ in His manhood, as the Lord and Head of all, and therefore naturally calls God *His* God. This is only what Christ said Himself. "I ascend to my Father, and your Father;

to *my God*, and your God." "The Father of glory." This is a somewhat unusual expression; it reminds us of the expression of S. James, "The Father of lights." This glory is the special glory of the divine nature manifested in Christ of which S. John says, "The Word was made flesh, and dwelt among us, and we beheld His glory." "The Father of glory," then, will mean the Father of our Lord Jesus Christ; the Father of the Glory in Him.

S. Paul's prayer was that they might know, that they might have full knowledge of, what was the hope of their calling. They had only the beginnings, only the germ, of this calling in them; what that calling was in its fulness was the object of hope; that they might know the riches of the glory of His inheritance in the Saints. S. Paul might well have prayed before, as he did pray, that God would give them the spirit of wisdom and revelation; for otherwise, without that heavenly wisdom, that spiritual enlightenment, they could not know, or even catch a glimpse of, the manifold grace of God.

If we think of what we are simply in ourselves, so sinful, so ignorant, so blind, we cannot possibly take in this boundless vista of glory: so S. Paul bids us look to Christ our Head, and see what the power of God has done for Him. And yet that power even in Him was only gradually exercised.

"The change wrought in Christ on His resurrection morning was but the first of a series of changes. During the forty days which He passed between His disciples on earth, and His work in Hades, the process of His glorification was going on. His ascension to Heaven only waited until Heaven and His humanity were brought into perfect accord.... Nor must we suppose that the last change was wrought in Him at His ascension.

There were yet sublimer and sublimer changes to be effected. For He had not only to enter Heaven, but to pass through all the Heavens, on His way to His Throne 'over all.' And as a series of transformations prepared His humanity to go up from Hades to Heaven; in like manner we must presume that other and higher transformations characterized His rise from Heaven to Heaven. His human nature would put on the glory of each successive Heaven. But in order to leave Heaven after Heaven behind Him, it would be necessary that His humanity should surpass the power, purity, and glory of each Heaven. We may be sure that there was nothing arbitrary in the movement of His Human Nature through the Heavens. If He found not His permanent throne and sphere of influence, until He was far above them all, it was for no other reason than that our nature in Him was being wrought up to a condition transcending anything that had been known throughout the Heavens. . . . . That our nature should be set on a level with the original thrones and dominions of heaven, is perhaps more than we should look for; but Paul asserts that God has raised it '*far above* all principality, and power, and might, and dominion.'. . . . . Alone before God, and looking forward to your own eternity, review the whole prayer and muse thereupon, until you feel the insanity of allowing anything in time or mortal life to becloud 'The Hope' with which 'The Father of Glory' is seeking to allure the children of men." (J. PULSFORD, *Christ and His Seed*.)

It has been already pointed out that there is a likeness, and yet a likeness in difference, between the Epistle to the Ephesians and that to the Colossians.

The main theme of the latter is the Person of

Christ; the main theme of the Epistle to the Ephesians is the life of Christ manifested in His Church. Here the Church is the fulness, the plenitude; there the fulness, the plenitude dwells in Christ.

Wonderful indeed is the Apostle's language respecting the Church.

"It is Christ's Body, the fulness of Him that filleth all in all." We must remember, of course, that S. Paul is speaking of the ideal Church, of the Church, that is, as it exists in the idea or thought of God, the Church as it was intended to be—all its members holy, and all holy ones its members.

Yet though the Church that the Apostle describes was an ideal Church, the working of God, in it was an actual reality, an accomplished fact. But all— S. Paul especially insists upon this—is of God's free grace. By grace we are saved through faith. The good works which God enables us to do, which He has prepared for us to walk in, in no sense obtain these unspeakable blessings for us. No, our salvation from first to last is all of free unmerited grace, undeserved kindness; such exceeding riches of grace and kindness, as shall be a blessed witness to God for all succeeding generations.

Then specially addressing the Gentile members of the Church, he reminds them of what Christ had done for them, that He had proclaimed a great covenant of peace between heaven and earth, of peace between man and man, between Jew and Gentile: that henceforth the dividing wall of partition was broken down; that they were no more strangers and aliens, but fellow-citizens with God's true Israel; that they were built upon the foundation of the Apostles and Prophets, to be a holy temple, the habitation of God in the Spirit.

Ch. ii. 11: Wherefore remember that ye ... Gentiles

were at that time separate from Christ, alienated from the commonwealth of Israel, and strangers from the covenants of the promise, having no hope, and without God in the world.

But now in Christ Jesus ye that once were afar off are made nigh in the blood of Christ. For He is our Peace, who made both (Jews and Gentiles) one, and brake down the middle wall of partition . . . that He might create in Himself of the twain one new man, so making peace; and might reconcile them both in one body unto God through the Cross, having slain the enmity thereby: and He came and preached peace to you that were far off (i. e. to the Gentiles), and peace to them that were nigh (i. e. to the Jews): for through Him we both (Jews and Gentiles) have our access in one Spirit unto the Father.

So then ye are no more strangers and sojourners, but ye are fellow-citizens with the saints, and of the household of God, being built upon the foundation of the Apostles and Prophets, Christ Jesus Himself being the chief cornerstone; in whom each several building, fitly framed together, groweth into a holy temple (or sanctuary) in the Lord; in whom ye also are builded together for a habitation of God in the Spirit.

In speaking of the breaking down the barriers that separated Jews and Gentiles, S. Paul speaks of the "middle wall of partition." This probably alludes to the low wall in the Temple enclosure which divided the court of the Gentiles from the court of Israel. On this wall were inscriptions in two or three languages warning all Gentiles, on pain of death, not to pass the barrier. The thought of this middle wall of partition naturally suggested the idea of the Temple itself, that is the Sanctuary, the innermost temple. Into this Holy of Holies both Jews and Gentiles had free access.

Indeed, they themselves constituted this Temple; into it both Jews and Gentiles were built; the

Jewish portion might seem to tend in one direction, and the Gentile portion in another: but Christ was the corner-stone, binding both into one; belonging to both, and because belonging to both, making both one. Thus Christ is both the foundation-stone upon which the whole fabric rests, and the corner-stone, the stone of unity, binding all together.

> "The Saints build up its fabric,
> And the corner-stone is Christ."

CHAPTER XXXII.

THE EPISTLE TO THE EPHESIANS
(*continued*).

THE Apostle has now traced out God's glorious and gracious Plan from its beginning, he has shown it to us in its origin and source. As S. John saw the river of water of life flowing out from the throne of God, so S. Paul shows us the full stream of the Divine purpose issuing out of the loving heart of the Father of all. This glorious and gracious Plan is nothing short of this, to regenerate human nature, and to reconstitute it in His Son, in whom it was originally constituted. It is often thought that God's purpose began at the Fall and was intended only to remedy the Fall, and to bring back man to the state from which he had fallen. But S. Paul teaches us something very different. According to him, the work of man's salvation is to bring him back to what God had purposed concerning him before the foundation of the world.

To work out this Plan God sent His Son into the world to take upon Him the nature of all men, and to taste death for every man, and by His death to reconcile the world unto Himself. To make this redemptive work possible for man, to bring men into this reconciliation, to recreate them in holiness, to change them into the image of Christ from glory to glory, God sent forth His Spirit to establish a spiritual kingdom upon earth, in which men might obtain the adoption of sons, and be trained for the sphere of glory which Christ went before to prepare for them.

And this kingdom, the Apostle has assured the Ephesians, is already founded, and they, Gentiles as well as Jews, have received their full citizenship in it ; they have been made members of the Body of Christ, the fulness of Him that filleth all in all; they have been builded together in Him as a holy temple, the habitation of God in the Spirit.

Having laid down this, the Apostle goes on to speak, in yet more ample terms, of the infinite extent and all-embracing influence of this great Plan; and of his own special part in proclaiming it.

This sublime mystery of God's purpose was not his own discovery, it was revealed to him by the Spirit of God. Hitherto it had been kept secret from the sons of men, but was now revealed to the Apostles and Prophets of the Church in the same Spirit. And this hidden but now revealed mystery was—that the Gentiles are fellow-heirs, and fellow-members of the body, and fellow-partakers of the promise in Christ Jesus through the Gospel: and of this Gospel he continues:—

Ch. iii. 7: I was made a minister according to the gift of that grace of God which was given me, according to the working of His power.

Unto me, who am less than the least of all saints, was this grace given, to preach unto the Gentiles the unsearchable riches of Christ; and to make all men see what is the dispensation of the mystery which from all ages hath been hid in God who created all things ; to the intent that now unto the principalities and the powers in the heavenly places might be made known through the Church the manifold wisdom of God, according to the eternal purpose which He purposed in Christ Jesus our Lord: in whom we have boldness and access in confidence through our faith in Him.

This was the Gospel which S. Paul had to preach, and of which he said, "Woe is me if I preach not the Gospel." It was really a Gospel, good news for all. Not a gospel which called upon men to separate themselves from a doomed race, and to secure safety for themselves, but a Gospel which proclaimed that God had redeemed the world, and reconciled all things to Himself; the good news that each might claim the grace that was meant for all.

It was the unsearchable riches of this grace that S. Paul believed himself sent to preach. His desire was to make all men see—not a select few, but all men—the truth which from all eternity had been hidden in God.

And this also the Apostle held, that "the effect of this revelation was not to be measured by the number of persons who might receive it, then or in any after age, among Jews and Gentiles, among any inhabitants of this planet. The revelation of God's love in Christ, of Christ's incarnation, and sacrifice, and resurrection, of the victory over fallen and rebellious wills, was a revelation to the whole universe, to the principalities and powers in heavenly places. The Church, however small its numbers, however insignificant its members, declared to them the manifold wisdom of God, according to the forearrangement of the ages which He made in Christ Jesus our Lord."

But how should he exercise this ministry? who was sufficient for these things? how was he to make all men see? Instruction, exhortation, seemed alike insufficient; there was nothing for it but prayer, and to prayer the Apostle betakes himself; and this is his prayer:—

Ch. iii. 14: For this cause I bow my knees unto the Father, from whom every family in heaven and on earth is named, that He would grant you, according to the riches of His glory, that ye may be strengthened with power through His spirit in the inward man; that Christ may dwell in your hearts through faith; to the end that ye, being rooted and grounded in love, may be strong to apprehend with all the saints what is the breadth and length and height and depth, and to know the love of Christ which passeth knowledge, that ye may be filled unto all the fulness of God.

It would be a good thing for us to study carefully the words of this prayer, and to turn it into a prayer for ourselves and for all men.

First notice the deep reverence of the address; though he had just before spoken of boldness and confidence of access, the Apostle begins in the attitude of the deepest reverence, "I bow my knees unto the Father."

Passing on to the prayer itself, we see that the heart and core of the prayer is for the strengthening power of God's Holy Spirit. He prays that they may be strengthened by the power of the Holy Spirit infused *into* the inner man, in order that Christ may dwell in their hearts by faith—by their faith. You see the Holy Spirit does not come instead of Christ; does not come to take the place of an absent Christ, but to bring about His Presence.

That, being rooted and grounded in *love*, they may be able to apprehend. So we see that *love*, not knowledge or intelligence, is the condition of this spiritual apprehension.

That they may be strong to apprehend the breadth and length and height and depth—the breadth and depth of what? S. Paul does not tell us that; the old fathers of the Church delighted to see in it the description of the Cross of Christ, in its four-fold extension.

And here I am going to quote the words of one whose character and teaching were highly appreciated in his life, and have been still more highly appreciated since his death. I mean Charles Kingsley.

"What is the breadth of Christ's Cross? It is as broad as the whole world; for He died for the whole world.

"And what is the length of Christ's Cross? The length thereof, says an old father, signifies the time during which it will last.

"How long, then, is the Cross of Christ? Long enough to last through all time; as long as there is a sinner to be saved; as long as there is ignorance, sorrow, pain, or death in the universe of God, so long will Christ's Cross last.

"And how high is Christ's Cross? As high as the highest heaven, and the throne of God, and the bosom of the Father.

"And how deep is the Cross of Christ? This is a great mystery, and one which people in these days are afraid to look at, and darken it of their own will, because they will neither believe their Bibles, nor the voice of their own hearts. But if the Cross of Christ be as high as heaven, then, it seems to me, it must also be as deep as hell, deep enough to reach the deepest sinner in the deepest pit to which he may fall.

"At all events, I believe, that we shall find S. Paul's words true when he says, that Christ's love passeth knowledge; and therefore that we shall find this also;—that however broad we may think Christ's Cross, it is broader still. However long, it is longer still. However high, it is higher still. However deep, it is deeper still."

And then follows the doxology, such a doxology as is a suitable finish to such a prayer!

Ch. iii. 20: Now unto Him that is able to do exceeding abundantly above all that we ask or think, according to the power that worketh in us, unto Him be the glory in the Church and in Christ Jesus unto all generations for ever and ever (or, unto all the generations of the age of the ages). Amen.

It might be thought that in praying as the Apostle did in this prayer, he was praying for the unattainable, the impossible: so he hastens on to transfer our thoughts to the all-subduing power that is working in us.

So far from having asked greater things than can be fulfilled, S. Paul asserts that what God will do in us, and for us, exceeds everything we can express or imagine.

We are started on a journey whose end is the fulness of God. The golden year of God's loving purposes has its seasons which are unfolded each in its proper turn. "Spring has its beauty, and summer its glory, but God's full idea is not realized till harvest."

And what that harvest will be is too full, too glorious for us to grasp. "We can no more imagine it than the catterpillar can imagine what its life will be when it will spread its painted wings, and flit from flower to flower."

But there is a power at work in us, to which nothing is impossible, which can bring us to this consummation.

And this power "offers no violence to our independence of action. It brings forth the powers and peculiarities of each soul as silently and with as little force as the flowers of spring are opened from their roots."

Ch. iii. 21: Unto the Father be the glory in the Church unto all the generations of the age of the ages. Amen.

"Christ's age is the age of the ages; but this age is made up of infinite periods, or generations. Christ has not only infinite power to work with, but infinite ages to work in. But these generations of the age of the ages are too much for our limited faculties. A child's hand might as well grasp the Pleiades, as we this vista of the ages. Thought is baffled, even hope is dazed, there is nothing for it but faith, and love, and trust in Him who is working out the good pleasure of His Will, in Him who will subdue all things to Himself."—(PULSFORD *on the Ephesians*.)

CHAPTER XXXIII.

THE EPISTLE TO THE EPHESIANS
(*continued*).

IN the opening sentence of the Epistle S. Paul records his thankfulness to God for the spiritual blessings with which He had blessed His people: and declares his belief that God had chosen them before the foundation of the world, that they should be holy and without blemish before Him in love, having received through Christ the adoption of sons.

In the chapters that follow S. Paul fills in this outline sketch, till the finished picture stands before us in all its matchless sublimity.

In sentence after sentence he unfolds the divine mystery which filled his mind, the mystery which had been hid from ages and generations, but was now being uttered in the Church, the truth that all things end in God, as they began in God: the truth—

> ". . . . That we and all men move
> Under a canopy of love
> As broad as the blue sky above."

Then he lets his whole soul flow out in fervent supplication for them, that they might know the love of Christ which passeth knowledge, that they might be filled with all the fulness of God.

After having thus laid the foundation, he proceeds in the fourth chapter to build up the superstructure of the Christian life: having set before them the vastness and the glory of their high calling, he urges them to walk worthy of it.

But what sort of walk would be worthy? In what spirit, in what frame of mind were they to advance towards it? There could not be much doubt about the answer. What was the mind in which Christ Himself advanced towards His boundless exaltation? It was humility. He emptied Himself, He humbled Himself even unto death. So it must be in a spirit of humility that we can walk worthy of our high calling.

The unspeakable glories of "the generations of the age of the ages" could only be reached by those who were content to become as little children.

And in this spirit of meekness they were to give diligence to keep the unity of the Spirit in the bond of peace.

But what is meant by the unity of the Spirit? It is that unity which is the work of the Holy Spirit.

The Holy Spirit is Himself the Spirit of unity. In the very being of God, the Father and the Son are one in the unity of the Spirit. In Him the all things of creation are one ordered whole. In Him the Church, with its many members, its ages and generations, is one. But though the Church is one in the Holy Spirit, and is kept one by His continual presence, we have our part to do in keeping it one; we are to keep it in the bond of peace, in the uniting power, that is, which peace produces. And this initial unity opens out into a sevenfold series of unities, which ends, as it began, in God—Father, Son, and Holy Ghost; the Father over all, the Son through all, the Holy Ghost in all.

Ch. iv. 1 : I therefore, the prisoner in the Lord, beseech you to walk worthily of the calling wherewith ye were called, with all lowliness and meekness, with long-suffering, forbearing one another in love; giving diligence to keep the unity of the Spirit in the bond of peace. There is one body, and one Spirit, even as also ye were called in one hope of your calling; one Lord, one faith, one baptism, one God and Father of all, who is over all, and through all, and in all.

But though the body is one, it consists of many members, and each member has his own place, and his own special gift.

But this assignment of a special gift to a particular member was not to be regarded as an accidental or capricious thing. When Christ ascended up on high, and first received, and then gave gifts to men, in that general giving He gave to each one his own special gift.

This leads the Apostle to think of the ascension of Christ, and this thought, in a mind so impregnated with the sacred scriptures as his was, naturally clothed itself in the language of prophecy. The words which he quotes are taken from the 68th Psalm. Whatever may have been the occasion of this Psalm he claims it as a witness to Christ. He felt, as has been beautifully said, that "every note struck on the lyres of the sweet singers of Israel is but part of a chord, deep and world-wide, sounding from the golden harps of redemption."

Ch. iv. 7: But unto each one of us was the grace given according to the measure of the gift of Christ. Wherefore he saith,

When he ascended on high, he led captivity captive,
And gave gifts unto men.

But the Apostle could not speak of Christ's ascension without thinking of His first coming down from heaven. The ascent implied a previous descent. For " no man hath ascended into heaven but he that descended out of heaven, even the Son of Man which is in heaven."

But the descent from heaven to earth did not constitute the whole descent; He descended into the lower parts of the earth, or, as we express it in the Creed, "He descended into hell." The full extent, then, of His triumphal ascent was not from earth to heaven, but from hades to heaven, from the lowest depth of the unseen world to the highest heaven.

"His descent into the earth, and thence into death and hades, and His ascension thence to a sphere above all the inhabited heavens, demonstrated to all angels, as He passed through the midst of them to His own Throne, that no power remained anywhere unsubdued."

So the Apostle continues:—

Ch. iv. 9: (Now this, He ascended, what is it but that He also descended into the lower parts of the earth? He that descended is the same also that ascended far above all the heavens, that He might fill all things.)

What immediately follows this is connected with what had been said a verse or two before.

The Apostle had been speaking of the spiritual gifts which had been given to each member of the Body of Christ. In what follows he expands this statement, and mentions the special gifts with which Christ had enriched His Church, and the purpose for which they had been given.

The gifts that he mentions, indeed, are not things, but persons; but this need not surprise us, since men are greater and more necessary than the gifts which they exercise.

But then it must be remembered that after all the Church, and the ministries of the Church, are not the end, but only means to an end; and that end, the attainment, in the Spirit, of the final unity, the unity of mankind in Christ, and in Christ with the universe, and with God.

Ch. iv. 11: And He gave some to be apostles; and some, prophets; and some, evangelists; and some, pastors and teachers; for the perfecting of the saints, unto the work of ministering, unto the building up of the body of Christ: till we all attain unto the unity of the faith, and of the knowledge of the Son of God, unto a full-grown man, unto the measure of the stature of the fulness of Christ.

In this list of the various ministries of the Church, Apostles, as we might expect, come first. They were first not only in importance, but in order of time. For a while the Apostles were the sole rulers, the sole pastors, the sole deacons of the flock. The fulness of their apostleship was such, that all the ministries which have since been exercised were stored up in them.

Next to Apostles come Prophets. As, I dare say you know, a prophet is not primarily one who foretells, but who forthtells, who speaks by the immediate impulse of the Holy Spirit. By Evangelists are meant, not evangelists in the stricter sense, as writers of the Gospel Story; but mission-preachers, who went from place to place delivering their message. Then come the ministries which are to consolidate, and build up the converts of the evangelists, pastors (i. e. shepherds) and teachers.

These ministries, the Apostle goes on to say, are the joints of the body by which it is fitly framed and knit together. Believers new born into this Body are to grow up into Christ, the Head, and thus, by the power of truth and the power of love, the Body grows, being built up in love.

As the coral island is built up by the toil of myriads of little insects, each working in its own place, so by little ministries of love the fabric of the Church is enlarged and consolidated.

Ch. iv. 14: That we may be no longer children, tossed to and fro and carried about with every wind of doctrine . . . . but speaking truth in love, may grow up in all things into Him, which is the Head, even Christ; from whom all the body fitly framed and knit together through that which every joint supplieth, according to the working in due measure of each several part, maketh the increase of the body unto the building up of itself in love.

In the passage which follows, S. Paul draws a contrast between the Gentile Christians and their still unbelieving countrymen; and between the new nature, the Christ-nature, which they had put on, and the old nature, the Adam-nature, in which the Gentiles still walked.

But you will notice that in doing this the Apostle is very careful to point out that the life which the Gentiles were living was not their proper life. The true light is in every man, though that light may be darkened: the life of God is in every man, though he be alienated from it. So S. Paul speaks of the heathen not as dark, but as *darkened*; not as aliens, but as *alienated*.

Also we should notice that S. Paul recognizes the possibility of Christians falling from their high calling, and walking as other Gentiles walked. Indeed, in very solemn words he warns them of their danger, and urges them to walk in newness of life.

Ch. iv. 17: This I say therefore, and testify in the Lord, that ye no longer walk as the Gentiles also walk, in the vanity of their mind, being darkened in their understanding, alienated from the life of God because of the ignorance that is in them, because of the hardening of their heart; who being past feeling gave themselves up to lasciviousness, to work all uncleanness with greediness.

But ye did not so learn Christ; if so be that ye heard Him, and were taught in Him, even as truth is in Jesus: that ye put away, as concerning your former manner of life, the old man, which waxeth corrupt after the lusts of deceit; and that ye be renewed in the spirit of your mind, and put on the new man, which after God hath been created in righteousness and holiness of truth.

In all the exhortations which follow, S. Paul assumes the great principles which he had before laid down.

He never forgets, and does not allow his readers to forget, that God is regenerating, and reconstituting humanity in Christ, according to that original purpose which He had purposed before the worlds, and that the true state of man is that which is revealed in Christ.

Thus, when he bids them to put away falsehood, it is on the ground that they are members one of another: when he bids the thief to steal no more, it is on the ground that by honest labour he may be able to give to a needy brother: when he warns them against impurity of speech, it is on the ground that their speech should build up their brethren's faith: when he enforces the duty of forgiveness, it is on the ground that God in Christ had forgiven them.

Ch. iv. 25: Wherefore, putting away falsehood, speak ye truth each one with his neighbour: for we are members one of another. Be ye angry, and sin not: let not the sun go down upon your wrath: neither give place to the devil. Let him that stole steal no more: but rather let him labour, working with his hands the thing that is good, that he may have whereof to give to him that hath need. Let no corrupt speech proceed out of your mouth, but such as is good for edifying as the need may be, that it may give grace to them that hear. And grieve not the Holy Spirit of God, in whom ye were sealed unto the day of redemption. Let all bitterness, and wrath, and anger, and clamour, and railing, be put away from you, with all malice: and be ye kind one to another, tender-hearted, forgiving each other, even as God also in Christ forgave you.

As this was probably a circular letter to the Churches of Proconsular Asia, there are no salutations. Tychicus the bearer of the letter would give all required information about the imprisoned Apostle.

The Epistle concludes as usual with a benediction.

Ch. vi. 23: Peace be to the brethren, and love with faith, from God the Father and the Lord Jesus Christ. Grace be with all them that love our Lord Jesus Christ in uncorruptness.

CHAPTER XXXIV.

THE PASTORAL EPISTLES.

THE FIRST EPISTLE TO TIMOTHY.

YEARS and years before this Epistle was written, when S. Paul, in company with S. Barnabas, made his first missionary journey, they visited Lystra, a city of the wild and uncivilized country of Lycaonia.

It was a memorable visit. The two Apostles were first taken for gods, and were about to have divine honours paid to them.

A little after S. Paul was stoned, and left for dead.

As the little band of disciples whom they had gathered stood around him, S. Paul rose up and returned with them to the city. One of that little band of disciples was a young man named Timotheus, or Timothy. His father was a Greek, but both his mother and grandmother had been devout Jews, and were now faithful believers in Christ.

On his second missionary journey S. Paul revisited Lystra, and found that Timothy had not belied his early promise, but was well reported of, not only in his own town of Lystra, but in the neighbouring city of Iconium.

S. Paul was evidently strongly attracted to him, and regarded him with a special and fatherly affection; and he never lost his place in the Apostle's heart.

After anxious thought and prayer, S. Paul determined to take Timothy with him as his companion, and to train him for the work to which he had devoted his own life.

From that time Timothy continued to be S. Paul's constant companion and fellow-labourer.

His name was joined with that of the great Apostle in the two Epistles to the Thessalonians, and in the Second Epistle to the Corinthians.

Timothy shared S. Paul's first imprisonment, and was again associated with the Apostle, in three of the Epistles which he wrote at that time.

After S. Paul's release from his first Roman imprisonment, it would appear that Timothy accompanied him to Ephesus, and when S. Paul had to leave for Macedonia he left him in charge of one of the most important Christian communities, the Church of the Ephesians.

It may be that S. Paul found that he was likely to be detained in Macedonia longer than he had expected, and that he felt therefore that Timothy would need more explicit instructions, and, perhaps, more ample authority; and so wrote the letter which we are now going to glance at.

It begins thus:—

1 *Tim.* i. 1: Paul, an apostle of Christ Jesus according to the commandment of God our Saviour, and Christ Jesus our hope; unto Timothy, my true child in faith: Grace, mercy, peace, from God the Father and Christ Jesus our Lord.

There is a slight peculiarity in this opening salutation, which is common to the pastoral Epistles. This is the addition of the word "mercy" to the ordinary salutation of "grace and peace."

S. Paul had grown older; he had suffered more; he found his work harder, his adversaries fiercer, and his opponents within the Church more insidious than of old.

This led him to realize more than he had done before the great need that he, and they, and all had of God's *mercy*. To bring them and himself to a true and lasting peace, they needed not *grace* only, but also *mercy*.

In the exhortations that follow, the Apostle carries out the same thought. He shows that to God's free *mercy* he owed his own conversion, and his call to be Apostle. He lays down as the foundation of the Church's existence and work the *mercy* of God to a fallen world, he declares the central truth on which Christianity rests that Christ Jesus came into the world to save sinners.

And what is the first superstructure of the Church's order, which he bases upon this foundation?

Ch. ii. 1 : I exhort therefore, first of all, that supplications, prayers, intercessions, thanksgivings be made for *all men* . . . . This is good and acceptable in the sight of God our Saviour; who willeth that *all men* should be saved, and come to the knowledge of the truth.

For there is one God, one mediator also between God and men, Himself man, Christ Jesus, who gave Himself a ransom for *all* . . . .

I desire therefore that the men pray in every place, lifting up holy hands.

You can easily see the connection. We are to pray for *all men*, because God loves *all men:* we are to care for *all* men, because God cares for *all* men, and wills *all* men to be saved, and because Christ gave Himself a ransom for *all*.

Upon this follows a discourse about the duties of the presbyters and deacons of the Church, about which I shall have something to say when we come to the Epistle to Titus.

We will pass on now to the instructions given to Timothy himself for his own guidance, in the difficult office which he was called to discharge.

Ch. iii. 14: These things write I unto thee.... that thou mayest know how thou [margin] oughtest to behave thyself in the house of God, which is the Church of the living God, the pillar and ground of the truth .....

Ch. iv. 12: .... Be thou an ensample to them that believe, in word, in manner of life, in love, in faith, in purity.

Till I come, give heed to reading, to exhortation, to teaching .... Take heed to thyself, and to thy teaching. Continue in these things; for in doing this thou shalt save both thyself and them that hear thee.

The evil tendencies which S. Paul had rebuked in his Epistle to the Colossians, and which he had sought to correct in his Epistle to this very Church at Ephesus, had grown and developed, and one of Timothy's greatest and most difficult tasks, to accomplish which he would have to stir up the gift of God which was in him, was to grapple with these false doctrines, and to contend with these false teachers.

It is of such teachers and teachings that he speaks in the following passage.

Ch. vi. 2: These things teach and exhort. If any man teacheth a different doctrine, and consenteth not to sound words, even the words of our Lord Jesus Christ, and to the doctrine which is according to godliness; he is puffed up, knowing nothing, but doting about questionings and disputes of words, whereof cometh envy, strife .... wranglings of men corrupted in mind and bereft of the truth, supposing that godliness is a way of gain.

This instruction is followed by an impassioned

appeal to the youthful bishop to walk worthy of the vocation with which he had been called.

The Apostle had been speaking of the sordid ambition to be *rich :* he now contrasts this grovelling ambition with that which ought to swell the heart of a chief Pastor of the Church.

The false teachers with whom he would have to deal, however lofty their pretended aims, however high-flown their utterances, were men whose ambition was to become rich, and who looked on religion as "a way of gain."

But he, the man of God, must have a higher and nobler ambition than this; his heart must be set upon the true riches, upon a heavenly treasure.

Timothy had embarked upon his ministry knowing well that it would not lead to riches or fame. He had counted the cost. He knew that he was called to be a soldier of Jesus Christ, and that he must be prepared, therefore, to endure hardship.

He had made a good confession when he was baptized. He had made a good confession when he was ordained.

As the sovereign gives the banner of his country to the standard-bearer, telling him to maintain untarnished the honour of his flag, so the great Apostle gives the most solemn charge to Timothy to keep the commandment without spot, without reproach, until the appearing of the Lord.

Ch. vi. 11 : But thou, O man of God, flee these things; and follow after righteousness, godliness, faith, love, patience, meekness.

Fight the good fight of the faith, lay hold on the life eternal, whereunto thou wast called, and didst confess the good confession in the sight of many witnesses.

I charge thee in the sight of God, who quickeneth all things, and of Christ Jesus, who before Pontius Pilate witnessed the good confession; that thou keep the commandment, without spot, without reproach, until the appearing of our Lord Jesus Christ: which in its own times He shall show, who is the blessed and only Potentate, the King of kings, and Lord of lords; who only hath immortality, dwelling in light unapproachable; whom no man hath seen, nor can see: to whom be honour and power eternal. Amen.

After this impassioned appeal and fervent doxology, and after an earnest exhortation to the rich not to trust in their riches, but to use them to the glory of God and the benefit of their brethren, S. Paul closes his letter with an appeal to Timothy not to be over-awed by the bold vauntings of those who gloried in their superior knowledge, who called themselves professors of the true knowledge (Gnosis), and were known in consequence—if the title had been invented as early as this—as *Gnostics*. This was the " philosophy and vain deceit " against which S. Paul had warned the Colossians, and against which the Bishop of Ephesus would have to protect his flock.

Ch. vi. 20 : O Timothy, guard that which is committed unto thee, turning away from the profane babblings and oppositions of the knowledge (Gnosis) which is falsely so called; which some professing have erred concerning the faith. Grace be with you.

CHAPTER XXXV.

THE PASTORAL EPISTLES.

THE EPISTLE TO TITUS.

THE Epistle to Titus was written much about the same time, and under much the same circumstances, as the First Epistle to Timothy.

Of Titus himself we know nothing but what we can gather from S. Paul's Epistles. His name is not once mentioned in the Acts.

The first notice that we have of him, is that he accompanied Paul and Barnabas to Jerusalem on the occasion of the great conference about circumcision.

He was a Gentile by birth, and in spite of the attempts of the Judaizing party, he remained uncircumcized.

S. Paul seems to have regarded him with great affection, and we cannot doubt that he deserved it.

During S. Paul's long stay at Ephesus, tidings were brought to him of the deplorable state of the Church at Corinth. As he could not go to Corinth himself, he sent Titus in his name, and with full authority to correct and amend the scandals which were so rife in the Corinthian Church.

It was a most difficult mission, and Titus seems to have been quite a young man. But he seems to have carried out his instructions with great tact and wisdom, and to a very great extent to have succeeded. He was evidently a man of great force of character, if he had not been he would not have been able to reduce the refractory Corinthians to submission.

He was just the sort of man for the difficult mission on which S. Paul sent him, namely, to organize the Christian Churches of Crete.

We have no record in the Acts of any missionary work done in Crete by S. Paul.

But this much is certain, that either a little before, or a little after Timothy's mission to Ephesus, S. Paul visited Crete, and left Titus there to carry on the work which he had begun.

It was certainly not altogether an eligible diocese. The Christian communities were disorderly and unruly, and required a strong hand to bring them into order.

Thus, then, we find S. Paul addressing himself to the Bishop or Vicar-Apostolic of Crete :—

Ch. i. 1 : Paul, a servant of God, and an Apostle of Jesus Christ .... to Titus, my true child after a common faith : Grace and peace from God the Father and Christ Jesus our Saviour.

For this cause left I thee in Crete, that thou shouldest set in order the things that were wanting, and appoint elders in every city. For a Bishop must be blameless, not self-willed, not soon angry .... but .... sober, just, holy, temperate.

As to the duties of Deacons we may read here a passage from S. Paul's letter to Timothy.

1 *Tim.* iii. 8 : Deacons in like manner must be grave, not double-tongued .... holding the mystery of the faith in a pure conscience.

And let these also first be proved ; then let them serve as deacons, if they be blameless. .... For they that have served well as deacons gain to themselves a good standing, and great boldness in the faith which is in Christ Jesus.

There has been a great deal of controversy as to what these Pastoral Epistles really teach about the ministry of the Church.

We must remember in discussing this subject, that the Christian Church did not start into life fully equipped in doctrine and discipline.

The Church was a living body, and because it was alive it *grew*, its doctrine grew, its order and discipline grew.

The Apostles were at first the sole ministers of the Church. They preached, they taught, they baptized, they organized, they administered relief, they exercised discipline as occasion demanded.

As the Christian society grew, the special work of relieving the poor was delegated to Church officers appointed for that purpose.

Soon we hear of "Elders" as existing in the Church of Jerusalem: and not in the mother Church only, we hear of S. Paul ordaining "Elders" in every Church among the Gentiles.

On his last journey to Jerusalem he gave a solemn charge to the Elders of Ephesus, to take heed to the flock over which the Holy Ghost had made them bishops or overseers.

From his Roman lodging he addresses a letter to the Saints at Philippi, with the bishops and deacons.

And now we find him leaving Titus in Crete, to appoint elders in every city.

It is clear therefore that the ministers of the Church over whom Timothy and Titus presided were called indifferently elders or bishops.

But it will naturally occur to you, as good Churchmen, to ask, Is not then Episcopacy of primitive origin, and Divine authority?

Is the presbyterian form of government, after all, the most ancient, and the most scriptural?

But this is not the case. By admitting that the same order of ministers are called indifferently elders and bishops, we by no means concede the point of the apostolical origin of the Episcopate.

Remember what I pointed out just now, that the Apostles were deacons before the establishment of the diaconate; they were elders and pastors before the appointment of presbyters; and they were bishops before the formation of the Episcopate.

Timothy was sent to Ephesus, Titus to Crete, with full apostolical authority, with power to ordain elders, to put candidates for the diaconate to the proof, to apportion the scanty pay of the elders, to rebuke, to exhort, with all authority.

Now what were Timothy and Titus? They were certainly not simple elders, for they had ample authority over the elders. What were they then? Well, whatever they might be called, they were obviously exercising the functions of what we call a bishop.

But it is said that Timothy and Titus exercised this authority as apostolic envoys, not as diocesan bishops.

To this we may say, was this Episcopal rule over presbyters and deacons a permanent necessity for the Church, or was it a temporary expedient only?

If it was not necessary, why did S. Paul leave the presbyters of Crete and Ephesus to manage their own affairs?

If it was necessary then, why should it have ceased to be necessary afterwards?

If the appointment of bishops, in our sense of the word, was necessary or even expedient for the

Church, we may be sure that it would be supplied: and that as the Apostles out of the fulness of their apostolate had drawn out in turn the diaconate and the presbyterate, they would also, when the necessity should arise, draw out the Episcopate also.

Besides, as a matter of fact, no other sort of government prevailed in the Church generally. And in many of the principal Churches, such as Rome, Antioch, and Alexandria, a list of the bishops was kept, going back to the days of the Apostles.

In this matter, then, we may confidently accept the declaration of our Prayer-book. "It is evident unto all men diligently reading the Holy Scripture and ancient authors, that from the Apostles' time there have been these Orders of Ministers in Christ's Church—Bishops, Priests, and Deacons."

In the passages which we read last, the Apostle speaks of the special duties, and special qualification, of presbyters and deacons.

It will probably strike us as we read them, that there is very little said of special or professional qualifications in the Ministers of the Church. There are nearly as many *negative* qualifications as *positive* ones. They have to do with the ordinary duties of life. The description would serve well enough for the portrait of a magistrate. No very unusual qualifications are insisted upon, no highly spiritual acquirements are spoken of.

The reason of this is not hard to find. S. Paul regarded the Church as a society, as a family, a society which was to show what ordinary human life ought to be, a society based upon family relationships. And accordingly S. Paul's notion was that the ministers of this society should be taken from those who were already husbands and fathers.

With regard to the deacons, they were intrusted

with the business matters of the community. They would have to obtain rooms for the religious assemblies of the faithful. They would have to provide the bread and wine, and to set out the Holy Table, and assist the presbyter in the distribution of the Sacred Elements. They would be responsible for the distribution of alms to the sick and poor. They would keep both the general roll of church members, and the roll of the widows who were supported by the offerings of the community.

With regard to the presbyters, their chief work was naturally teaching and preaching, conducting the public services of the Church, and celebrating the Holy Communion.

Accordingly we find the Apostle directing Titus to give such directions as these to the presbyters or bishops of the Cretan Churches. The presbyter was to hold

Tit. i. 9: To the faithful word which is according to the teaching, that he may be able both to exhort in the sound doctrine and to convict the gainsayers.

And then, having spoken more at large of the evils wrought in the Church by these gainsayers, these deceivers and unruly men, the Apostle continues:—

Ch. ii. 1: But speak thou the things which befit the sound doctrine.

This sound or healthy doctrine related to such matters as the duties of aged men and women, the duties of young men, the special duties of Christian slaves. These last he exhorts to adorn the doctrine of God their Saviour in all things. Then he continues:—

Ch. ii. 11: For the grace of God hath appeared, bringing salvation to all men, instructing us, to the intent that, denying ungodliness and worldly lusts, we should live soberly, and righteously, and godly in this present world...

Ch. iii. 4: [For] when the kindness of God our Saviour and His love toward man appeared, not by works done in righteousness, which we did ourselves, but according to His mercy He saved us, through the washing (or laver) of regeneration and renewing of the Holy Ghost, which He poured out upon us richly, through Jesus Christ our Saviour; that, being justified by His grace, we might be made heirs according to the hope of eternal life.

There is an expression in this passage which is peculiar to these Pastoral Epistles, which I must on no account omit to notice.

Frequently in these Epistles we come across the expression, " God our Saviour," where the reference is not to the Son, but to the *Father*.

If our attention has not been specially called to this, it comes upon us as a sort of surprise, that by God our Saviour is meant, not our Lord Jesus Christ, but our Father in Heaven.

The Father is as much our Saviour as Jesus is. If we had this well in our minds, we could never harbour such a notion as that Jesus saves us from the Father.

It really amounts to this, that not this Person in the Godhead, or that Person, exclusively is our Saviour, but that God in His Divine completeness— Father, Son, and Holy Ghost—is our only Saviour.

So in this very passage, we have put before us the kindness and the "philanthropy" of *the Father*, the renewing of *the Holy Ghost*, and the gift of the Spirit through *our Lord Jesus Christ*, by whose free grace we are justified, or renewed to righteousness.

This is also a most important passage, as showing what is the real doctrine of grace.

In some quarters we hear a great deal about the doctrines of grace; as these doctrines are sometimes stated, they appear to teach that a man who is once in a state of grace, may live as he will; and that the grace of God is most signally displayed in the salvation of a handful of souls out of a reprobate and perishing race.

But widely different is what S. Paul means by the doctrine of grace. According to him, the grace of God hath appeared, bringing salvation *to all men.* According to him, salvation is not the liberty to live as we will, but the power to live as the children of God.

Salvation, S. Paul teaches, is of free, unmerited grace; "according to *His mercy* He saved us."

But the Apostle tells us also how this salvation is made ours, how it is brought home to us. "According to His mercy He saved us by *the washing of regeneration and the renewing of the* Holy Ghost."

God saves us, then, by bringing us, by baptism, into a state of salvation; as S. Peter also teaches that "Baptism doth also now save us."

Without any merit on our part, entirely irrespective of good works which we have done, or may do, God brings us into a state of salvation, a state of God's favour and of forgiveness of sins.

This is S. Paul's teaching on salvation by grace.

With a few directions to Titus to meet him at Nicopolis, and to speed on other travellers on their way, the Apostle thus concludes:—

Ch. iii. 15: All that are with me salute thee. Salute them that love us in faith.

Grace be with you all.

CHAPTER XXXVI.

THE PASTORAL EPISTLES.

THE SECOND EPISTLE TO TIMOTHY.

WE come now to the last of the Epistles of S. Paul. We are about to read the last message of the great Apostle of the Gentiles to the Church, the last warning, the last consolation spoken by one who was not only an inspired Apostle, but was now on the confines of the eternal world, and whose crown of martyrdom was near.

Since he wrote his letter to Titus, the whole aspect of his life was altered.

Then he was free, settling his plans for the coming winter; now he is once more a prisoner.

Whether at Nicopolis, or elsewhere, he had been apprehended and sent to Rome, probably on the capital charge of being concerned in the burning of the imperial city.

As I have pointed out in the tenth Chapter of this book, his second imprisonment was very different from his first. Then he was allowed to live in his own lodging with the soldier who guarded him: now he was consigned to a dark and probably filthy dungeon. Then he was regarded as the victim of unreasoning malice, now he was regarded as a dangerous criminal.

It was in this dark dungeon that S. Paul dictated,

no doubt to S. Luke, for "only Luke was with him," this second letter to Timothy.

Whether the Apostle's main object was to entreat his child in the faith to come to him with all speed, or whether his first thought was that Timothy required some special help and encouragement, it is hard to say.

It is possible that Timothy may have written to his father in the faith, and poured out his difficulties and discouragements; or it may have been that some hint had been given to the imprisoned Apostle that Timothy was not taking such a resolute line as the circumstances of the case demanded, and was not holding the reins of government with a sufficiently firm hand.

However this may be, there are certainly indications, in the opening sentences of the Epistle, that there had been great discouragement in the mind of Timothy, and something perhaps of the timidity which is the natural result of discouragement.

After expressing his earnest and affectionate care for him, and his remembrances of the unfeigned faith which he had shown, a faith which was almost an hereditary faith, S. Paul goes on to warn him, that neither his early zeal, nor the lessons that he had received from others, could enable him to sustain his position at Ephesus.

He reminds him of the gift of God which was in him, with which he had been endowed at his ordination; he would have Timothy remember that the Spirit which he had received was not a spirit of cowardice, but of power, love, and a sound mind.

Ch. i. 1 : Paul, an Apostle of Christ Jesus .... to Timothy, my beloved child; Grace, mercy, peace, from God the Father, and Christ Jesus our Lord.

I thank God .... how unceasing is my remembrance

of thee in my supplications, night and day longing to see thee .... having been reminded of the unfeigned faith that is in thee; which dwelt first in thy grandmother Lois, and thy mother Eunice; and, I am persuaded, in thee also.

For the which cause I put thee in remembrance that thou stir up the gift of God, which is in thee through the laying on of my hands. For God gave us not a spirit of fearfulness, but of power, and love, and discipline.

In the firm assurance that Timothy has this mighty Friend and Helper with him, he can bid him not to be ashamed either of the Gospel, or of its imprisoned ambassador, but to suffer hardship for its sake.

Nor does S. Paul hesitate to use his own example to brace up the flagging spirit of his friend. "*I* am not ashamed," therefore be not *thou* ashamed. "*I* am persuaded that God is able to guard that which I have committed unto Him," do *thou* share the same confidence.

Ch. i. 8: Be not ashamed therefore of the testimony of our Lord, nor of me His prisoner; but suffer hardship with the gospel according to the power of God .... whereunto I was appointed a preacher, and an Apostle, and a teacher. For the which cause .... I am not ashamed; for I know Him whom I have believed, and I am persuaded that He is able to guard that which I have committed unto Him against that day.

Hold the pattern of sound words which thou hast heard from me, in faith and love which is in Christ Jesus. That good thing (or the good deposit) which was committed unto thee guard through the Holy Ghost which dwelleth in us.

The pattern of sound words which Timothy was exhorted to hold for himself, and the good deposit which he was to guard in the power of the Holy Spirit, was almost certainly the baptismal confession of faith, which became afterwards, varying in form indeed in each Church, the venerable compilation known as the Apostles' Creed.

The primitive Creed was not only a *form* of sound words, but a *pattern*, according to which the aftergrowth of Christian truth must be conformed.

But Christian teaching, if it is to have any vital power, must have something more than bare orthodoxy; the faith must be held not only according to the standard pattern, but in "faith and love;" the good deposit must be guarded not merely with strictness, but through the Holy Ghost, the Spirit of love and freedom.

The Apostle then goes on to indicate one cause of Timothy's depression and discouragement.

There had been a lamentable falling away among the members of the Churches of S. Paul's planting in the province of which Ephesus was the centre and capital.

In such a crisis Timothy must play the man, and show himself to be a good soldier of Jesus Christ; and then he concludes this section of his letter with what sounds like a quotation from some Christian hymn.

Ch. i. 15: This thou knowest, that all that are in Asia turned away from me....

Ch. ii. 1: Thou therefore, my child, be strengthened in the grace that is in Christ Jesus.... Suffer hardship with me, as a good soldier of Christ Jesus... (Ver. 11) Faithful is the saying: For if we died with Him, we shall also live with Him: if we endure, we shall also reign with Him: if we shall deny Him, He also will deny us: if we are faithless, He abideth faithful; for He cannot deny Himself.

A little before this, when speaking of the desertion of so many of his friends and adherents in Asia, the

Apostle's thoughts turned to one friend from Asia who had remained faithful to his doctrine, and loyal to his person.

This was Onesiphorus, who, when visiting Rome, had with great perseverance, and at great personal risk, found out the imprisoned Apostle, and often came to see him and cheer him in his lonely prison.

Since that time, so it would seem, Onesiphorus had died, and entered into rest, for S. Paul invokes mercy upon his house, and sends a greeting, not to Onesiphorus himself, as he would naturally have done had he been living, but to his *household*.

This makes the prayer which the Apostle offered doubly interesting, as it shows that S. Paul did not recognize death as any barrier—as, indeed, why should it be?—to free supplication and spiritual communion.

Ch. i. 16: The Lord grant mercy unto the house of Onesiphorus: for he oft refreshed me, and was not ashamed of my chain; but when he was in Rome he sought me diligently and found me (the Lord grant unto him to find mercy of the Lord in that day); and in how many things he ministered at Ephesus, thou knowest very well.

After having endeavoured to strengthen Timothy's own faith, and to brace him up to fight the good fight, S. Paul goes on to describe in greater detail the course that he would have to take in meeting the various heresies of these false teachers.

From what the Apostle says, we see how fully his sad forebodings as to the future of the Ephesian Church, to which he gave expression to the elders of Ephesus, were fulfilled. "I know," he had said, "that after my departing from among your own selves shall men arise, speaking perverse things, to draw away the disciples after them."

And in instructing Timothy how he ought to prepare himself for this encounter with error, S. Paul, in a very famous and important passage, refers him to the Sacred Scriptures of the old covenant.

Ch. iii. 14: But abide thou in the things which thou hast learned . . . . [even] the sacred writings which are able to make thee wise unto salvation, through faith which is in Christ Jesus.

Every Scripture inspired of God is also profitable for teaching, for reproof, for correction, for instruction which is in righteousness : that the man of God may be complete, furnished completely unto every good work.

From this, his complete equipment in the possession of the Old Testament Scriptures, the Apostle proceeds to make one last solemn appeal, in which he sums up all that he had previously said.

Ch. iv. 1 : I charge thee, in the sight of God, and of Christ Jesus . . . . preach the word; be instant in season, out of season; reprove, rebuke, exhort, with all long-suffering and teaching. . . . .

(Ver. 5) Be thou sober in all things, do the work of an evangelist, fulfil thy ministry.

And this solemn and affecting charge, S. Paul makes more solemn, and more touching, by connecting it with the now nearly accomplished work of his ministry.

Earlier in his Christian life, earlier in his apostolical career, S. Paul had expressed himself as uncertain as to the issue of the conflict; he had admitted the possibility that, having preached to others, he himself might be a castaway. But now no cloud, even the thinnest, dimmed the full assurance of his hope. His crown was sure, it was waiting for him.

And what sort of a crown? Not of course a material crown: but what sort of spiritual crown?

It was the crown of righteousness, the crown which was itself righteousness. Righteousness is the reward of righteousness: pureness is the reward of purity, love is the reward of love, God is the reward of godliness.

Nor was it a *selfish* crown, a crown peculiar to himself that he looked forward to: it was the crown which should be given to all who loved the Lord's appearing.

Ch. iv. 6: I am already being offered, and the time of my departure is come. I have fought the good fight, I have finished the course, I have kept the faith: henceforth there is laid up for me the crown of righteousness, which the Lord, the righteous Judge, shall give to me at that day: and not only to me, but also to all them that have loved His appearing.

Then follow personal directions to Timothy, and allusions to his recent trial and temporary deliverance.

Several names are mentioned that have become familiar to us. Demas, who had been his companion in his first imprisonment, had now forsaken him. Luke, a friend constant to death who was with him then, was with him still. Mark, who at one time had lost S. Paul's good opinion, had now nobly retrieved his character, and was reckoned by him as profitable for the ministry.

The names of some Roman Christians are mentioned as sending kind messages to Timothy, among them, Claudia, perhaps a British princess, and Linus, who was afterwards one of the earliest bishops of Rome.

Ch. iv. 9: Do thy diligence to come shortly unto me; for Demas forsook me, having loved this present world... only Luke is with me. Take Mark, and bring him with thee: for he is useful to me for ministering.... (Ver. 19) Salute

Prisca and Aquila and the house of Onesiphorus..... Do thy diligence to come before winter. Eubulus greeteth thee, and Pudens, and Linus, and Claudia, and all the brethren.

The Lord be with thy spirit. Grace be with you.

Whether Timothy was able to reach Rome in time to see the Apostle before his martyrdom, we can only guess. From an allusion to Timothy in the Epistle to the Hebrews, it may be plausibly gathered that he did reach Rome in time to see his friend and father in the faith, and perhaps that he shared his imprisonment. We can only hope that it was so.

What was the after-life of Timothy we have no means of knowing. It is sufficient to know that he, no less than the great Apostle whose life and Epistles we have been considering, is numbered with the saints.

May we all have grace to follow S. Paul, even as he followed Christ, that so we too may finish our course with joy, and receive from the Master's hands—S. Paul's Master and ours—the crown of righteousness; that being faithful unto death, we too may receive the crown of life.

CHAPTER XXXVII.

THE EPISTLE TO THE HEBREWS.

I DARE say you know that very many eminent biblical scholars, both in ancient and modern times, have come to the conclusion that the Epistle to the Hebrews, though a book of the greatest value, and the most undoubted inspiration, is not the work of S. Paul. Yet so many others have come to an opposite conclusion, that we may include it in our readings on the Life and Epistles of this great Apostle.

As to the question to whom it was written, there can be no doubt that it was written to Hebrew Christians; and but little doubt that these Hebrew Christians were members of the Mother Church of Jerusalem, of whom we read in the early chapters in the Acts of the Apostles.

Nor can there be much doubt that this Epistle was written only two or three years before the destruction of Jerusalem, and when the Jewish war had begun. The time of which our Lord had warned His disciples had come. Jerusalem was already being surrounded by armies, the great tribulation was at hand, tribulation such as had not been from the beginning of the world, nor ever should be.

It was the time when, as our Lord had forewarned them, they should be hated of all men; when many should stumble, and should deliver up one another, and should hate one another; when many false prophets should arise, and lead many astray; when, because iniquity should abound, the love of the many should wax cold.

It is in full accord with these solemn warnings spoken before by Christ, that the writer of this Epistle addresses the Churches of Judea and Jerusalem. We can hardly fail to mark the specially earnest tone of its exhortation, nor to perceive that its warnings are directed not against heresy, but against *apostasy*.

The history of the Church of Jerusalem is a very sad one. Its first beginnings were like a lovely morning of which we say it is too bright to last. Who has not read with delight the description of their simple life in the Acts of the Apostles? And who can think without sorrow of the fearful calamities through which they had to pass, and of the terrible apostasy into which so many of them fell?

It was not so much that they had shifted their ground, that they had given up their belief, as that they had made no advance. They remained stationary when they ought to have "gone on unto perfection." They were like a pool of water cut off by the receding tide, which feels no longer the ebb and flow of the great ocean, and becomes day by day shallower and more bitter.

They were in extreme peril; as spiritual beings, there was before them "a boundless better, a boundless worse." And a crisis was at hand which would bring them to the test, which would show that though nominally Christians, many of them were in reality Jews, and regarded their faith in Christ as a mere appendage, and that a separable appendage to their Judaism. A crisis was at hand which would shake not *earth* only, but also *heaven*; not the earthly polity of the nation only, but their divine polity as the Israel of God.

If they would only be warned in time, if they would but rise to a higher and truer faith in Christ, as the Son of God, they would pass unscathed through the great tribulation, they would find that though the old Jerusalem was gone, the new Jerusalem was still their home; though the temple was destroyed, there remained a temple not made with hands; though the daily sacrifice had ceased, they would find that in the Christian Church "they had still an altar."

But unless they rose to a higher and truer faith in Jesus as the Son of God, they would not be able to keep the faith they had. They would begin, nay, they had begun, to think of Him merely as man, as a great Prophet, as the Reformer and Restorer of the Old Covenant: they thought of Jesus as the Messiah, they did not doubt that, but they had lost, or were beginning to lose, the belief that He was the Son of God.

They seem to have thought more of their circumcision than their baptism, more of the temple sacrifices than of the Eucharist, more of their standing in the law than of their standing in the Gospel, more of the intervention of angels than of the mediation of the Eternal Son.

The writer of this Epistle had as his object in writing it, to show that in every respect their position and privileges as Christians were far higher, far nobler, than their former position as Jews. That the Jewish Covenant, the Temple, the Sacrifices, might all pass away, but that the New

Covenant, the New Jerusalem, the "pure offering," would be for them, and for all, abiding realities.

It would seem that the current belief of the Hebrew Christians, as it regarded Christ more and more as a man, was beginning to settle down into a belief in angels as controlling the spiritual world, and as guiding and guarding the children of the Covenant. With these thoughts in his mind, and with these objects in view, the writer of the Epistle, without any preamble, plunges into the midst of his subject.

He begins by reminding these Hebrew Christians that God had revealed Himself gradually to man.

Ch. i. 1: God, having of old time spoken unto the fathers in the prophets by divers portions and in divers manners, hath at the end of these days spoken unto us in His Son [or in a Son], whom He appointed heir of all things, through whom also He made the worlds; who being the effulgence of His glory, and the very image of His substance, and upholding all things by the word of His power, when He had made purification of sins, sat down on the right hand of the Majesty on high; having become by so much better than the angels, as He hath inherited a more excellent name than they.

Then follows the first of the solemn warnings of the Epistle.

Ch. ii. 1: Therefore we ought to give the more earnest heed to the things that were heard, lest haply we drift away from them. For if the word spoken through angels proved steadfast, and every transgression and disobedience received a just recompense of reward; how shall we escape, if we neglect so great salvation?

Then, again, speaking of the angels, he declares that whatever may have been the case in the Jewish age, the Christian age, the New Dispensation, is in no way subject unto angels. For the Psalmist had said of old, that not to angels but to *man* had God subjected all things; to man, even to that Perfect Man, to Christ Jesus, who is crowned with glory and honour, and under whose feet all things are in subjection.

Ch. ii. 5: For not unto angels did He subject the world to come, whereof we speak. But one hath somewhere testified, saying,

What is man, that thou art mindful of him?
Or the Son of Man, that thou visitest Him?
Thou madest Him a little lower than the angels;
Thou crownedst Him with glory and honour,
And did'st set Him over the works of Thy hands;
Thou did'st put all things in subjection under His feet.

But now we see not yet all things subjected to Him.

But we behold Him who hath been made a little lower than the angels, even Jesus, because of the suffering of death, crowned with glory and honour; that by the grace of God He should taste death for every man.

For it became Him, for whom are all things, and through whom are all things, in bringing many sons unto glory, to make the Author of their salvation perfect through sufferings. . . . .

(Ver. 17) Wherefore it behoved Him in all things to be made like unto His brethren, that He might be a merciful and faithful High Priest in things pertaining to God, to make propitiation for the sins of the people. For in that He Himself hath suffered being tempted, He is able to succour them that are tempted.

(iii. 1) Wherefore, holy brethren, partakers of a heavenly calling, consider the Apostle and High Priest of our confession, even Jesus.

If the Hebrew Christians had got into the way of thinking that Christ had come to reform the Old Covenant, and to rest the law upon a firmer basis, they might not unnaturally think that the Reformer of the Law could not be greater than the Giver of the Law; that Moses, whom they saw through the long vista of the ages of the past, in the dim religious light of age-long veneration, was at any rate not to be surpassed by the Prophet of Nazareth, who had lived to within forty years of the time then present.

In the next passage of his Epistle the writer contrasts the inferior and temporary position of Moses with the supreme and abiding position of Christ. Moses, he argues, though faithful in his position in God's house, was faithful only as a servant, whereas Jesus was faithful to Him that appointed Him as a Son over God's house. And as the Lord had Himself said, the servant abideth not in the house for ever, but the Son abideth ever.

As Moses had been over God's house in former times, so Christ was over God's house now. But the same danger that existed then, existed now. Those who were placed under Moses in God's household hardened their hearts, and provoked God, so that He was constrained to say, "They shall not enter into My rest." So also they who were now, in Christ, and under His authority, adopted into God's family, were in danger of falling away, and so of coming short of His rest. For He with whom they had to do, the Word which would try them, was not indeed a word spoken, as was the Law, from the lightnings and thunderings of Sinai, but was a living Word, piercing asunder to the very thoughts and intents of the heart.

Ch. iii. 1: Wherefore, holy brethren, partakers of a heavenly calling, consider the Apostle and High Priest of our confession, even Jesus; who was faithful to Him that appointed Him, as also was Moses in all God's house. For He hath been counted worthy of more glory than Moses, by so much as He that built the house hath more honour than the house. For every house is builded by some one; but He that built all things is God. And Moses indeed was faithful in all God's house as a servant . . . . . ; but Christ as a Son, over God's house; whose house are we, if we hold fast our boldness and the glorying of our hope firm unto the end. . . . . . .

(Ver. 12) Take heed, brethren, lest haply there shall be in any of you (as in Israel of old) an evil heart of unbelief, in falling away from the living God. . . . . . (iv. 1) Let us fear, therefore, lest haply, a promise being left of entering into His rest, any of you should seem to have come short of it. . . . .

(Ver. 11) Let us therefore give diligence to enter into that rest, that no man fall after the same example of disobedience.

For the word of God is living, and active, and sharper than any two-edged sword, and piercing even to the dividing of soul and spirit, of both joints and marrow, and quick to discern the thoughts and intents of the heart. And there is no creature that is not manifest in His sight: but all things are naked and laid open before the eyes of Him with Whom we have to do.

CHAPTER XXXVIII.

THE EPISTLE TO THE HEBREWS
(*continued*).

WE must constantly have in mind that the Hebrew Christians to whom this letter was written were in danger of losing their Christian faith altogether; and that the main object of the writer is to show that the things which they most valued in the Jewish Covenant were but shadows of the good things which were to be found in Christ and His Church.

He has already shown that the New Covenant in Christ, the Son of God, was as immeasurably greater than the old law which was ordained by angels, as Christ the God-man was greater than the angels. He has also shown that Moses, in whom they were so inclined to trust, was only over God's household as a servant, whereas Christ was a Son in His Father's house.

In the passage which we are now going to read, the writer applies this principle to the Priesthood of Christ, and shows how, through His perfect intercession and mediation, believers in Him had a free access to the throne of God; and how, though so exalted, the Lord of angels and men, the Son of the Most High God, He was yet a merciful and sympathizing High Priest, One who having Himself suffered, and been Himself tempted, was able to succour them in their temptations and sufferings.

The writer had already called upon his fellow Christians and fellow Israelites to fix their thoughts upon Jesus, the Apostle and High Priest of their confession.

He now urges them to hold fast to that confession, the confession which they had made when they were baptized into the name of the Father, the Son, and the Holy Ghost, for that their true High Priest, even Jesus the Son of God, was passed into the heavens.

Then, before he goes on, he meets an objection that might arise in their minds. They might say, It is all very grand and wonderful what you say of the Son of God, who has passed through all heavens, being our High Priest; but how can One who is so high, and so highly exalted, feel for us in our weakness and sinfulness? we want for our High Priest one who is one of us, and one with us, who can feel for us, and understand us.

Yes, but, continues the Apostle, Jesus our High Priest does feel for us, and feels with us; He has been tempted as we have, tempted in all points just as we are tempted.

It is true that He is without sin, it is true that He is the Son of God, it is true that He sits at the right hand of God; but that is just the reason why He is able to introduce us to the very throne of God Himself, that there, in the Fatherly heart of God Himself, we may find peace and grace.

Ch. iv. 14: Having then a great High Priest, who hath passed through the heavens, Jesus the Son of God, let us hold fast our confession. For we have not a High Priest that cannot be touched with the feeling of our infirmities; but One that hath been in all points tempted like as we are, yet without sin. Let us therefore draw near with boldness unto the Throne of Grace, that we may receive mercy, and may find grace to help us in time of need.

In the passage that follows this, the Apostle describes at length the qualifications which any high priest must possess, and the manner in which all high priests must be appointed. The high priest must (1) be taken from among men, he must share the nature of those for whom he is to minister; (2) he must act for men, as their representative; (3) the sphere of his ministry is in things pertaining to God; (4) he must be qualified in office, to offer for sins; (5) he must be qualified in person, as being himself compassed with infirmity, to deal gently with the ignorant and the erring; (6) he is bound on this account for himself, no less than for the people, to offer for sins; and (7) he must be called by God, and not assume the office himself.

Ch. v. 1: For every high priest, being taken from among men, is appointed for men in things pertaining to God, that he may offer both gifts and sacrifices for sins: who can bear gently with the ignorant and erring, for that he himself also is compassed with infirmity; and by reason thereof [i.e. of this infirmity] is bound, as for the people, so also for himself, to offer for sins. And no man taketh the honour unto himself, but when he is called of God, even as was Aaron. So Christ also glorified not Himself to be made a high priest, but He that spake unto Him,

> Thou art My Son,
> This day have I begotten thee.

As He saith also in another place,

> Thou art a Priest for ever,
> After the order of Melchisedek.

As in this last passage the Apostle speaks of the qualifications which a high priest must possess, if he is rightly to discharge his office, so in the passage that follows, he shows how Christ was not only not self-appointed, but appointed by the Father Himself, and how He was trained and disciplined by the Father, to fit Him to be a perfect High Priest.

It was by no easy method that Jesus was taught, it was along no easy road that He had to walk. He prayed in agony, with strong crying and tears, to Him that was able to save Him out of death, that the cup might pass from Him. And because of His pious resignation His prayer was heard: for this seems to be the true meaning of the expression in the A. V. "and was heard in that He feared."

Christ Himself had to learn obedience; and He learnt it by the things which He suffered. But His suffering was not thrown away; no suffering is: it brought Him, as it is intended to bring us, to perfection, and the issue of that perfection was that He is able to save those who obey Him with an eternal salvation.

Ch. v. 7 : Who in the days of His flesh, having offered up prayers and supplications with strong crying and tears unto Him that was able to save Him from death, and having been heard for His godly fear, though He was a Son, yet learned obedience by the things which He suffered; and having been made perfect, He became unto all them that obey Him, the Author of eternal salvation; named of God a High Priest after the order of Melchisedek.

Here follows a long digression, in which the Apostle upbraids the Hebrew Christians with their backwardness and infantile intelligence. The truths which he had to teach them were deep and mysterious, solid food for matured Christians; whereas they had need to be fed with the milk of simple doctrine, such as they had learnt years before at the beginning of their Christian course.

This digression is incidentally very valuable, as it shows us what, in the opinion of this profound writer and unimpeachable witness, were the chief points of primitive Church teaching in those early days, what were reckoned to be the first rudiments, the very alphabet of Christian teaching. These rudimentary principles are the following:—Repentance from dead works; faith towards God; teaching of baptisms; laying on of hands; resurrection of the dead; and eternal judgment. (Ch. vi. 1, 2.)

Now what is this laying on of hands? Whatever it is, it is obviously most important, for it is classed with faith and repentance, with the resurrection and the judgment. The position which it occupies, immediately following repentance, faith, and baptism, clearly shows it to be that special ordinance which we know as Confirmation, or the laying on of hands. We have, then, in this Epistle an authoritative statement that Confirmation is one of the first principles of the doctrine of Christ.

This digression ended, the Apostle resumes his argument in the seventh chapter. He had already said, as you remember, that Christ was named of God a High Priest after the order of Melchisedek.

He proceeds, then, to show that by the recorded fact of this mysterious Personage having blessed Abraham, the Head and Father of the Jewish race; and even by his very name, and by the name of his city, Melchisedek was a type of the Son of God, and—whatever may be the meaning of this confessedly difficult expression—"abideth a priest continually."

He then shows the superiority of the Melchisedek priesthood to that of Aaron.

When therefore it is said that "Christ is a Priest for ever after the order of Melchisedek," it follows not only that Christ's priesthood is not the Levitical priesthood; but that His priesthood is infinitely higher and nobler, and more efficacious than that of the Jewish Law.

The Jewish high priest was made after the law of a carnal commandment, that is, made not in the nature of things, but by an external ordinance, founded on the existing fleshly and decaying state of things: Christ, the Melchisedek Priest, was constituted High Priest by the power of an endless life.

The Jewish high priest was consecrated without any oath: but the Melchisedek Priest with an oath, according to that which was written—"The Lord sware and will not repent Himself, Thou art a Priest for ever."

The Jewish high priests were many in number, because by death they were hindered from continuing: but Christ, because He abideth for ever, hath His priesthood unchangeable.

And because of this unchangeable priesthood He is able to save to the uttermost them that draw near unto God through Him.

The word that the Apostle uses to describe the extent of our Lord's saving work is a very remarkable one: it means literally "to the last," it might be rendered, as in the margin of the A. V., "for evermore;" and it carries with it the notion of perfection, as if it said, He is able to carry the work of salvation to the full perfection of which regenerated humanity is capable. He can save to the last, His mercy can reach the case of the most hopeless, the last of sinners, the farthest from God's presence; He can save to the last fibre of the bruised reed, to the last flicker of the smoking flax. He can save for evermore. His hand will never be shortened that it cannot save, His ear will never be heavy that it cannot hear. He will be able to save the generations of the future, as He has saved the generations of the past. He will save us to perfection; He will purge and purify us seven times in the fire of His love; He will never hold His hand while evil and imperfection have a hold upon us. And we must notice that this salvation to the uttermost is connected, not, as we might expect, with Christ's past work, but with His present work. We, perhaps, should have supplied some such words as these—He is able to save to the uttermost, seeing that He once died for them on the Cross, and made atonement for them: but it is not so written. The Apostle's words are:—

Ch. vii. 25: Wherefore also He is able to save to the uttermost them that draw near unto God through Him, seeing He ever liveth to make intercession for them.

Then follows a description of the qualifications of Christ as our High Priest, which exhibits another side of His perfect priesthood.

The Apostle had before spoken of His oneness with sinners, as having been tempted, as being able to deal gently with the ignorant and erring, as having learned obedience by the things which He suffered, and as being touched with the feeling of our weakness: now he goes on to speak of Christ as separate from sinners, as holy and undefiled, as having no occasion to offer sacrifice daily like the Jewish priesthood, but as One who was perfected for evermore.

"Only One, holy, harmless, separated from sinners, could really be so touched with the feeling of their infirmities, as to be the needful Intercessor for them.

Only One who has been on earth, and suffered death, and passed into the heavens: only One who is now at the right hand of God, could exercise that permanent Priesthood, which the legal succession in the family of Aaron had indicated. Only One who had actually gone out of the visible world into the presence of the unseen God, could lead men into it."

Ch. vii. 26: For such a High Priest became us, holy, guileless, undefiled, separated from sinners, and made higher than the heavens; who needeth not daily, like those high priests, to offer up sacrifices, first for His own sins, and then for the sins of the people: for this He did once for all, when He offered up Himself. For the law appointeth men high priests, having infirmity; but the word of the oath, which was after the law, appointeth a Son, perfected for evermore.

CHAPTER XXXIX.

THE EPISTLE TO THE HEBREWS
(*continued*).

MUST repeat here what I reminded you of at the beginning of the last chapter, that if we wish to understand the drift and bearing of this Epistle, we must keep in mind the object which the writer of it had in view. He was anxious to convince these Jewish Christians that they must not fix their faith and hope upon the continuance of their national life, and their national worship. Their nation might be scattered to the four winds of heaven; not one stone of their temple might be left upon another; the sacrifices might cease, and the priesthood cease with them; but if only they would fix their faith upon the Lord Jesus, and properly estimate the privileges of the Christian Covenant, none of these things would affect them, because in Jesus they had a greater High Priest, the Mediator of a better Covenant; and in His Church a more enduring city, a kingdom which could not be shaken, a purer worship, a more spiritual altar.

With this object in view, the writer of the Epistle has shown the superiority of Christ as the High Priest over the Levitical priesthood; and in the section of the Epistle which we are now about to consider, goes on to show that this involves the bringing in of a New Covenant, and the establishment of a higher and more spiritual worship, of which the temple service was but a shadow and type. Christ, he says, being ascended on high, has become the Mediator of a New Covenant.

Now the Covenant of Israel was of all things the most sacred in the eyes of a Jewish Christian. He might acknowledge that the coming of Christ made it more comprehensive, that the Gentiles had been admitted into some of the privileges of it. But it was made expressly with his fathers, and with him. But here the Apostle would have them see, that as the Levitical priesthood was not, and could not be permanent or final, so neither could the Jewish Covenant be final and lasting; but must yield place to a new and better Covenant. Their prophets had spoken of such a new Covenant; and the very fact of there being a new Covenant, involved the passing away of the old.

Ch. viii. 1 : Now in the things which we are saying the chief point is this : we have such a High Priest, who sat down on the right hand of the throne of the Majesty in the heavens, a minister of the sanctuary, and of the true tabernacle, which the Lord pitched, not man.

(v. 6.) [Who] obtained a ministry the more excellent, by how much also He is the Mediator of a better Covenant, which hath been enacted upon better promises. For if that first Covenant had been faultless, then would no place have been sought for a second.

For finding fault with them, he saith,—

Behold the days come, saith the Lord, that I will make a new Covenant with the house of Israel and with the house of Judah. . . . . .

[And] this is the Covenant that I will make with the house of Israel after those days, saith the Lord; I will put my laws into their mind,

And on their heart also will I write them;

. . . And their sins will I remember no more.

In that He saith, a new Covenant, He hath made the first

old. But that which is becoming old and waxeth aged is nigh unto vanishing away.

In the previous passage the Apostle had said that Christ as the true High Priest was a Minister of the Sanctuary, and of the true Tabernacle. Of this Sanctuary, and of the worship offered there, he now goes on to speak.

"The ark which had gone along with the Jews in the desert, the temple which was raised upon Mount Zion, had testified to them from generation to generation that the Lord was in the midst of them. Their disbelief of it had been their greatest sin, the ground of all other sins. And yet this temple had itself borne witness that there was something hidden from the view of the worshipper. There had been a veil over the mercy-seat. They had been reminded by those very figures which they prized so much, that into the pure and perfect presence of Him whom they served, they were not yet admitted. And yet everything in their Covenant and their discipline had been teaching them to be satisfied with nothing less than this. Everything had been meant to draw away their minds from the visible to the invisible, from the shadowy to the real. If they had entered into the temple-worship—if they had really sought the Unseen Presence—they could not be content until the figures were exchanged for the reality; until they had the power of entering into that reality—of holding actual and awful communion with the living God."—(MAURICE *on the Hebrews*.)

Ch. ix. 1: Now even the first Covenant had ordinances of divine service, and its sanctuary, a sanctuary of this world. [In contrast with the heavenly sanctuary of the new Covenant.]

For there was a tabernacle prepared; the first, wherein

were the candlestick, and the table, and the shew-bread; which is called the Holy place. And after the second veil, the tabernacle which is called the Holy of Holies; having a golden censer, and the ark of the Covenant overlaid round about with gold, wherein was a golden pot holding the manna, and Aaron's rod that budded, and the tables of the Covenant; and above it cherubim of glory overshadowing the mercy-seat; of which things we cannot now speak severally.

Now these things having been thus prepared, the priests go in continually into the first tabernacle, accomplishing the services; but into the second the high priest alone, once in the year, not without blood, which he offereth for himself, and for the errors of the people: the Holy Ghost this signifying [i.e. indicating by signs], that the way into the Holy place hath not yet been made manifest, while as the first tabernacle is yet standing; which is a parable for the time now present; according to which are offered both gifts and sacrifices that cannot, as touching the conscience, make the worshipper perfect, being only (with meats and drinks and divers washings) carnal ordinances, imposed until a time of reformation.

But Christ having come a High Priest of the good things to come, through the greater and more perfect Tabernacle, not made with hands, that is to say, not of this creation, nor yet through the blood of goats and calves, but through His own blood, entered in once for all into the Holy place, having obtained eternal redemption. For if the blood of goats and bulls, and the ashes of a heifer sprinkling them that have been defiled, sanctify unto the cleanness of the flesh, how much more shall the blood of Christ, who through the eternal Spirit offered Himself without blemish unto God, cleanse your conscience from dead works to serve the living God................
(v. 24) For Christ entered not into a Holy place made with hands, like in pattern to the true; but into heaven itself, now to appear before the face of God for us; nor yet that He should offer Himself often: as the high

priest entereth into the Holy place year by year with blood not his own; else must He often have suffered since the foundation of the world: but now once at the end of the ages hath He been manifested to put away sin by the sacrifice of Himself.

In treating of the Mosaic ritual, and of the worship of the sanctuary, the Apostle fixes the minds of his readers on the services of the great day of Atonement, when the high priest, after undergoing the most elaborate ceremonial purification, entered into the Holy of Holies and sprinkled the blood of the sacrifice seven times before the mercy-seat.

The high priest did not remain in the most Holy place, the mercy-seat of God's Presence was not permanently made open. In fact, the material sanctuary and mercy-seat so carefully veiled off was a sign that the real Priest had not yet come, that the real Sacrifice had not been yet offered. It was a sign that there was something overshadowing the heart of the worshipper, which separated it from Him to whom it would draw nigh. All the appointed ceremonies for the purification of the flesh reminded him of the fact, but could not change it. They only touched the flesh, they could not reach the conscience.

But now, in the end of the ages of the Jewish dispensation, Christ the true Priest had come, had offered Himself with His spotless life, and willing death, as the one perfect all-sufficient sacrifice.

As the Jewish high priest went into the Holy of Holies, with the blood of the typical sacrifice, and sprinkled it before the mercy-seat: so Christ entered into heaven itself, into the very Presence of God, with His own blood, pleading, that is, the efficacy of His one perfect Sacrifice, and thus obtained an eternal redemption for us.

The sacrificial act of the Jewish high priest was

twofold. First he killed the appointed victim outside the Holy place, and next carried its blood into the Holy of Holies, and sprinkled it seven times before the mercy-seat. So also is the sacrificial act of Christ our great High Priest twofold.

The first part was accomplished on earth when He yielded up His departing spirit into the Father's hands. This can never be repeated, Christ being raised from the dead dieth no more. He entered into the Heavenly Sanctuary once for all. But the second part of the sacrificial act is going on still. The high priest sprinkled the blood not once, but seven times. Christ continually does that which the sprinkling of the blood typified. He presents Himself continually before the throne of God for us; and He will remain there till the mysterious sevenfold sprinkling of His blood is accomplished. And what He does in heaven in His own proper Person, that He effects on earth by the ministry of His Church. As He continually presents Himself as the One Sacrifice in the courts of Heaven: so does He present Himself, in a mystery, in the courts of His Church on earth.

It is only when we grasp this twofold action of Christ's Sacrifice, only when we see that the Sacrifice which was once offered for the sins of the whole world is being perpetually presented before God in heaven, that we can understand the true meaning of the Eucharistic Sacrifice, freed alike from Roman additions and Puritan defects.

For can we think that because the one true Sacrifice has been offered, therefore sacrificial worship must cease? Is it not rather the precise reason why it should continue?

"Must not," asks one whose guidance I have been following throughout this book, and whom no one can accuse of fondness for Roman superstition,

"Must not this idea of sacrifice penetrate even more deeply into this dispensation than it did into the old? Must not the presentation of the one real perfect Sacrifice to the Father, the continual thanksgiving for that Sacrifice, be the central act of all worship to God—of all fellowship among men? Must not the offering of the worshipper's soul and body as living sacrifices to God be the necessary fruit and accompaniment of this act?"—(MAURICE *on the Hebrews*.)

But the Apostle goes on to show in what the essence of Christ's sacrifice, and its infinite superiority over the legal sacrifices, consisted.

The Psalmists and Prophets of Israel had been led to see the insufficiency of the sacrifices of the law: but by the very same process they had been led to look forward in faith and hope to a real and perfect sacrifice, and to see, as it were, behind the ineffectual sacrifices of the law, One who should come to offer the real, acceptable sacrifice, One who could say, "Lo! I come to do Thy will, O God."

Ch. x. 1 : For the law having a shadow of the good things to come, not the very image of the things, they can never with the same sacrifices year by year, which they offer continually, make perfect them that draw nigh. . . . . For it is impossible that the blood of bulls and goats should take away sins. Wherefore when He cometh into the world, He saith,

Sacrifice and offering thou wouldest not. . . . .

Then said I, Lo, I am come . . . . to do Thy will, O God. Saying above, Sacrifices and offerings . . . . thou wouldest not, . . . then hath He said, Lo, I am come to do Thy will. He taketh away the first, that He may establish the second. By which will we have been sanctified through the offering of the body of Jesus Christ once for all. . . . .

Having therefore, brethren, boldness to enter into the Holy place by the blood of Jesus, by the way which He dedicated for us, a new and living way, through the veil, that is to say, His flesh; and having a great Priest over the house of God ; let us draw near with a true heart in fulness of faith, having our hearts sprinkled from an evil conscience, and our bodies washed with pure water.

This whole passage is one of the most important in the whole Bible on the subject of sacrifice. From the sacrifice of Cain and Abel downwards, the whole Bible is full of the doctrine of sacrifice; in the tangled skein of human history the scarlet thread of sacrifice can be traced throughout. And as the sacrifices were consummated in the Sacrifice of Christ, so the doctrine of sacrifice culminates in this passage of the Epistle to the Hebrews, and in this its central thought, "Lo! I am come to do Thy will, O God."

This is the highest teaching of the Bible about sacrifice.

Men have too often thought of sacrifice as a human device to propitiate an angry deity, as an attempt to change the Divine Will, and avert the Divine vengeance: the Bible, on the other hand, teaches that sacrifice is not a human device, but a Divine ordinance : not something which changes God's will, but that which removes the obstacles to the fulfilment of His will.

We do not read, I come to change Thy will, O God; but "*I am come to do Thy will, O God.*"

The sacrifice which the Great High Priest offered was the sacrifice of absolute submission, of entire surrender, of perfect obedience. In other words, it was the sacrifice of Himself, it was the perfect doing of the Father's will, even that good will, that perfectly righteous will, on which the government of the universe is based.

CHAPTER XL.

THE EPISTLE TO THE HEBREWS
(continued).

IN our last chapter we reached that point in the Apostle's argument, in which he demonstrates that, as the Lord Jesus in the dignity of His Person was infinitely greater than Moses, so in the excellency of His High Priesthood He excelled the high priests of Israel who succeeded one another in their high office, and so also the efficacy of His Sacrifice infinitely exceeded the efficacy of the sacrifices of the Law, and His own blood was far more precious than the blood of bulls and goats.

Moses ruled in God's household as a servant, a faithful servant no doubt, but still a servant: Christ ruled in God's household as a Son in His Father's house.

The Jewish high priest was compassed with infirmity; was constrained to offer sacrifice for his own sins, as well as for the sins of the people; was not allowed to continue long in his office by reason of death. Christ, the real High Priest, was holy, harmless, undefiled, separated from sinners; and yet could be touched with the feeling of our infirmities, and save all that came to Him to the uttermost. He exercised His priestly office not by the authority of a carnal commandment, but by the power of an endless life.

The Jewish sacrifices could not take away sins; at the best they sanctified unto the cleanness of the flesh; but the sacrifice which Jesus offered, the supreme sacrifice of Himself, was able to cleanse the conscience from dead works to serve the living God, and to make perfect for ever them that are sanctified.

Upon this instruction in Divine truth the Apostle bases his invitation to his Hebrew brethren in Christ, to draw near to God with a true heart, in fulness of faith, having their hearts sprinkled from an evil conscience and their bodies washed with the pure water of holy baptism.

Then the invitation passes into an appeal, and the appeal into a most solemn warning.

These things being so, let them hold fast their Christian profession, and cling in faith to their Divine King, their Heavenly Priest; and, remembering the dangers of the times in which they lived, dangers of which Jesus had himself warned them, let them stir one another up to love and devotion, and let them not, as they were beginning to do, absent themselves from the solemn assemblies of the Church, where they could draw near to God by a better way than the temple service, and partake of a better altar than the reeking altars of a dying religion.

If they fell away wilfully there was no more sacrifice for sins,—how could there be if they rejected the one only Sacrifice? There remained nothing for them but the terrible judgment which was then hanging over the apostate city, 'the fierce fire of God's wrath which would shortly be poured forth on the Jerusalem which had rejected its King, and crucified its Christ.

Ch. x. 23: Let us hold fast the confession of our hope

that it waver not; for He is faithful that promised: and let us consider one another to provoke unto love and good works; not forsaking the assembling of ourselves together, as the custom of some is, but exhorting one another; and so much the more, as ye see the day drawing nigh.

For if we sin wilfully after that we have received the knowledge of the truth, there remaineth no more a sacrifice for sins, but a certain fearful expectation of judgment, and a fierceness of fire, which shall devour the adversaries.
.... For yet a very little while,
He that cometh shall come, and shall not tarry.
But my righteous one shall live by faith:
And if he shrink back, my soul hath no pleasure in him.
But we are not of them that shrink back unto perdition; but of them that have faith unto the saving of the soul.

Ch. xi. 1: Now faith is the assurance of things hoped for, the proving of things not seen. For therein the elders [i.e. the worthies of the Old Testament] had witness borne to them.

The prophet Habakkuk had spoken of faith as that power in which the true Israelite should live. But what was this faith? Was it a looking backward or a looking forward? Was it to rest contented in the present, or to press on to what was still beyond? The Apostle answers these questions in the words which are so familiar to us. Faith he declares is the assurance, or confidence of things *hoped for*, the evidence, the proving of things *not seen*.

The faith by which the elders lived, and pleased God, was a faith which forbad them to rest in their present state of knowledge or privilege. The highest hope of the true Israelite was in something which would issue from his calling, not in the calling itself. That which the faithful Israelite looked forward to was not a selfish privilege, but a universal blessing. The hope of Israel was not held as a possession, but as a trust, held in trust for the world. Faith did not begin with Abraham, and therefore the object of his hope was not limited to Abraham's seed.

Abel, Enoch, Noah, walked by faith also, and what they hoped for, what they looked forward to, was that in which the whole race, and not one portion of it, had an interest.

Abraham's faith was shown in this, that he pressed onward; what he sought always lay before him, he never reached it. Being called by God, he went out not knowing whither he went. In the very land of promise he was but a sojourner, and a dweller in tents; he had there no continuing city, for he looked for the city which hath foundations, whose builder and maker was God; he desired a better country, that is a heavenly.

Ch. xi. 13: These all died in faith, not having received the promises, but having seen them and greeted them from afar, and having confessed that they were strangers and pilgrims on the earth. For they that say such things make it manifest that they are seeking after a country of their own. And if indeed they had been mindful of that country from which they went out, they would have had opportunity to return. But now they desire a better country, that is, a heavenly: wherefore God is not ashamed of them, to be called their God: for He hath prepared for them a city.

And then having spoken of the power of faith in Abraham, Isaac, and Jacob, in Moses, in the judges, in the prophets, and of others innumerable who through faith wrought righteousness, endured torture and persecution, of those who had been stoned, sawn asunder, slain with the sword, who had had to wander in deserts and mountains and caves, he continues:—

Ch. xi. 39: And these all, having had witness borne to them through their faith, received not the promise, God having provided some better thing concerning us, that apart from us they should not be made perfect. Therefore let us also, seeing we are compassed about with so great a cloud of witnesses [i.e. those before enumerated], lay aside every weight, and the sin which doth so easily beset us, and let us run with patience the race that is set before us, looking unto Jesus the Author and Perfecter of our faith, who for the joy that was set before Him endured the Cross, despising shame, and hath sat down at the right hand of the throne of God.

This great Epistle is no formal, passionless treatise on theology, to be calmly studied by students in the quiet of their libraries; it was written for men who were about to pass through the most terrible crisis that ever city or nation had to meet. It was written for men who were about to pass through "the great tribulation," "the fiery trial" of which S. James had spoken; "the day of the Lord revealed in fire," of which S. Paul had written. It was written as a last warning to men who were tottering on the brink of apostasy.

It is not difficult to see the drift of the section of the Epistle which we have been reading.

It was not enough to prove the unapproachable superiority of Christ over Moses, of the Gospel over the Law, of the Sacrifice of Christ over the sacrifices of bulls and goats.

The Hebrew Christians would be taunted with the reproach that they were renegades from their religion, that they had renounced their fellowship with the saints of the Old Testament, with the fathers of Israel; they would be subjected not only to taunts, but to cruel persecution, from which the impartial rule of the Roman law existed no longer to protect them; they were at the mercy of the fierce fanatics, the blood-thirsty zealots of whom Josephus tells us. Their bishop, S. James the Just, either had been or was about to be foully murdered. It is clear, then, that the Apostle would arm them to meet this taunt, to endure this persecution, and to resist unto blood.

So far from their Christian profession cutting them off from the great company of the saints and martyrs of Israel, it really brought them into fuller communion with them. They had not been blessed in what they possessed, but in what they looked forward to; they had died not in fruition, but in faith; they had not received the promise, they could not be made perfect in themselves, they could only be made perfect in the Communion of Christ and His Church.

What the elders of the Old Covenant, what Abraham, and Moses, and David had looked forward to, believers in Christ and members of Christ's Church had as their present possession.

And, moreover, if these Jewish believers in Christ would pass through the fiery trial that was in store for them, unharmed, it could only be in the power of the same faith. It was as true for them as it had ever been for the saints of old—*My righteous one shall live by faith.*

They must be prepared to resist unto blood striving against sin, as the saints of old had resisted. They must be prepared to endure torture and death, mockings and scourgings, bonds and imprisonments, even as God's faithful ones of old had had to endure.

Let them remember, then, that they were compassed about with such a cloud of witnesses, that they were surrounded by such a vast multitude of God's saints, who by their lives and deaths had been witnesses for God. The words do not mean, as they have often been taken to mean, that we are called upon to run the race which is set before us, because we are compassed about with such a cloud of spectators, who witness our struggle and rejoice in our victory. Such a thought may be as true as it is beautiful; but it is not what the Apostle meant.

Above all, let them remember that Jesus Himself, their Lord and Master, the Apostle and High Priest of their profession, for the joy which was set before Him, endured the Cross, and despised the shame, and had entered into His glory; and if they would be faithful to Him, as they had borne His cross and endured shame for His sake, so also should they share in His glory, and sit with Him in His throne, even as He had overcome, and was set down with His Father on His throne.

But now let us remember that this solemn appeal of the Apostle, though it had this special, local application, has a wider, an universal application.

The character of our lives, the nature of our temptations, may be widely different from those of these Hebrew Christians. But we, too, have a race set before us, upon the issue of which our eternity depends. Each one of us has his own special sin, that sin that doth so easily beset him; each one is more or less heavily weighted by the things of time and sense.

And we, too, are compassed about with a great cloud of witnesses for the truth, with the great multitude which no man can number, the great company of all saints, who have fought the good fight, and have entered into their rest.

And we, too, must run our race, ever looking unto Jesus; the whole attitude of our minds, the whole current of our lives, being set to Him, who, as He has been the Beginner, will be also the Finisher, the Perfecter of our faith.

Christ has gone before us, and has set us an example that we should follow His steps. Let us, then, not shrink from taking up His Cross, let us not hesitate to confess Him before men, and openly to take His side. And then His joy will be ours; not a selfish happiness,—that could be no joy to Him; but the joy of being at peace with God, the joy of working under the Master's eye, the joy of having a share in bringing on the Golden Year, "the dim far-off event to which the whole creation moves."

CHAPTER XLI.

THE EPISTLE TO THE HEBREWS
(*continued*).

AMONG the many opinions that have been held about the authorship of this Epistle, is one that ascribes it to S. Barnabas. Whether the writer was indeed S. Barnabas it is impossible to say; but at any rate he was "a Son of Consolation." Though his warnings are most solemn, and his exhortations urgent, he follows them up with the tenderest consolation.

He reminds them of the exhortation of the Divine Wisdom in the Book of Proverbs, in which God reasons with His people, as a father with his sons, and calls upon them to endure His Fatherly chastisements.

He would have them remember for their comfort that whom the Lord loveth He chasteneth, and scourgeth every son whom He receiveth: and that the end and purpose of this loving discipline is for their eternal profit, that they might be partakers of God's holiness. And though all chastening must needs for the time be not joyous, but grievous, yet let them remember that it will work for their good, and will yield peaceable fruit, even the fruit of righteousness.

This passage not only brought comfort, as we may well believe, to those to whom it was addressed, but has comforted many thousands of afflicted souls from that day to this; and has found a most suitable setting in the office for the Visitation of the Sick.

Then follows a warning against worldliness and a life of sense. Our Lord had solemnly warned his Apostles, that they should not allow themselves to be overcharged with surfeiting and drunkenness and cares of this life, and so that day should come upon them suddenly.

So the Apostle cautions these Hebrew Christians against low aims of life, against unspirituality and earthliness of mind, by the example of Esau, who for one morsel of meat sold his birthright.

Ch. xii. 14: Follow after peace with all men, and the sanctification without which no man shall see the Lord: looking carefully lest there be any man that falleth short of the grace of God; lest any root of bitterness springing up trouble you, and thereby the many be defiled; lest there be any fornicator or profane person, as Esau, who for one mess of meat sold his own birthright. For ye know that even when he afterward desired to inherit the blessing, he was rejected (for he found no place of repentance), though he sought it diligently with tears.

This last sentence has sometimes been twisted to mean, that Esau repented of his sin, repented earnestly with tears, and yet that a place of repentance was denied to him.

Esau sold his birthright because he did not value it: he did not value it, because it was purely a spiritual thing, and he did not care for spiritual things; but when he found that the blessing of the first-born went with it, then he was sorry enough, not sorry that he had done wrong, but sorry that he had sacrificed his interests, and cried out piteously, My father, hast thou but one blessing? Bless me, even me also, O my father.

He found no place of repentance, that is, he found that he could not alter what had been done.

It ought to be remembered that God dealt very mercifully with Esau. It is true he forfeited the special blessing; but for that special blessing he did not really care, he was not fit for it. Such a blessing as he was fit for, such a blessing as he would value, was freely given him, a blessing which, in temporal matters, was nearly as desirable as his brother's.

Why, it may be asked, does the Apostle barb the arrow of his warning with the example of Esau? It was because these Hebrew Christians were tempted to commit the very same sin as Esau committed. They were tempted to despise their birthright, their spiritual calling, their privileges as Christians, and to barter them for material advantages, for immunity from persecution and ridicule.

And this naturally leads the Apostle to speak of what their spiritual birthright was, and how immeasurably it exceeded the vaunted privileges of Israel after the flesh.

The whole passage is one of the most striking in the New Testament. It opens with a description of the giving of the law, the establishment of the Mosaic Covenant, and of the terrors which accompanied it. In contrast with this, and expressed in the most glowing terms, is described the nature and privileges of the Christian Covenant.

The tangible, sensible mountain of Sinai, is contrasted with the spiritual mountain of Zion. The rigorous fencing of the bounds of the mountain of the law are implicitly contrasted with the free and joyful approach to the Mount Zion, the Spiritual Jerusalem.

Ch. xii. 18: For ye are not come unto a mount that

might be touched, and that burned with fire, and unto blackness, and darkness, and tempest, and the sound of a trumpet, and the voice of words ; which voice they that heard intreated that no word more should be spoken unto them : for they could not endure that which was enjoined. If even a beast touch the mountain, it shall be stoned; and so fearful was the appearance that Moses said, " I exceedingly fear and quake:" but ye are come unto Mount Zion, and unto the city of the living God, the heavenly Jerusalem, and to innumerable hosts of angels, to the general assembly and Church of the first-born who are enrolled in heaven, and to God the Judge of all, and to the spirits of just men made perfect, and to Jesus the Mediator of a New Covenant, and to the blood of sprinkling, which speaketh better than that of Abel.

You will notice, of course, that this is spoken of, not in the future, but in the present. It is not a description of the blessedness of "heaven," as we phrase it ; but a description of the Christian's spiritual heritage on earth.

Not " we shall one day come:" but " we are come." This is very wonderful, but it is true.

But if it sounds wonderful to us, how wonderful it must have sounded to the Hebrew Christians, who in their solemn assembly heard it for the first time.

To the Jew, Jerusalem was the joy of the whole earth, the City of the Great King; Mount Zion was the Lord's delight, where it pleased Him to dwell.

With what wonder and awe, then, would the Hebrew Christian hear what was told him, that there was for him another Zion than the city of David, another Jerusalem than that which was about to be destroyed ; that there was for him what was denied to Abraham, an abiding city, a city which had foundations, whose Builder and Maker was God, a kingdom which could not be shaken; that in this city of God, in this kingdom of Christ, he had a real and true communion with the spirits of just men made perfect; that he had to do with the festal assemblies of angels, not as his masters and mediators, but as his friends and fellow-servants; that in it, above all, he had communion with Jesus, the Mediator of a New Covenant, whose blood called not as Abel's did for vengeance, but pleaded for his pardon.

But if this calling was his, how fearful to come short of it! If these were the privileges and blessings of the Christian Covenant, what terrible retribution would overtake him who should tread the Son of God under foot, and account the blood of the Covenant an unholy and common thing!

Ch. xii. 25 : See that ye refuse not him that speaketh. For if they escaped not, when they refused Him that warned them on earth [i.e. speaking from Sinai], much more shall not we escape, who turn away from Him that warneth from heaven : whose voice then shook the earth : but now He hath promised, saying, Yet once more will I make to tremble not the earth only, but also the heaven [i.e. not the earthly polity of the Jews only, but also the religious polity of Judaism] . . . . . .

Wherefore, receiving a kingdom that cannot be shaken, let us have grace, whereby we may offer service well-pleasing to God with reverence and awe ; for our God is a consuming fire.

These last words are very startling—"Our God is a consuming fire ;" startling as well as awful, for we at once ask ourselves, Is it not said again and again that " God is love "?

But there is really no contradiction. He is a consuming fire, just because He is love. The fire consumes up everything that is capable of being burnt, what is not changed into another form is purified. Because God is perfect love He will be to us the consuming fire, to burn up all that is bad and shameful in us, to burn out of us our unlovingness, our untruthfulness, our impurity, our meanness and selfishness. If God were less loving, He would be less strict. His fire is eternal, because His love is eternal.

This solemn warning is followed by sundry exhortations to faith and holy living, of which it must suffice to mention one or two.

The writer of the Epistle exhorts the Christian community at Jerusalem to pay a reverent regard to the bishop, and elders, and deacons of the Church. It is possible that the Epistle may have been written at the time of the murder of S. James, their first bishop, when they would need special encouragement and warning, and when the presbyters of the Church would specially need to have their authority strengthened. It may be even that it was to S. James that the words I am going to quote were intended in the first instance to apply:—

Ch. xiii. 7 : Remember them that had the rule over you, which spake unto you the word of God; and considering the issue of their life, imitate their faith. Jesus Christ is the same yesterday, and to-day, yea, and for ever.

This last assertion, so suitable at all times, and so comforting under all circumstances, would be doubly welcome and necessary at a time of such a terrible crisis as then existed; when perhaps the Christian community were lamenting the deaths of some of their spiritual rulers who had won the crown of martyrdom, by reason of which they were left in a measure as sheep without shepherds.

But that there were some of their spiritual leaders

and pastors left, appears from a similar exhortation a little further on.

Ch. xiii. 17 : Obey them that have the rule over you, and submit to them : for they watch in behalf of your souls, as they that shall give account, that they may do this with joy, and not with grief : for this were unprofitable for you.

Such words as these could hardly have been written by one, who repudiated the existence of the Christian ministry, and rejected the idea of a Christian priesthood.

It is often asserted that to say that Christ's ministers are in any real and true sense priests, is to place an order of men between the soul and God, and is to interfere with the belief in the priesthood of Christ.

So far from interfering with the priesthood of Christ, the existence of a human priesthood is a witness for the truth and reality of Christ's priesthood. If Christ were not the One only real Priest, there could not by any possibility be a human priesthood. Instead of there being any opposition between the two, the true way of stating it is to say, that Christ the true Priest exercises some of His priestly functions through the ministry of His Church.

Let me quote again the words of one whom no one can accuse of what is called sacerdotalism. He says:—" If the argument of the Epistle signify anything, for a high priest there could be no place. He who should assume to be *the* Priest of the Universe, would by that claim interfere not with some accident of the New Dispensation, but with its primary idea. .... But are we therefore to say, The idea of priests upon earth, of men witnessing of that filial High Priest who has ascended into the heavens ... would be incompatible with any maxim of the new economy? Can we think that it would interfere with the heavenly and perfect character of the Head, or with the privileges of the body, or with the distinctness of any one of its members? Are we to say that such an order would have only a figurative, not a real, right to the name of priests? Must we not rather think, that if the priestly idea dropped out of the circle of Christian ideas, the sense of what mankind had gained by the ascension of Christ would disappear also; that if it were limited to Him who has fully realized, and can alone fully realize it, the belief in His union with the creatures whom He has called His brethren, would grow feeble?"—(MAURICE *on the Hebrews.*)

Much the same thing may be said about the sacrificial worship of the Church. The writer of this Epistle declares :—

Ch. xiii. 10: We have an altar, whereof they have no right to eat which serve the tabernacle.

The application of this to the Commemorative Sacrifice of the Holy Eucharist has been as resolutely denied as it has been firmly asserted. But it is difficult to see what else it can mean. Now it is sometimes thought that to assert that the Holy Communion is in any sense a sacrifice, is to make it into a substitute for the Sacrifice of Christ. But it is only prejudice that can make such an assertion seem reasonable. It may be freely allowed that, in the highest and strictest sense of the words, there is and can be but one sacrifice, as there is and can be but one priest.

But, as has been shown, the human priesthood of the Church does not interfere with the true Priesthood of Christ, but rather derives its sole efficacy from it: so also the fact that the Holy Eucharist is a Commemorative Sacrifice does not interfere with the supreme and sole position of the Sacrifice of Christ.

The Holy Communion as a Commemorative Sacrifice has simply no existence apart from the Sacrifice of Christ, of which it is the memorial.

And now, having reviewed some of the chief points which the Apostle has insisted on in this Epistle, we may conclude our readings on this Epistle to the Hebrews, and indeed our readings on the life and letters of S. Paul, to whom the authorship of this Epistle has been traditionally assigned, with the prayer that, with the exception of a few parting words, closes it :—

Ch. xiii. 20 : Now the God of peace, who brought again from the dead the great Shepherd of the sheep, with the blood of the eternal covenant, even our Lord Jesus, make you perfect in every good thing to do His will, working in us that which is well pleasing in His sight, through Jesus Christ ; TO WHOM BE THE GLORY FOR EVER AND EVER. AMEN.

Printed at the University Press, Oxford
By HORACE HART, *Printer to the University*

Society for Promoting Christian Knowledge.

Publications on
THE CHRISTIAN EVIDENCE.

BOOKS. Price.

Christianity Judged by its Fruits. *s. d.*
By the Rev. C. Croslegh, D.D.   Post 8vo ......*Cloth boards* 1 6

The Great Passion-Prophecy Vindicated.
By the Rev. Brownlow Maitland, M.A.   Post 8vo.
Limp cloth 0 10

Natural Theology of Natural Beauty (The).
By the Rev. R. St. John Tyrwhitt, M.A.   Post 8vo.
Cloth boards 1 6

Steps to Faith.
Addresses on some points in the Controversy with Unbelief.
By the Rev. Brownlow Maitland, M.A.   Post 8vo.
Cloth boards 1 6

Scepticism and Faith.
By the Rev. Brownlow Maitland.   Post 8vo.   *Cloth boards* 1 4

Theism or Agnosticism.
An Essay on the grounds of Belief in God.   By the Rev.
Brownlow Maitland, M.A.   Post 8vo.............*Cloth boards* 1 6

Argument from Prophecy (The).
By the Rev. Brownlow Maitland, M.A., Author of
"Scepticism and Faith," &c.   Post 8vo. ....*Cloth boards* 1 6

Some Modern Religious Difficulties.
Six Sermons preached, by the request of the Christian
Evidence Society, at St. James's, Piccadilly, in 1876;
with a Preface by his Grace the late Archbishop of Canterbury.   Post 8vo. ....*Cloth boards* 1 6

Some Witnesses for the Faith.
Six Sermons preached, by the request of the Christian
Evidence Society, at St. Stephen's Church, South Kensington, in 1877.   Post 8vo. ....*Cloth boards* 1 4

Publications on the Christian Evidence.

Price. *s. d.*

Being of God, Six Addresses on the.
By C. J. Ellicott, D.D., Bishop of Gloucester and Bristol. Small Post 8vo. .... *Cloth boards* 1 6

Modern Unbelief: its Principles and Characteristics. By the Right Rev. the Lord Bishop of Gloucester and Bristol. Post 8vo. .... *Cloth boards* 1 6

When was the Pentateuch Written?
By George Warington, B.A., Author of "Can we Believe in Miracles?" &c. Post 8vo. .... *Cloth boards* 1 6

The Analogy of Religion.
Dialogues founded upon Butler's "Analogy of Religion." By the late Rev. H. R. Huckin, D.D., Head Master of Repton School. Post 8vo. .... *Cloth boards* 3 0

"Miracles."
By the Rev. E. A. Litton, M.A., Examining Chaplain of the Bishop of Durham. Crown 8vo. .... *Cloth boards* 1 6

Moral Difficulties connected with the Bible.
Being the Boyle Lectures for 1871. By the Ven. Archdeacon Hessey, D.C.L., Preacher to the Hon. Society of Gray's Inn, &c. FIRST SERIES. Post 8vo. ...*Cloth boards* 1 6

Moral Difficulties connected with the Bible.
Being the Boyle Lectures for 1872. By the Ven. Archdeacon Hessey, D.C.L. SECOND SERIES. Post 8vo.
Cloth boards 2 6

Prayer and recent Difficulties about it.
The Boyle Lectures for 1873, being the THIRD SERIES of "Moral Difficulties connected with the Bible." By the Ven. Archdeacon Hessey, D.C.L. Post 8vo.
Cloth boards 2 6
The above Three Series in a volume ....*Cloth boards* 6 0

Historical Illustrations of the Old Testament.
By the Rev. G. Rawlinson, M.A., Camden Professor of Ancient History, Oxford. Post 8vo .... *Cloth boards* 1 6

Can we Believe in Miracles?
By G. Warington, B.A., of Caius College, Cambridge. Post 8vo.. *Cloth boards* 1 6

The Moral Teaching of the New Testament
VIEWED AS EVIDENTIAL TO ITS HISTORICAL TRUTH. By the Rev. C. A. Row, M.A. Post 8vo...................*Cloth boards* 1 9

Publications on the Christian Evidence.

	Price s. d.

The Witness of the Heart to Christ.
Being the Hulsean Lectures for 1878. By the Right Rev. W. Boyd Carpenter, Bishop of Ripon. Post 8vo. *Cl. boards* — 1 6

Thoughts on the First Principles of the Positive
PHILOSOPHY, CONSIDERED IN RELATION TO THE HUMAN MIND. By the late Benjamin Shaw, M.A., late Fellow of Trinity College, Camb. Post 8vo. .... *Limp cloth* — 0 8

Thoughts on the Bible.
By the late Rev. W. Gresley, M.A., Prebendary of Lichfield. Post 8vo. .... *Cloth boards* — 1 6

The Reasonableness of Prayer.
By the Rev. P. Onslow, M.A. Post 8vo. .... *Paper cover* — 0 8

Paley's Evidences of Christianity.
A New Edition, with Notes, Appendix, and Preface. By the Rev. E. A. Litton, M.A. Post 8vo. .... *Cloth boards* — 4 0

Paley's Natural Theology.
Revised to harmonize with Modern Science. By Mr. F. le Gros Clark, F.R.S., President of the Royal College of Surgeons of England, &c. Post 8vo. .... *Cloth boards* — 4 0

Paley's Horæ Paulinæ.
A new Edition, with Notes, Appendix, and Preface. By J. S. Howson, D.D., Dean of Chester. Post 8vo. *Cloth boards* — 3 0

Religion and Morality.
By the Rev. Richard T. Smith, B.D., Canon of St. Patrick's, Dublin. Post 8vo. .... *Cloth boards* — 1 6

The Story of Creation as told by Theology
AND SCIENCE. By the Rev. T. S. Ackland, M.A. Post 8vo. *Cloth boards* — 1 6

Man's Accountableness for his Religious Belief.
A Lecture delivered at the Hall of Science, on Tuesday, April 2nd, 1872. By the Rev. Daniel Moore, M.A., Holy Trinity, Paddington. Post 8vo. .... *Paper cover* — 0 3

The Theory of Prayer; with Special Reference
TO MODERN THOUGHT. By the Rev. W. H. Karslake, M.A., Assistant Preacher at Lincoln's Inn, Vicar of Westcott, Dorking. Post 8vo. .... *Limp cloth* — 1 0

Publications on the Christian Evidence.

The Gospels of the New Testament: their Genuineness and Authority. By the Rev. R. J. Crosthwaite, M.A. Post 8vo. ....*Paper cover* — 0 3

Analogy of Religion, Natural and Revealed, to the Constitution and Course of Nature: to which are added, Two Brief Dissertations. By Bishop Butler. New Edition. Post 8vo. ....*Cloth boards* — 2 6

Christian Evidences: intended chiefly for the young. By the Most Reverend Richard Whately, D.D. 12mo. .... *Paper cover* — 0 4

The Efficacy of Prayer. By the Rev. W. H. Karslake, M.A., Assistant Preacher at Lincoln's Inn, &c. &c. Post 8vo. .... *Limp cloth* — 0 6

Science and the Bible: a Lecture by the Right Rev. Bishop Perry, D.D. 18mo. *Paper cover* 4d., or *Limp cloth* — 0 6

A Lecture on the Bible. By the Very Rev. E. M. Goulburn, D.D., Dean of Norwich. 18mo. *Paper cover* — 0 2

The Bible: Its Evidences, Characteristics, and Effects. A Lecture by the Right Rev. Bishop Perry, D.D. 18mo. ....*Paper cover* — 0 4

The Origin of the World according to Revelation and Science. A Lecture by Harvey Goodwin, M.A., Bishop of Carlisle. Post 8vo. ....*Cloth boards* — 0 4

How I passed through Scepticism into Faith. A Story told in an Almshouse. Post 8vo. ......*Paper cover* — 0 3

On the Origin of the Laws of Nature. By Sir Edmund Beckett, Bart. Post 8vo. ....*Cloth boards* — 1 6

What Is Natural Theology? Being the Boyle Lectures for 1876. By the Rev. Alfred Barry, D.D., Bishop of Sydney. Post 8vo. ....*Cloth boards* — 2 6

*** For List of TRACTS on the Christian Evidences, see the Society's Catalogue B.

LONDON:
SOCIETY FOR PROMOTING CHRISTIAN KNOWLEDGE,

www.ingramcontent.com/pod-product-compliance
Lightning Source LLC
Chambersburg PA
CBHW030811230426
43667CB00008B/1170